I.B.TAURIS SHORT HISTORIES

I.B.Tauris Short Histories is an authoritative and elegantly written new series which puts a fresh perspective on the way history is taught and understood in the twenty-first century. Designed to have strong appeal to university students and their teachers, as well as to general readers and history enthusiasts, *I.B.Tauris Short Histories* comprises a novel attempt to bring informed interpretation, as well as factual reportage, to historical debate. Addressing key subjects and topics in the fields of history, the history of ideas, religion, classical studies, politics, philosophy and Middle East studies, the series seeks intentionally to move beyond the bland, neutral 'introduction' that so often serves as the primary undergraduate teaching tool. While always providing students and generalists with the core facts that they need to get to grips with the essentials of any particular subject, *I.B.Tauris Short Histories* goes further. It offers new insights into how a topic has been understood in the past, and what different social and cultural factors might have been at work. It brings original perspectives to bear on the manner of its current interpretation. It raises questions and – in its extensive bibliographies – points to further study, even as it suggests answers. Addressing a variety of subjects in a greater degree of depth than is often found in comparable series, yet at the same time in concise and compact handbook form, *I.B.Tauris Short Histories* aims to be 'introductions with an edge'. In combining questioning and searching analysis with informed history writing, it brings history up-to-date for an increasingly complex and globalized digital age.

www.short-histories.com

'This is a short and pithy book by an outstanding scholar at the top of her game. Prioritizing literature, it uses newly-discovered or unfamiliar writings to re-describe social classes, as well as topics like individualism and gender. Its innovative chapters on "Renaissance Man" and – especially – "Renaissance Woman" help to reset the agenda for understanding the Italian Renaissance, making this book an invaluable twenty-first-century guide, not only for students but for the rest of us as well.'

– *Alison Brown, Emerita Professor of Italian Renaissance History, Royal Holloway, University of London, author of* **The Renaissance**

'Virginia Cox's short history of the Italian Renaissance is an exemplary introduction – concise, lucid, elegant, balanced, perceptive and accessible. It summarizes traditional views of the Renaissance, especially Jacob Burckhardt's, criticizes them, and offers a revised interpretation of the movement. Cox's Renaissance is, in her own words, "broader and deeper" than its predecessors. She places more emphasis than usual on the coexistence and conflict between different ideas and styles. She re-interprets Burckhardt's idea of Renaissance "individualism" with the aid of recent work on social psychology. Her book includes discussions of the applied arts, notably fashion, as well as a chapter on "the Renaissance woman", based on the author's own research. Students will be grateful for this book, general readers will enjoy it, and fellow-scholars will be appreciative of the knowledge and thought underlying its apparently effortless production.'

– *Peter Burke, FBA, Emeritus Professor of Cultural History, University of Cambridge, author of* **The Italian Renaissance**

'Virginia Cox's creative, original, and well-argued study of the Italian Renaissance should be on the bookshelf of every reader interested in the period. Cox gives attention not only to classical scholarship and those who practised it, but also to those who used it in their everyday lives. She presents short, judiciously chosen case studies that illuminate Renaissance art-making and collecting. And she writes with an expert hand about what it was like to live as a man or woman in the Renaissance, again by limiting her focus to exemplary cases that illuminate much larger realities. This short volume should be a go-to book for scholars teaching courses in the Renaissance as well as for general readers who want an introduction to the period that wears its considerable scholarship lightly. The writing throughout is crisp and elegant, with not a wasted word in sight.'

– *Christopher S Celenza, Charles Homer Haskins Professor of Classics and German and Romance Languages and Literatures, Johns Hopkins University, author of* **Machiavelli: A Portrait** *and* **The Lost Italian Renaissance: Humanists, Historians, and Latin's Legacy**

'Virginia Cox's rich, thought-provoking and elegantly written introduction to the Italian Renaissance conceives the cultural movement widely and inclusively, and encourages us to see it in new ways. Cox shows how it was rooted in an emulative and endlessly inventive dialogue with the models of ancient Rome and Greece that responded to, and was made more urgent by, the new needs of expanding cities and commerce. The cultural production that she considers includes of course literature, fine art, music and thought, but also material culture (including cooking and fashion), geography and science. Cox argues convincingly that the Renaissance in Italy should be seen as lasting until as late as the start of the seventeenth century, and as multipolar, with important developments emerging as much from princely courts as from the republics of Florence and Venice. Her approach enables her to go beyond the cultures of the social elites to study those of the literate urban classes in general. Perhaps most strikingly, she can devote equal space to Renaissance man – merchants, courtiers and artists in a broad sense – and to Renaissance woman, the secular and religious figures whose engagement with culture flourished most fully towards the end of the period. This finely judged book achieves much more than one might expect from a short history. It should be read and pondered by anyone interested in the Italian Renaissance, whether they are experienced scholars, students or non-specialists.'

– ***Brian Richardson, Emeritus Professor of Italian Language, University of Leeds, author of*** **Manuscript Culture in Renaissance Italy**

A Short History of . . .

the American Civil War	Paul Anderson (Clemson University)
the American Revolutionary War	Stephen Conway (University College London)
Ancient China	Edward L Shaughnessy (University of Chicago)
Ancient Greece	P J Rhodes, FBA (Durham University)
Ancient Rome	Andrew Wallace-Hadrill (University of Cambridge)
the Anglo-Saxons	Henrietta Leyser (University of Oxford)
the Byzantine Empire	Dionysios Stathakopoulos (King's College London)
the Celts	Alex Woolf (University of St Andrews)
Christian Spirituality	Edward Howells (Heythrop College, University of London))
the Crimean War	Trudi Tate (University of Cambridge)
English Renaissance Drama	Helen Hackett (University College London)
the English Revolution and the Civil Wars	David J Appleby (University of Nottingham)
the Etruscans	Corinna Riva (University College London)
the Hundred Years War	Michael Prestwich (Durham University)
Irish Independence	J J Lee (New York University)
the Italian Renaissance	Virginia Cox (New York University)
the Korean War	Allan R Millett (University of New Orleans)
Medieval Christianity	G R Evans (University of Cambridge)
Medieval English Mysticism	Vincent Gillespie (University of Oxford)
the Minoans	John Bennet (University of Sheffield)
the Mongols	George Lane (SOAS, University of London)
the Mughal Empire	Michael H Fisher (Oberlin College)
Muslim Spain	Alex J Novikoff (Rhodes College, Memphis)
New Kingdom Egypt	Robert Morkot (University of Exeter)
the New Testament	Halvor Moxnes (University of Oslo)
Nineteenth-Century Philosophy	Joel Rasmussen (University of Oxford)
the Normans	Leonie Hicks (Canterbury Christ Church University)
the Ottoman Empire	Baki Tezcan (University of California, Davis)

the Phoenicians	Mark Woolmer (Durham University)
the Reformation	Helen Parish (University of Reading)
the Renaissance in Northern Europe	Malcolm Vale (University of Oxford)
Revolutionary Cuba	Antoni Kapcia (University of Nottingham)
the Risorgimento	Nick Carter (Australian Catholic University, Sydney)
the Russian Revolution	Geoffrey Swain (University of Glasgow)
the Spanish Civil War	Julián Casanova (University of Zaragoza)
the Spanish Empire	Felipe Fernández-Armesto (University of Notre Dame) and José Juan López-Portillo (University of Oxford)
Transatlantic Slavery	Kenneth Morgan (Brunel University)
Venice and the Venetian Empire	Maria Fusaro (University of Exeter)
the Vikings	Clare Downham (University of Liverpool)
the Wars of the Roses	David Grummitt (University of Kent)
the Weimar Republic	Colin Storer (University of Nottingham)

In memory of Frank Woodhouse,
who helped set me off on the Renaissance path

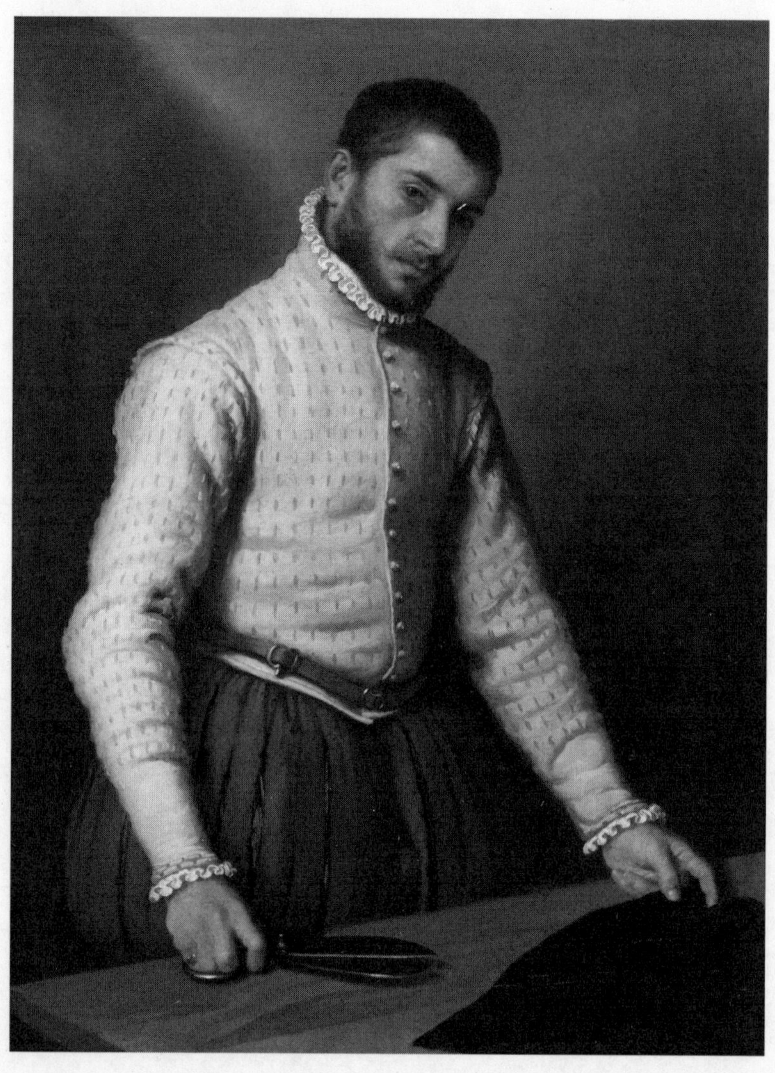

Frontispiece: Giovanni Battista Moroni, *The Tailor* (*Il Tagliapanni*), *c.*1565–70.

A SHORT HISTORY OF THE ITALIAN RENAISSANCE

Virginia Cox

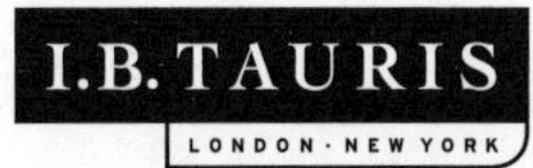

Published in 2016 by
I.B.Tauris & Co. Ltd
London • New York
www.ibtauris.com

ISBN: 978 1 78453 077 8 (HB)
ISBN: 978 1 78453 078 5 (PB)
e ISBN: 978 0 85772 974 3

A full CIP record for this book is available from the British Library
A full CIP record is available from the Library of Congress

Library of Congress Catalog Card Number: available

Typeset by Freerange
Printed and bound in Great Britain by T.J. International, Padstow, Cornwall

Contents

List of Maps and Illustrations

Acknowledgements

This work synthesizes knowledge gained and ideas developed over thirty years of research and teaching on Italian Renaissance literature and culture, at the universities of Cambridge, Edinburgh, and London (UCL), and at New York University. It would be impossible to acknowledge all those mentors, colleagues, peers, friends, and students who have contributed to this process through personal interaction and dialogue, let alone the countless scholars whose published work has helped to shape my thinking on the Renaissance, only a limited number of whom I have been able to cite in the relatively sparing notes to this book.

In view of this, I will limit myself in these acknowledgments to mentioning only those who participated directly in the production of the present volume. A major debt is due to Shannon McHugh and Anna Wainwright, who helped me with fact-checking and chasing up references in the final stages of preparation of the manuscript, doing an excellent job to a very tight deadline; and to Melissa Swain, who showed admirable patience and initiative in sourcing the images and permissions for the book. Clément Godbarge provided valuable help with the section on anatomy in Chapter 3, and Bruce Edelstein kindly read and commented on the various passages of the book that touch on art history. Paul Greene was an ideal beta reader and a patient sounding-board for ideas as I was writing the book.

Finally, I am grateful to Alex Wright for having invited me to write this book and for having proved such a supportive and engaged editor. Writing a synthesis of this kind is not the kind of thing that I can imagine would have occurred to me spontaneously; yet pulling together my ideas on the Italian Renaissance has been a remarkably rich experience, and I have learned far more than I would have anticipated along the way.

Introduction

It may be useful to start this book by making clear what it is *not*. The term 'Renaissance' is used in academic and everyday discourse in two senses. First, it is used to denote a cultural movement or tradition, centring on the recuperation of classical literature, art, and thought. Secondly, it is sometimes used to denote a period of time (in the case of Italy, generally from the fourteenth to the sixteenth century; in northern Europe generally later). This book takes 'Renaissance' in the first sense of the term. No attempt is made here to summarize the social, economic, religious or political history of Italy from the fourteenth to the sixteenth century in any systematic way, although mention is made of salient developments that impacted on cultural production. Works that attempt this kind of general overview are listed in the *Further Reading* section.

Although this book takes as its remit to narrate and analyse a cultural movement rooted in engagement with classical antiquity, it is not a history of Renaissance 'humanism' in the narrow sense in which that term is often used. *A Short History of the Italian Renaissance* does not merely survey the activities of those men and (very few) women who engaged with Latin and Greek literature, history, and thought, reading classical works in their original languages. It also gives space to material culture, including art, inspired by antiquity in respect of its subject-matter or form; and, where textual culture is concerned, it encompasses the vernacular reception of classical ideas and literary works. Nor does this book limit itself to describing the contributions of great scholars and thinkers and artists who forged the 'headline' culture of this period. Instead, it looks beyond the headlines, to the mass of men and women who participated in the cultural movement of the Renaissance in a quieter, secondary way. Petrarch, Boccaccio, Alberti, Castiglione, Machiavelli have a place here, as do Masaccio, Leonardo, Raphael, and Titian, but there is also space for mapmakers, mining engineers, lace designers, anatomists, tailors, chefs, courtesans, and celebrity meat carvers, along with a street poet who claims he made his first acquaintance with Ovid through a greasy page used to wrap food. The later phases of the cultural movement of the Renaissance coincided with a revolution in information technology, as printing and visual reproduction techniques such as woodcuts and engraving disseminated high culture as never before. Renaissance humanism touched a far wider segment of the population than earlier intellectual movements such as medieval scholasticism had done; yet its story is often told in a manner that stops at the study door.

Chapter 1 of the book ('What? Where? When? Whose?') sketches out the main parameters of the Renaissance as it is understood in this book, defining the movement, establishing its chronology, calling attention to the fundamental fact of Italy's political disunity and regional diversity in this period, and underlining the breadth and social diversity of the 'stakeholders' in the movement. A key argument in this chapter is that traditional periodizations that locate the end of the Renaissance in the first half of the sixteenth century fail to capture the movement's full arc.

Chapter 2 ('The Renaissance and the Ancient') traces the history of Renaissance Italy's long and passionate love affair with the textual and material remnants of classical antiquity, tracing classical influences in literary and intellectual history, art history, and material culture. A major focus of the chapter is the way in which a society deeply invested in Christianity responded to the philosophical challenges posed by its interactions with pagan antiquity.

Chapter 3 ('The Renaissance and the Modern') looks at responses to the material innovations that reshaped the world at the time when the Renaissance was gathering pace as a cultural movement, notably the introduction of printing into Europe and the geographical 'discoveries' of the period, especially that of the New World. In addition, the chapter examines the sense of novelty and progress that was such a marked feature of the later Renaissance, through case studies of the histories of geography and cartography; of anatomy; and of art-historical writing.

Chapter 4 ('Identity and the Self') re-examines the famous contention of the great nineteenth-century cultural historian Jacob Burckhardt that the Italian Renaissance saw the birth of a new and modern form of selfhood, which Burckhardt captured with the formula of 'individualism'. While acknowledging the findings of more recent scholarship, which has emphasized the massive weight that collective, group identities continued to have in the period, the chapter argues that Burckhardt's formula still has value in capturing aspects of the Italian Renaissance culture of identity. Considerable energies were invested in the period in crafting attractive and distinctive social selves, and practices of self-fashioning attained a high degree of sophistication in this period; yet this was not universal, nor did Renaissance individualism map on to modern individualism in any easy way.

Chapter 5 ('Renaissance Man') examines three distinctive Renaissance social and cultural types: the merchant, the courtier, and the artist. The latter term is understood in the broadest possible sense, to encompass not only painters, sculptors, and architects, but performance artists and skilled artisans of all kinds. The chapter looks at self-descriptive writings produced by each of these professional groups, with a special focus, where performance artists are concerned, on the vast and articulated professional sector of the 'table arts' associated with the courts: cooks, stewards, virtuoso carvers. The chapter makes the case that the much-studied rise of painting and sculpture from a lowly craft status to a much more elevated status as 'liberal arts' across the course of the fifteenth and sixteenth centuries was one instance of a much broader phenomenon.

Chapter 6 ('Renaissance Woman') traces two important, related developments in this period which profoundly affected women's cultural standing. The first is the emergence of the figure of the secular female creative artist or *virtuosa*, understood in a broad sense, to encompass writers, musicians, painters, actresses, composers, engravers. The second is the development of new ways of thinking about sex and gender, framed to counter traditional arguments for women's inferiority to men. Like many of the cultural innovations discussed in this book, the emergence of the *virtuosa* and the new attitudes to women were initially elite phenomena, but they migrated down to lower reaches of urban society in the course of the sixteenth century. The traditional periodization of the

Renaissance, focused on the fifteenth and early sixteenth centuries, and the tendency of twentieth-century studies of the Renaissance to focus disproportionately on Florence—a highly conservative society in gender terms—have led to a vast underestimation of the degree to which women may be considered stakeholders in the movement alongside men.

A few technical points, in conclusion. To enhance this book's utility for more specialized readers, I have cited the original text for most quotations from primary sources, especially in those sections of Chapters 5 and 6 which incorporate previously unpublished primary research. Where secondary literature is concerned, I have given preference to works in English where possible; and I have indicated English translations of primary sources where available. All translations in the body of the text are mine, unless otherwise stated in the notes.

Timeline

In addition to events in Italy, this timeline incorporates select material from elsewhere for comparison and calibration.

1303 Giotto begins work on Arena Chapel frescoes in Padua, continuing to 1306

c. 1308 Dante begins work on *Divine Comedy*, continuing to his death in 1321

1309 Papacy under Clement V (Raymond Bertrand de Got) transfers from Rome to Avignon

c. 1314 Albertino Mussato, *Ecerinis*, the first humanist tragedy

1320s Petrarch (Francesco Petrarca) begins work on his love poetry, continuing to his death in 1374

1337 Beginning of Hundred Years' War between England and France

1341 Petrarch crowned poet laureate in Rome, with the support of Robert of Anjou, king of Naples

1345 Petrarch discovers Cicero's letters to Atticus in the cathedral library of Verona and launches post-classical tradition of the private, or 'familiar' letter

1347 Black Death arrives in Europe, lasting until 1353 and killing at least a third of the continent's population

1353 Giovanni Boccaccio completes *Decameron*, which opens with a description of the plague in Florence

1360s Boccaccio, *Famous Women* (*De claris mulieribus*), the first humanist treatise on women

1376 Catherine of Siena sent by Florence as ambassador to Pope Gregory XI (Pierre Roger de Beaufort) in Avignon during 'War of the Eight Saints' between Florence and papacy

1377 Gregory XI returns papacy from Avignon to Rome
1378 Start of 'Great Schism' in the Church, with two and eventually three competing claimants to papacy; revolt of the wool-workers (*ciompi*) in Florence
1381 Peasants' revolt in England
c. 1387 Geoffrey Chaucer begins work on *Canterbury Tales*
1397 Manuel Chrysoloras invited to teach in Florence by Coluccio Salutati, marking the beginning of humanistic Greek studies
1401 Lorenzo Ghiberti wins competition to design the Florentine Baptistery doors
1413 Accession of Henry V in England
1414 Opening of Church Council of Constance
1415 Council of Constance posthumously declares English reformer John Wycliffe a heretic and orders execution of Bohemian reformer Jan Hus; Leonardo Bruni starts writing his ground-breaking *History of Florence*, continuing to 1442
1417 Great Schism resolved at Council of Constance; Poggio Bracciolini discovers complete text of Quintilian's *Education of the Orator* and Lucretius's *On the Nature of Things*
1419 Beginning of Hussite Wars in Bohemia
1420 Brunelleschi begins work on the dome of Florence cathedral, continuing to 1436
1421 Gerardo Landriani discovers complete text of Cicero's dialogue *On the Orator*
1423 Vittorino da Feltre establishes prototypical humanist school in Mantua
1424 Masaccio and Masolino da Panicale begin work on the Brancacci Chapel frescoes in Santa Maria del Carmine, Florence, continuing to 1427–8
1434 Return from exile of Cosimo de' Medici marks beginning of *de facto* Medici rule in Florence
c. 1435 Leon Battista Alberti writes *On Painting*, the first humanist art treatise
1438 Delegation sent from Byzantium to papal Council of Ferrara (Council of Florence after 1439), in a failed attempt to negotiate conciliation of Eastern and Western churches

1439–40 Lorenzo Valla writes *On the False Donation of Constantine* in Naples, proving the main document underpinning the papacy's claim to temporal sovereignty to be a fake

1442 Alfonso V of Aragon crowned Alfonso I of Naples, confirming Aragonese rule there after a long power struggle with the Angevin dynasty

1443 Alberti begins writing *On Architecture*, continuing to 1457

1447 Election of the first humanist pope, Nicholas V, who begins to plan the architectural reconstruction of Rome; Leonello d'Este, duke of Ferrara, plans first princely decorated *studiolo* in the palace of Belfiore, completed *c.* 1463

1450 Sforza dynasty established in Milan

1453 Fall of Constantinople to the Ottoman Turks, resulting in an exodus of Byzantine scholars to Italy

1455 Johannes Gutenberg completes printing of the Bible in Mainz, the first major work to be printed in Europe using moveable type

1465 First books printed in Italy, at the monastery of Subiaco, near Rome (Cicero's *On the Orator* and Lactantius's *Works*)

1468 Byzantine-Italian Cardinal Basilios Bessarion donates his remarkable library to the senate of Venice, forming nucleus of the Biblioteca Marciana

1469 Marriage of Ferdinand of Aragon and Isabella of Castile, uniting the principal powers of Spain; Lorenzo di Piero de' Medici ('Lorenzo the Magnificent') assumes *de facto* control in Florence after the death of his father

1475 First female-authored books printed in Italy (works by Saints Catherine of Siena and Catherine of Bologna); first dated Hebrew book published in Italy (a commentary on the Torah, published in Reggio Calabria); Angelo Poliziano begins his epic *Stanzas for the Joust* (*Stanze per la giostra*), abandoned in 1478 after the murder of its protagonist Giuliano de' Medici in the Pazzi conspiracy; Vatican Library founded by Sixtus IV (Francesco della Rovere)

1476 First Greek book published in Italy (a grammar text by Constantine Lascaris)

1478 Pazzi conspiracy in Florence; murder of Giuliano de' Medici and attempt on the life of Lorenzo de' Medici in Florence cathedral; Inquisition introduced in Spain

1480 Ottoman siege of Otranto in Puglia; threat of Ottoman invasion of the south of Italy, cut short by death of Sultan Mehmet II in 1481

1482–3 Publication of the first two books of Matteo Maria Boiardo's romance, *Orlando innamorato* (*Orlando in Love*), generally considered the greatest vernacular poem of the fifteenth century, together with Poliziano's *Stanzas*

1484 Marsilio Ficino's Latin translation of Plato's dialogues printed in Florence

1485 Accession of the first Tudor monarch, Henry VII, in England

1488 First secular work by a female author printed in Italy (an oration by Cassandra Fedele)

1492 Columbus's first voyage to New World; fall of last Muslim stronghold in Spain, in Granada; expulsion of Jews from Spain; death of Lorenzo de' Medici; accession of Pope Alexander VI (Rodrigo Borgia)

1494 Charles VIII of France invades Italy, marking beginning of Wars of Italy; Medici family exiled from Florence and republic restored

1495 Naples falls briefly into French hands; French expelled by a league formed by Alexander VI; Leonardo da Vinci begins painting *Last Supper* in Milan; Aldo Manuzio begins publication of complete works of Aristotle in Greek in Venice

1497 Vasco da Gama embarks on what is to prove the first sea voyage from Europe to India, via Cape of Good Hope

1498 Execution of politically influential fundamentalist preacher Girolamo Savonarola in Florence; Cesare Borgia, son of Alexander VI, renounces cardinalate to become leader of his father's troops

1499 Louis XII of France occupies Milan, ousting Lodovico Sforza; Cesare Borgia begins his campaigns in the Romagna, capturing Imola and Forlì

1500 Louis XII and Ferdinand II of Aragon agree in the Treaty of Granada to split Naples and southern Italy between them, after forcing out the king of Naples, Federico IV d'Aragona

1501 Aldo Manuzio launches first small-format (*octavo*) series of literary classics with an edition of Virgil; Michelangelo begins work on *David*, the first free-standing colossal nude sculpture of the Renaissance (completed 1504)

1503 Death of Pope Alexander VI; election of Julius II (Giuliano della Rovere); first publication of Amerigo Vespucci's *The New World*, a Latin translation of a letter describing his voyage to Venezuela and Brazil

1504 Louis XII relinquishes Naples to Spanish rule in Treaty of Lyon; Jacopo Sannazaro's *Arcadia* published in Naples, the first Renaissance pastoral romance

1506 Julius II initiates rebuilding of St Peter's in Rome, continuing to 1615

1508 Formation of the papal-led League of Cambrai against Venice; Michelangelo starts work on Sistine Chapel ceiling for Julius II, continuing to 1512; Lodovico Ariosto writes *La Cassaria* [*The Play of the Strongbox*], initiating the Renaissance tradition of vernacular comedies based on classical models

1509 Venetian defeat at Battle of Agnadello results in complete (though temporary) loss of Venice's mainland empire; Raphael begins work on the Stanza della Segnatura for Julius II, continuing to 1512; accession of Henry VIII of England

1511 First edition of Erasmus's *Praise of Folly*

1513 Death of Julius II; accession of Leo X (Giovanni de' Medici); return of Medici to Florence; Niccolò Machiavelli writes *The Prince*; first comedy involving a cross-dressed female character performed at Urbino (Bernardo Dovizi da Bibbiena, *La Calandra*)

1515 Baldassare Castiglione completes first version of *Book of the Courtier* (published in a revised version, 1528); accession of François I as king of France

1516 First publication of Ariosto's romance *Orlando furioso* (revised 1521 and 1532); publication of Thomas More's *Utopia* and Pietro Pomponazzi's *On the Immortality of the Soul*; accession of Charles I, of the Hapsburg dynasty, to throne of Spain

1517 Martin Luther posts 95 theses in Wittenberg, initiating Protestant Reformation

1519 Accession of Charles I of Spain as Holy Roman Emperor Charles V; Ferdinand Magellan embarks on voyage of circumnavigation of the globe, completed by a handful of survivors in 1522

1520 Titian starts work on *Bacchus and Ariadne*, the first of his great mythological paintings for the *studiolo* of Alfonso I d'Este in Ferrara

1521 Hernán Cortes completes overthrow of the Aztec Empire in Mexico, following the death of Moctezuma II in 1520

1524 First publication of Machiavelli's *The Mandrake Root*, the most famous Italian Renaissance comedy (written *c.* 1518)

1525 French defeat at Battle of Pavia; François I taken prisoner by the Spanish; foundation of Accademia degli Intronati in Siena, the first formal literary academy; publication of Pietro Bembo's *Prose della volgar lingua (Dialogues on the Vernacular)*, establishing the Tuscan of Petrarch and Boccaccio as the basis for literary Italian

1526 Sannazaro's *De partu Virginis (On the Virgin Birth)* published, the most important Latin religious epic of the period

1527 Sack of Rome by German mercenaries; Medici family exiled from Florence; last Florentine republic, continuing to 1530

1529 Siege of Vienna by the Turks under Suleiman I 'the Magnificent', marking the furthest reach of Turkish aggression in central Europe

1530 Coronation of Charles V by Pope Clement VII in Bologna; Girolamo Fracastoro publishes the Latin epic *Syphilis*, coining the modern term for an illness that first appeared in Europe in the 1490s

1532 First volume of François Rabelais's *Gargantua and Pantagruel* published

1534 Act of Supremacy in England seals Henry VIII's break with Rome

1536 Michelangelo begins work on *Last Judgment* in the Vatican (to 1541); Tuscan architect Jacopo Sansovino begins his transformation of St Mark's Square in Venice

1538 Pirated edition of Vittoria Colonna's poems published, the first secular verse collection by a woman to appear in print; Pietro Aretino publishes first volume of *Letters*, the first vernacular letter-collection in print

1540 Jesuit order approved by Pope Paul III (Alessandro Farnese)
1543 Andreas Vesalius publishes *On the Fabric of the Human Body*, the most important Renaissance anatomical work; Veronica Gambara admitted to Bolognese Accademia dei Sonnacchiosi, the first woman to be admitted to a literary academy
1545 Opening of Council of Trent to debate reform of Roman Catholic Church (continuing to 1563); first recorded *commedia dell'arte* company formed; Benvenuto Cellini casts the bronze statue *Perseus and Medusa* for Cosimo I de' Medici, duke of Florence
1546 First monographic publication of Vittoria Colonna's *Spiritual verse*, the founding work of the tradition of Petrarchist religious verse
1548 First recorded instance of actresses appearing on stage, in an Italian troupe performing Bibbiena's *La Calandra* in Lyon
1549 First European missionary visit to Japan led by Basque Jesuit Francis Xavier
1550 First edition of Giorgio Vasari's *Lives of the Artists* published (revised edition 1568); Giovanni Battista Ramusio begins publishing *Navigations and Voyages*, continuing to 1559
1554 First three parts of Matteo Bandello's *Novellas* published: along with Sannazaro's *Arcadia*, the most influential vernacular narrative work of the period and the source for Shakespeare's *Romeo and Juliet*
1556 Accession of Philip II of Spain
1558 Accession of Elizabeth I of England; posthumous publication of the works of Giovanni della Casa, author of an influential verse-collection and the conduct text *Galateo*
1559 Treaty of Cateau-Cambrésis marks definitive end of Wars of Italy; Pope Paul IV issues first papal Index of Prohibited Books
1560 First, partial publication of Luigi Tansillo's *Le lagrime di San Pietro (The Tears of St Peter)* (complete edition 1585), launching vogue for vernacular religious narrative in the style of Ariosto
1561 Posthumous publication of Francesco Guicciardini's influential *History of Italy*, centred on the period of the Wars of Italy

1562 Beginning of French Wars of Religion, continuing to 1598

1563 Foundation of Accademia delle Arti del Disegno in Florence, the first artistic academy in Italy

1564 Jacopo Tintoretto begins painting the Scuola di San Rocco in Venice, continuing to 1588

1568 Maddalena Casulana, *First Book of Madrigals*, the first printed volume of music composed by a woman

1570 Publication of Andrea Palladio's *Four Books of Architecture*, the most influential Renaissance architectural treatise

1571 Fall of Cyprus to the Turks, followed by Christian naval victory at Battle of Lepanto

1572 St Bartholomew's Day Massacre in France

1573 First performance of Torquato Tasso's *Aminta*, the most famous pastoral drama of the Renaissance (first published 1581)

1575 Torquato Tasso completes his great epic of the crusades, *Gerusalemme liberata (Jerusalem Delivered)* (first published 1581)

1580 First edition of Michel de Montaigne's *Essays* published; Alfonso II d'Este forms the *concerto delle donne* in Ferrara

1582 Jesuit Matteo Ricci's first mission to China

1584 Tipografia Medicea Orientale founded under the patronage of Cardinal Ferdinando de' Medici to publish religious and scientific texts in Arabic translation, and to search out manuscripts in Arabic and Persian

1585 Teatro Olimpico in Vicenza inaugurated: the first purpose-built permanent theatre in Italy, built to a design by Palladio

1588 Defeat of Spanish Armada; publication of Isabella Andreini's *Mirtilla*, and Maddalena Campiglia's *Flori*, the first two secular plays by women to appear in print

1589 Galileo Galilei appointed to his first academic post, at University of Pisa

c. 1590 William Shakespeare begins career as playwright

1598 Jacopo Peri's *Dafne*, often considered the first opera, performed in Florence; Edict of Nantes ends French Wars of Religion; Ferrara devolves to papal rule after the death of Duke Alfonso II d'Este

1599 Michelangelo Merisi da Caravaggio's first major commissions in Rome

1600 Philosopher Giordano Bruno executed for heresy in Rome
1602 Giovanni Battista Marino's verse published, marking beginning of literary Baroque movement
1603 Foundation of Accademia dei Lincei (Academy of the Lynx-Eyed) in Rome, the most important scientific academy of early modern Italy
1605 First part of Miguel de Cervantes's *Don Quijote* published
1607 Claudio Monteverdi's first opera, *Orfeo*, performed in Mantua; initial foundation of Jamestown, the first permanent English settlement in North America

1

WHAT? WHERE? WHEN? WHOSE?

THE AGE OF REBIRTH

The language of historical periodization is so much part of common currency that it is easy to use terms such as 'medieval' and 'Renaissance' without particularly pondering their meaning. These are complex terms, however, with complex histories, and they carry a good deal of invisible ideological baggage. 'Renaissance', of course, literally signifies 'rebirth'. But what exactly are we claiming was reborn?

This deceptively simple question is best answered by revisiting the history of the notion of 'Renaissance' as we use it today. Although the term was first coined by Jules Michelet in his *History of France* (1855), it was conceptually crystallized in the Swiss historian Jacob Burckhardt's *The Civilization of the Renaissance in Italy*, a pioneering work first published in German in 1860 and in English in 1878. In a manner that reflects the philosophical influence of Hegel, Burckhardt sought to produce an account of Italian fifteenth- and sixteenth-century culture that embraced political, social, and intellectual history, all seen as reflections of the same unifying *Zeitgeist*, or 'spirit of the age'.[1]

Burckhardt's answer to the question of what was reborn in Renaissance Italy was most fundamentally the human spirit. In Burckhardt's representation, medieval culture was informed by abstraction and unworldliness, deriving from a transcendental, religious worldview. Men looked upwards to heaven, scorning or ignoring the material world around them. The Renaissance, by contrast, was marked by a reprise of the kind of vigorous attention to the world that had characterized classical antiquity; in Burckhardt's dramatic metaphor, the 'veil' that had obfuscated medieval man's vision 'melted into air' (p. 98). The natural and social worlds came into focus and became an object of a new and inexhaustible curiosity, manifested in phenomena such as the development of anatomical study and the growth of a new science of politics. At the same time, the inner world of the self became a focus of scrutiny; 'man became a spiritual individual and recognized himself as such' (p. 98).

This emphasis on the individual has an important part to play in Burckhardt's conception of the novelty and modernity of this period, and it led him to hail the Italian of the Renaissance as the 'first-born among the sons of modern Europe' (p. 98). In the Middle Ages, for Burckhardt, men conceived of themselves only as part of some larger social group, such as a family, a religious order, a guild or corporation. The Renaissance saw the birth of the self-conscious individual: proud of his quiddities, confident of his self-mastery, abounding with intellectual vigour. In his finest guise, this individual incarnates the type of the universal 'Renaissance man', perhaps Burckhardt's most lasting conceptual legacy. As an example, Burckhardt cites the Florentine intellectual Leon Battista Alberti, author of the first modern treatises on painting, sculpture, and architecture, and of dark, witty philosophical satires imitating the Syrian-Greek sophist Lucian. Alberti was also a practising sculptor and architect, a talented musician, a key figure in the early history of cryptography, and, in Burckhardt's endearingly eccentric account, a man of such remarkable physical prowess that he could flick a coin to the height of the dome of Florence cathedral and leap over a man's head from a standing start (p. 102).

Not all was quite so solar in Burckhardt's vision of the Renaissance. The titanic individuals that stride through his pages include not only artists and scientists, but also despots like Cesare Borgia, possessed of an amoral, Nietzschean will to power (Nietzsche was a colleague of Burckhardt's at the university of Basel and an admirer of his work). The Italian Renaissance was for Burckhardt the crucible of modernity in its disturbing, as well as its admirable, aspects: godless, cynical, zestfully Promethean, possessed of an inexhaustible, explosive, all-encompassing creativity. Even the political world became subject to this creativity, for Burckhardt; the Renaissance prince crafted his state as a 'work of art'.

The imaginative power of Burckhardt's construction of the Italian Renaissance was such as to leave a long shadow. For much of the twentieth century, scholarly descriptions of the period remained largely Burckhardtian in flavour, and, even today, popular accounts of the tour-guide type retain some Burckhardtian commonplaces intact. Within scholarship, meanwhile, Burckhardt's majestic Victorian edifice has been meticulously demolished, brick by brick. Today's scholarly 'Renaissance man' is less atomistically individualistic than Burckhardt's and distinctly more corporate, his identity inflected to a large extent by affiliations of kinship and *amicitia* (a term with a meaning somewhere between 'friendship' and 'networking'). He is also godlier than Burckhardt's figure, his faith providing a strong vein of continuity with his medieval forebears, so that sharp distinctions between 'medieval' and 'Renaissance' become increasingly difficult to maintain.

More than the mystical rebirth of the human spirit, it is the phenomenon that Burckhardt relegates to second place in his description of the Renaissance, the revival of interest in classical antiquity, that today seems more robust and defensible as a way of capturing and defining the cultural novelties of the age. That 'the individual' was born between 1300 and 1500 is a generalization most modern historians would find problematic. That artistic and literary style changed radically over this period is a matter of fact. The same may be said of styles of thought and argument, and of the range and variety of conceptual tools available to thinkers. Italians—or elite Italians—asked different questions of the world in 1500 than they did in 1300, and they came up with different answers. Their imagination was furnished differently, as were their cities and houses. They represented the world to themselves in different ways. Much of this cultural transformation was due to their intense and prolonged engagement with classical culture, and the extraordinarily vibrant dialogue this triggered between ancient models and modern needs.

Of course, the new and keen interest in the classical world that characterized the Renaissance did not 'just happen'. Italian readers turned with new curiosity and urgency to classical texts, artefacts and ruins, because the world of Greece and Rome had a relevance and a resonance for them that had not been so obvious in the earlier Middle Ages. Europe in general had witnessed an economic reprise from the eleventh century onwards, and trade, communications, and infrastructure steadily improved across the following centuries, despite the catastrophe of the Black Death in the fourteenth. In Italy, the twelfth and thirteenth centuries in particular saw massive commercial expansion and a sharp trend towards urbanization, especially in the centre and north (Fig. 1). The most rapidly growing city of all, Florence, had to expand the reach of its city walls to accommodate its burgeoning population in the 1170s and again from the 1280s. The second of these expansion projects, concluded in the 1330s, increased the size of the city to three or four times its previous extent.[2] An urbanization rate of 27 per cent has been calculated for Tuscany in 1300, at a time when the average across Europe was 10 per cent.[3]

Northern Italy's precocious urbanization was only one of the features that distinguished it from most European territories in this period. The wealth of the northern Italian cities derived principally from trade and commerce, and also increasingly from banking and financial services, a sector in which Florence took the lead. By the fourteenth century, the ruling class of a city like Florence was made up of wealthy merchants and merchant-bankers, flanked by well-educated notaries and lawyers. This was a very different world from most of northern Europe, where power lay predominantly in the hands of a landed feudal aristocracy under a king. In the thirteenth century, most of the cities of northern Italy governed themselves as independent city-republics on the model of ancient Greece or Rome, having wrested political independence from their nominal political overlord, the Holy Roman Empire, late in the previous century. These republics or 'communes' (*comuni*) were governed first by consuls, then later, increasingly, by guild-based governments, in a manner that reflects the importance of trade and the professions within late-medieval Italian civic life.

It is understandable that this wealthy, urban, and precociously proto-capitalistic society would not find itself fully reflected or expressed in medieval Christian culture, which had evolved largely in monastic and other ecclesiastical contexts. It seems predictable, as well, that in Italy, on lands saturated in classical reminiscences and surrounded by the impressive physical remains of classical culture, it

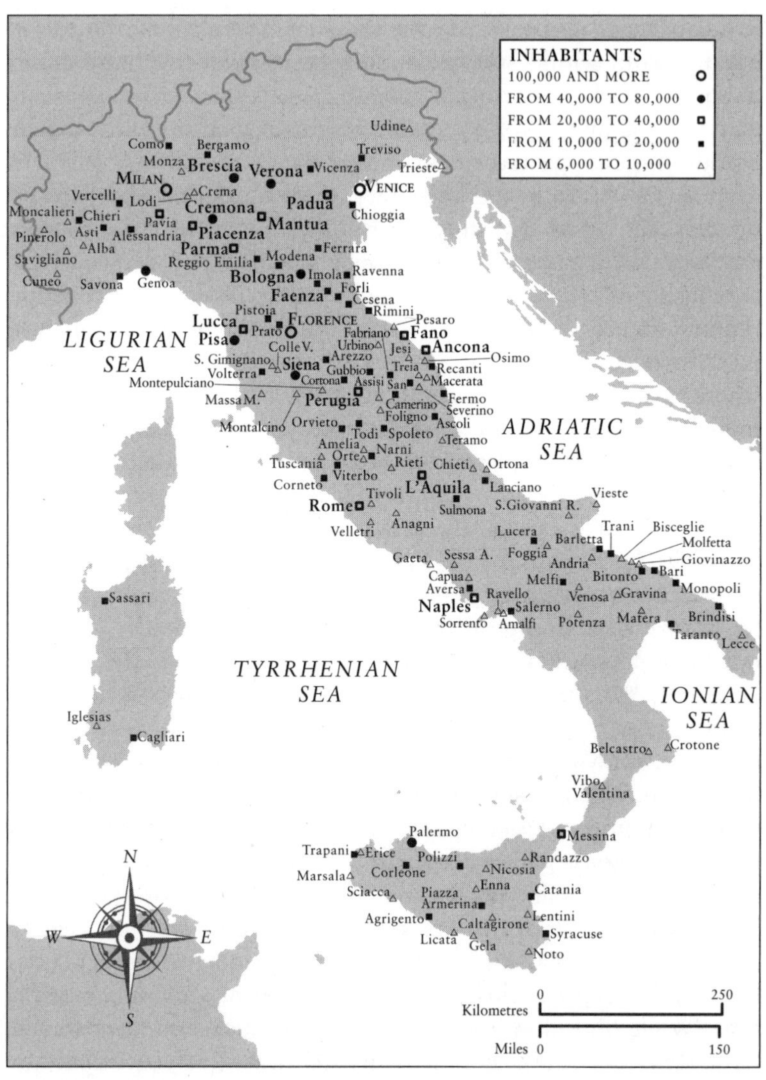

Fig 1: Map of Italy, *c.* 1300, showing extent of urbanization

would be to the ancient world that this society would look. Already in the thirteenth century, we find an impressive number of translations of ancient works appearing in Italy, suggesting that classical learning had a strong appeal for constituencies far beyond the Latin-literate worlds of the clergy and the notariate.[4]

It is the breadth and the practical bent of this attraction to the classical world that distinguishes the Italian Renaissance from the previous, medieval classical 'renaissances' that scholars have identified. Impressive though the Carolingian and the twelfth-century French renaissances were in their output, they remained the province of a limited elite.[5] This was not the case in Italy, where, from the later thirteenth and fourteenth centuries onwards, pioneering scholarly work on the classics was accompanied by a more grassroots interest in how classical learning might be appropriated and deployed in everyday life. The extraordinarily high literacy rate of Italy's merchant cities is an important consideration here. The fourteenth-century Florentine chronicler Giovanni Villani estimated that, when he was writing, in the 1330s, around 8,000 to 10,000 boys and girls were in elementary school in Florence, out of a population he estimates at around 90,000 (by modern estimates, 120,000). A further 1,000 to 1,200 adolescents were studying the business curriculum at abacus schools, and 550 to 600 were studying Latin.[6] Remarkable though these figures are for the period, Villani's statistics find confirmation in other evidence. Fifteenth-century Florentine census results confirm that 80 per cent of heads of household had sufficient literacy to sign their names.[7]

Reorienting our understanding of the Renaissance from Burckhardt's mystical 'human spirit' interpretation to one centred on the revival of classical culture has the advantage of bringing our modern-day analysis closer to the perception of intellectuals at the time. While fifteenth-century Latin has no exact equivalent for the term 'Renaissance', the notion existed and was clearly articulated by the early fifteenth century that a new and superior age was opening in cultural terms, defined by a return to the insuperable norms of classical culture after a long parenthesis of ignorance and 'darkness'. This represented an inversion of the historiographical narrative that had dominated within medieval Christian culture, which represented the classical world, despite its cultural sophistication, as benighted on account of its ignorance of the salvific truths of Christian revelation, and which saw the passage from 'darkness' to illumination as coinciding with the incarnation of Christ. This fifteenth-century historiographical revision effectively invented the modern narrative of the successive eras of 'classical', 'medieval', and 'Renaissance' (or 'modern'), as well as laying the conceptual foundation for a term such as the 'Dark Ages', a notion that would have perplexed the medieval mind.

Although any account of the Italian Renaissance must give centrality to the phenomenon of classical study and imitation, it would be reductive to see the extraordinary energies of this period as arising from classicism alone. As we have already seen, Renaissance Italy's imaginative engagement with the classical world may be seen more appropriately as a symptom than a cause, within a rapidly changing society that had in a sense begun to outgrow its own culture. Further dramatic changes were in store for fifteenth- and sixteenth-century Italians, as for Europeans in general. By the 1450s, the great communications revolution triggered by the introduction of print technology in the West was underway. In the 1490s, the known world dramatically expanded with the discovery of the 'new' lands beyond the Atlantic. By 1520, medieval Christendom was undergoing what would prove a permanent religious schism, with the coming of the Reformation.

It was against this dynamic and challenging background that the classicizing movement of the Italian Renaissance grew to maturity, and we should not perhaps be surprised that what resulted was so strikingly dynamic in turn. Although they took their cue from the classical world, Italian Renaissance art, thought, and literature were very far from being backward looking or tritely derivative. In some ways, the metaphor of 'rebirth', applied to the Renaissance, is misleading, in that it suggests a revivification of something that has already existed in the past. More than a simple 'rebirth' of classical culture in its pristine, ancient form, what we see in this period is something incorporating elements of both recovery and creative dialogue—both patient archeological work addressed to piecing together an understanding of the powerful legacy of antiquity, and a re-appropriation and reworking of the resulting discoveries to create something equally powerful, yet new.

THE CULTURAL GEOGRAPHY OF THE ITALIAN RENAISSANCE

Vital to any understanding of Italian Renaissance culture is the fact that there was no such thing, strictly speaking, as an 'Italian' Renaissance. Rather, there were as many Italian Renaissance cultures as there were Italian Renaissance cities. Art historians are, of course, familiar with this principle, and we are used to seeing anonymous works in galleries attributed to the Tuscan or the Venetian school, rather than simply the Italian. The same is true also to a remarkable extent for literary and intellectual history, with the result that the first question scholars in these fields ask in approaching a new writer or thinker tends to be 'where is he (or she) from'?

The importance that regionalism assumed in Italian culture was a result of the peninsula's distinctive political history. In northern and central Italy, throughout much of the Middle Ages, each city and town was effectively self-governing: a city-republic exerting sway over a surrounding country area (*contrada*). Only in the south could a pattern of political authority be observed more reminiscent of that found elsewhere in Europe, that of a united kingdom ruled by a single royal dynasty, presiding over a feudal hierarchy of barons. These southern dynasties were invariably foreign. After a failed attempt in the thirteenth century by the German imperial dynasty of the Hohenstaufen to establish a power base there, southern Italy and Sicily were ruled for most of the fourteenth and fifteenth centuries by the French dynasty of Anjou and by the Iberian dynasty of Aragon, which took over definitively in 1442.

The twelfth and thirteenth centuries were the high point of medieval Italian republicanism, but, by 1300, this political model was already beginning to manifest its precariousness. Over the course of the following century, most of the Italian city-republics devolved into *signorie* or lordships, as powerful local families profited from the political factionalism endemic to these small republican regimes. Twentieth-century scholarship often represented this shift in strongly negative terms, and the Italian lords were frequently referred to as 'despots', a term suggestive of cruel and arbitrary rule. Perspectives have shifted on this point, however, and it is now more usual to emphasize the continuities between republican and seigneurial rule, and the advantages the latter offered urban populaces in terms of security and stability.[8]

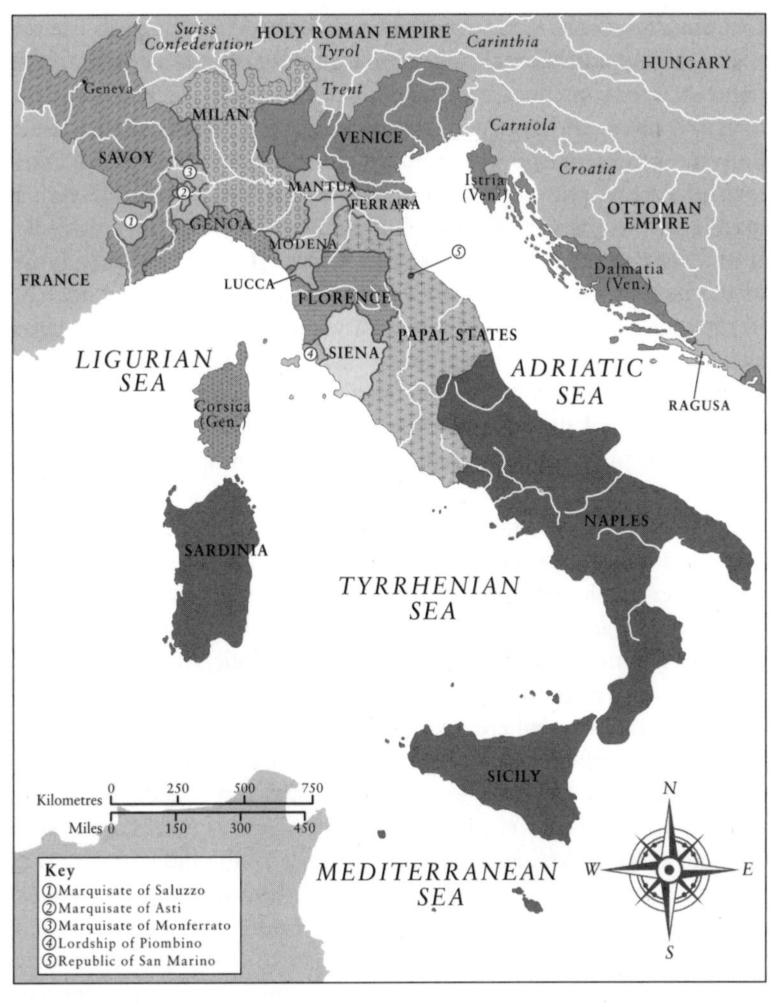

Fig 2: Map of Italy, *c.* 1494, showing main political divisions

Although *signorie* were generally established by warlords, those that survived consolidated over the centuries into quasi-monarchic regimes, acquiring the trappings of legitimate rule, such as imperial or papal titles, and marrying into families that could enhance their prestige. This could be an expensive business. In 1305, Azzo d'Este, lord of Ferrara, invested the huge sum of 51,000 ducats to buy a marriage alliance with the daughter of the king of Naples, Charles II of Anjou. In 1539, still in Ferrara, Ercole II d'Este paid the pope of the day 180,000 ducats to be reconfirmed in his title as duke.[9]

Although northern and central Italy began the thirteenth century as a genuine mosaic of miniature states, its political geography simplified over the course of the next two centuries, as larger cities began to extend their power over the surrounding territory and to subjugate nearby towns. By the later fifteenth century, seven principal regional powers may be observed in the peninsula, along with a few smaller independent states (Fig. 2). The northernmost of the great powers were the duchies of Savoy and Milan, along with the seafaring mercantile republics of Genoa and Venice, the latter of which had acquired an extensive mainland empire in the fifteenth century. South of Milan stood Florence, officially a republic, though under the informal sway of the Medici family for much of the fifteenth century. South of Tuscany, where Florence stood, were the Papal States, extending northwards on the Adriatic coast up to the Romagna, south of Venice. These lands were nominally under the rule of the popes, though in fact they were farmed out to vicarious rulers who were in some cases so well established as to be virtually indistinguishable from independent princes. To the south of the Papal States extended the vast kingdom of Naples, by this point under Aragonese rule.

Once this political background is grasped, it becomes clear why central and northern Italian cities, even small ones, are often so culturally distinctive. Most cities of any size had spent a period of some centuries in the late Middle Ages as independent, self-governing states, often at war with their neighbours. Even those that were subjugated and absorbed by those neighbours retained a keen sense of their own civic identity and history and culture. Indeed, it may well be that the loss of political independence led the former ruling elites of those cities to invest more—literally and metaphorically—in culture, as a form of compensation or displacement. By the mid-sixteenth century, even relatively small towns in central and northern

Italy generally had at least one publishing house, and very often an academy that organized plays and spectacles and fostered literary and sometimes musical production. Their elites spent lavishly on architecture, adding to an already impressive medieval urban legacy. All this cultural activity was conducted with an eye on neighbouring towns, in the emulative spirit that Italians evoke by the term *campanilismo* (literally, 'bell-towerism'—a fierce attachment to the town of one's birth).

The emulative dynamic just noted goes far to explain the extraordinary speed with which cultural novelties were generated and diffused in the Italian Renaissance. In an important work of 1993, the economic historian Richard Goldthwaite argued that the startling rate of stylistic innovation that characterized fifteenth-century Florentine artistic production could be explained by conditions of patronage, and notably the presence in Florence of numerous wealthy families of equal or near-equal status competing with one another for cultural prestige. This created a lively demand for art to which workshops responded increasingly by differentiating their products in formal and stylistic terms. As a result, the capacity to innovate gained a sharp premium, at least at the top end of the market.[10]

Something of a similar dynamic may be observed on a far vaster scale at a national level. Italy's disunity revealed itself a political and military liability in an age in which nation-states were consolidating elsewhere in Europe, but it was an undoubted strength in cultural terms. Rather than a country possessed of a sole capital city, Renaissance Italy was a land of competing capitals. The competitors at this national level were not merely the great powers listed earlier (Milan, Genoa, Venice, Florence, Rome, Naples). Smaller *signorie* such as Ferrara, Mantua, and Urbino, and smaller republics such as Siena, can also be numbered among Italy's key cultural protagonists, as can the larger cities of the Venetian mainland, such as Padua, Verona, Vicenza, and Brescia. Many of these cities ranked much higher in terms of cultural prestige than they did in terms of size or population or wealth. Each had a similar internal competitive patronage market to that described by Goldthwaite in the case of Florence. Even in *signorie*, where the ruling dynasties dominated the patronage of their cities, other elite families and courtiers contributed, eager to enhance the prestige of the city as well as their own prestige within it.[11] 'Magnificence' (*magnificentia*)—sumptuous and tasteful expenditure—was theorized by philosophers as a virtue and even accorded a cautious welcome by preachers as a duty of the civic-minded elite.[12]

The multipolar character of the Italian Renaissance is a point worth underlining, as there has been a tendency in both academic and popular culture to place undue emphasis on Florence, which is often given credit for initiating the movement. This has some justification in art-historical terms, but the notion of Florence as 'cradle of the Renaissance' is far less tenable in the case of literary and intellectual history; as Chapter 2 will make clear, the cities of the Veneto, such as Padua and Verona, have a better claim than Florence to this title. Nor is it easy to see, more generally, why Florence should be regarded as representing the apex of Italian Renaissance culture. Even in the fifteenth century, Florence's moment of greatest glory, the city was in competition with other culturally innovative cities, principally Milan, Naples, and the rapidly ascendent power of Rome. In the sixteenth century, Renaissance culture was even more dispersed. Histories of specific facets of Renaissance culture—poetry, drama, music, scientific culture, warfare—each have their own distinctive geographies, in which Florence features to a greater or a lesser extent. Early fifteenth-century art aside, only in a few of these narratives does Florence have a clear claim to precedence, perhaps most notably the history of political thought.

WHEN WAS THE RENAISSANCE?

The question of when the Renaissance began is reasonably well established, though the answer will differ somewhat depending on whether it is considered from the perspective of literary and intellectual history or art history. Where literary history is concerned, current scholarship tends to point to the late thirteenth and early fourteenth centuries for first stirrings, the later fourteenth century for something that may comfortably be called a movement, and the early fifteenth century for the moment when the concerted study of the classics went from being a minority and avant-garde interest to something more approaching mainstream. Art history has a similar trajectory, though less linear, with the impact of classical art and architecture most apparent from the early fifteenth century and important anticipations apparent from the later thirteenth century onwards. Needless to say, this chronology is remarkably precocious by comparison with other countries in Europe, where Renaissance classicism came much later. In England, Geoffrey Chaucer, born in 1343, is conceived of as squarely medieval, as is his successor John Lydgate, born around 1370. In Italy, Francesco Petrarca (b. 1304) and Giovanni Boccaccio (b. 1313) already have good claims to be 'Renaissance men'.

The question of when the Renaissance in Italy ended is a far more difficult and ideologically charged one than the question of when it began. One traditional periodization, largely based on art history, posited an 'Early Renaissance' in the fifteenth century, followed by a 'High Renaissance' in the early sixteenth, the latter encompassing the remarkable period in artistic production culminating in Michelangelo's decoration of the Sistine Chapel ceiling (1508–12), and encompassing also the works of Leonardo (d. 1519) and Raphael (d. 1520). Within this narrative, after this insuperable moment, the Renaissance essentially burnt itself out, even though some scholars were prepared to admit the notion of a 'late Renaissance', sometimes referred to as 'mannerism' in art-historical terms. Some extreme versions of this traditional periodization even dramatically posited an exact moment for the end of the Renaissance, with the Sack of Rome in 1527, when Lutheran mercenaries in the service of the Emperor Charles V brutally trashed the city, desecrating its relics, killing and mutilating many of its inhabitants, and provoking a diaspora among those artists who survived.

Among literary and intellectual historians, there has been less of a temptation to posit such an early date as the end of the Renaissance. In these fields, the tendency has been to see a date of around the mid-sixteenth century as the key turning point, at the time of the Council of Trent (1545–63), the great, decades-long meeting of Catholic clerics at which the reform imperatives of the movement known as the Counter-Reformation were defined. The Council of Trent was summoned in part as a defensive response to the Protestant Reformation, but in part also as a response to widespread calls for reform within the Catholic Church itself. The Council's remit was principally doctrine and church discipline, but, in the second half of the sixteenth century, under a series of reforming popes, concerted attempts were also made to bring secular culture under some kind of moral control. The most striking manifestation of this was the introduction on a national level of print censorship, resulting in the banning or bowdlerization of texts that were perceived as immoral or licentious, or which voiced anti-clerical views.

Because of this element of repression, the Counter-Reformation has traditionally been regarded in Italy as marking the end of the Renaissance and the beginning of a new age of cultural retrogression that would endure throughout the *ancien régime*. This narrative was soldered into place in Italy shortly after unification in 1861, when new, national histories of Italian literature began to be written. To a figure like Francesco De Sanctis, the founder of the modern Italian tradition of literary history, the Counter-Reformation represented a brutal end-point for the great explosion of creative energies Italy had seen during the period of the Renaissance.[13] The free, questing spirit of intellectual inquiry that had characterized the Renaissance was gradually replaced, through the agencies of church censorship and the Inquisition, with something much meaner and more timorous and convention-bound. Those thinkers who dared still to speculate were executed (like the philosopher Giordano Bruno) or silenced through censorship (like the scientist Galileo Galilei). In literature, too, the sensuous, world-embracing, classicizing works of the Renaissance were replaced by a literature of bigoted and superstitious religiosity. The Counter-Reformation cast Italy, culturally at the forefront of Europe during the Renaissance, back into the outer darkness of a belated Middle Ages.

Forged by Italian scholars but largely accepted by scholars elsewhere, this narrative has essentially maintained its currency almost down to the present day, despite its oddly anachronistic, nineteenth-century character. As a result, the literature and thought of later sixteenth-century Italy have remained significantly under-investigated by comparison with that of the fifteenth and early sixteenth centuries. Indeed, the flourishing and inventive tradition of Counter-Reformation religious literature is still virtually a 'lost continent', despite some signs of interest in recent years.[14] This model of cultural periodization has endured in Italian literature even as the 'black legend' of the repressive and backward-looking Counter-Reformation has been dispelled within the discipline of religious history. Most religious historians now see the Protestant

Reformation in the North and the Catholic Reformation in the South as parallel movements, rather than regarding the first as a grassroots religious movement and the second as an institutionally orchestrated campaign of spiritual and societal discipline, as was common until a few decades ago.[15]

Curious anomalies have resulted from the historiographical situation just outlined. As an example, the relative cultural prominence of women in Italian elite society in the fifteenth and especially the early sixteenth century has always been seen as a striking sign of the open-mindedness and 'modernity' of the Italian Renaissance. In a breathtaking exaggeration, Burckhardt even went so far as to assert that during this golden period 'women stood on a footing of perfect equality with men' (p. 250). Within traditional scholarly accounts, this extraordinary moment of female cultural emergence came to an end with the patriarchal and conservative social policies of the Counter-Reformation, which forced women back into traditional domestic roles and drove them from their tentative foothold in the cultural sphere.

What is odd about this view is that it flies entirely in the face of the empirical evidence, which shows Italian women's literary activity not only continuing but also actively flourishing after 1560. The decades from around 1580 to 1610, at the height of the Counter-Reformation's influence on Italian culture, mark the time when Italian women writers were at their boldest and most experimental (see Chapter 6 for further discussion). Women were also active during this period as painters, as musicians, and as actresses. A figure like the actress Isabella Andreini, author of a witty and sensual pastoral drama and a volume of sometimes faintly salacious lyric poems, is hard to square with traditional notions of the Counter-Reformation as an age of bigotry and obscurantism; yet Andreini was born as the Council of Trent was closing, and she ended her life in 1604.

Bearing in mind evidence such as this, it seems wise to define the chronological boundaries of the Italian Renaissance with sufficient elasticity to encompass the later sixteenth century—and perhaps even the first decade of the seventeenth century, when it becomes more illuminating to speak of the Baroque. Like later sixteenth-century music and art, so later sixteenth-century literature drew liberally on earlier Renaissance traditions, at the same time that it experimented with newer, proto-Baroque aesthetics and sensibilities. A term like 'late-Renaissance' makes perfect sense for this cultural production. It is true that religious subject matter became more common during the Counter-Reformation in art, music, and literature, but it flourished alongside secular subject matter, instead of replacing it. Besides, once we have disposed of the last remnants of the nineteenth-century myth of a neo-pagan Renaissance (see Chapter 2), there seems no reason to suppose that, because a work is religious, it cannot be 'Renaissance' as well.

WHOSE WAS THE RENAISSANCE?

At the time when the modern notion of the Renaissance was forged in the nineteenth century, talk of an undifferentiated 'man' to designate humanity was not regarded as problematic, even when that 'man', on closer inspection, generally meant 'elite, literate, urban man with the money to afford books and the leisure to study'. Talk of 'man' undergoing a spiritual revolution in this period, as was common in the nineteenth century, reveals this cultural myopia distinctly.

Modern historiographical trends have quite rightly debunked this tendency to a universalism blind to considerations of race, class, and gender. An essay of the 1970s, famous in the field, by the American historian Joan Kelly-Gadol, asked 'Did women have a Renaissance?'[16] Similar questions might be framed about non-elite men, or about racial or religious outsiders such as Italy's fairly large Jewish population. The nature of these questions has, of course, changed with the changing definition of what 'having a Renaissance' might mean. As Burckhardt's 'transformation of the human spirit' and 'birth of the individual' have given way to a less mystical conception of the Renaissance as a cultural movement, the question has become less whether a given subject-group metamorphosed in this period into a cohort of free, questing, self-defining individuals, cut loose from the constraints of collective identity, but rather whether a given subject-group participated in the cultural transformation of the Renaissance, with all the legacy of intellectual enrichment that implies. When we speak of a cultural transformation brought about through a galvanizing encounter with the classical world, are we speaking of something that affected only an extremely narrow—and male—social elite?

The answer to this changes somewhat depending on the periodization we posit for the Renaissance, which is one reason why chronological questions are so crucial. A cut-off point of 1527 or 1560 produces one answer, a cut-off point of 1600 a rather different one. Similarly, a methodology that isolates a small number of outstanding works of 'high' art and literature and concentrates on issues of authorship and patronage, rather than reception, produces a different answer from a methodology that extends its purview to 'secondary', imitative, more popular works and includes readers and users as well as authors and patrons. If we limit our consideration of Renaissance culture to the former, we will find ourselves inhabiting a world largely composed of dukes, marquises, popes and cardinals, of refined intellectuals and avant-garde artists. If we extend our consideration to the latter, we find ourselves in a more diverse and motley and distinctly more populous universe, whose denizens include merchants, printers, intellectually aspirant artisans, actors, courtesans, lesser artists, jobbing writers for the press.

Considerations of language and communications media are vital in understanding the diffusion of Renaissance culture. Latin was the dominant language of high culture down to the end of the fifteenth century, and texts tended to circulate largely in manuscript or in the relatively expensive printed books produced in the early decades of print technology. Both these factors limited the extent of the dissemination of the literary and intellectual novelties of the Renaissance. From the turn of the sixteenth century, as the cost of printing came down and print-runs increased, books began to become accessible to ever-larger segments of the public. At the same time, the vernacular grew in status as a viable and dignified alternative to Latin, not merely for creative writing, but also for works of philosophy, technical treatises, and other didactic literature. This vernacular turn drew momentum from the commercial considerations of printers keen to exploit the ample market of readers from outside Latin-literate milieus.

As a result of the greater availability of books and printers' attentiveness to the needs of their vernacular readership, classical learning became considerably more accessible in the later sixteenth century. Already in the fifteenth century, vernacular translations had played an important role in disseminating classical and humanistic literature in manuscript.[17] In the sixteenth, the volume of printed translations vastly increased, making a very substantial portion of classical literature accessible to a broad literate public, including women, who were rarely educated in Latin. At the same time, editions of vernacular classics such as Lodovico Ariosto's great chivalric romance *Orlando furioso* (*The Madness of Orlando*) began to appear with commentaries identifying their allusions to and imitations of classical texts, allowing non Latin-literate readers to participate in Italian elite culture's rich dialogue with the classical past.[18] By the late sixteenth century, it was possible for an adept writer to give a decent impression of classical learning with no acquaintance whatsoever with Latin.

It was not, of course, through books alone that the innovations of the Renaissance permeated the broader urban culture of Italy. A Venetian in 1550 wandering down the Piazzetta by the Ducal Palace to lay a bet at the gambling stalls that stood there would pass Jacopo Sansovino's newly constructed Loggetta, with its statues of Minerva, Mars, and Apollo. A Florentine of 1600 walking through the main piazza of her city could muse on such edifying tales in stone as Benvenuto Cellini's *Perseus with the Slain Medusa* of 1545, or Giambologna's recent *Abduction of the Sabine Woman*, completed in 1582. In addition to these fixtures, Renaissance cities regularly transmuted into stage sets to celebrate events such as dynastic marriages and diplomatic visits, their streets and piazzas filled with elaborate temporary architecture, which often served as a vehicle for allegorical or historical messages, helpfully spelled out in vernacular print texts that served as souvenirs for these events. For the 1589 wedding of Ferdinando I de' Medici and Christine of Lorraine in Florence, no fewer than seven triumphal arches were constructed in the city, all lavishly painted with images representing the glories of the two dynasties and the history of Florence. If medieval church paintings served as the 'bible of the unlettered', the streets of Renaissance cities must have similarly tutored intellectually curious observers in the classical past.

A vivid account of this filtering down of classical learning may be found in the verse autobiography of the Bolognese popular poet and street performer Giulio Cesare Croce (1550–1609). Croce was the son of a blacksmith and began life in his father's trade. In his verse autobiography, he constructs a paradigmatic tale of his transformation from blacksmith into poet, which he wryly represents as the result of an encounter with Ovid's *Metamorphoses*, the classical world's greatest epic of mutation. Croce recounts how a grocer neighbour lent him an ancient copy of Ovid, which he had bought along with other scrap paper (*scartafacci*) to wrap lard and cheese in his shop. His attention first caught by the book's illustrations of shape-shifting gods, the young blacksmith soon found himself enthralled.[19] Transfigured by this experience, Croce launched a poetic career that would fascinatingly contaminate low and high culture. His works range from pastoral idylls and high-flown compliments to local dignitaries to songs in dialect celebrating the clamour of the piazza, with its raucous street cries, or dramatizing a dialogue between a mother and daughter as they delouse their hair. We are far here from the sublimity of Michelangelo's Sistine Chapel or from the dazzling attainments of Burckhardt's Renaissance hero Leon Battista Alberti. Arguably, however, a more capacious Renaissance, capable of embracing also a figure like Croce, can capture the dynamics of this remarkable cultural movement more accurately than one that remains on the heights.

2

THE RENAISSANCE AND THE ANCIENT

THE BIRTH OF HUMANISM

In the autumn of 1416, the Tuscan intellectual Poggio Bracciolini was in Switzerland, attending the Council of Constance in his capacity as papal administrator. During his leisure time, he pursued his hobby of book-hunting, scouring monastic collections in the hope of unearthing rare manuscripts. In a visit to the ancient Benedictine monastery of St Gall, he struck gold.

> There amid a tremendous quantity of books, which it would take too long to describe, we found Quintilian still safe and sound, though filthy with mould and dust. For these books were not in the library, as befitted their worth, but in a sort of foul and gloomy dungeon at the bottom of one of the towers, where not even men convicted of a capital offence would have been stuck away.[1]

Poggio's letter, to the classical scholar Guarino da Verona, vividly conveys the excitement and sense of drama that surrounded discoveries of this kind. The principal work Poggio discovered on this occasion was Quintilian's *The Education of the Orator*, the most complete classical treatise on rhetoric and a major source for Roman education, aesthetics, and values. Up to this point, Quintilian's text had been known only in *mutili*, as philologists evocatively call incomplete manuscripts. The previous texts were, in Poggio's words, 'so fragmentary ... so cut down by the action of time ... that the shape and style of the man had become unrecognizable'. Poggio presents his discovery in dramatic terms, as a last-ditch rescue: 'By Heaven, if we had not brought help, [Quintilian] would surely have perished the very next day.'

At the time of Poggio's great discovery, Italian intellectuals' quest to reconstruct the culture of classical antiquity was already more than a century old, and the movement was finally on the cusp of translating from a private, scholarly obsession, pursued by a dedicated network of enthusiasts, into something more institutionalized and widespread. The Renaissance started small. The origins of this classicizing movement—often known as 'humanism', for reasons explained below—can be traced to a small clique of late thirteenth-century intellectuals based in the university city of Padua, near Venice. The leading figures were Lovato Lovati, a judge, and Albertino Mussato, a notary, politician, and diplomat. Lovati and Mussato and their circles sought out classical texts, studied their metre and diction, and produced new Latin works in imitation of them, treading self-consciously in the 'footsteps of the ancient poets' (*veterum vestigia vatum*).[2] Lovati composed a series of metrical verse letters closely echoing Ovid and Horace, and produced an edition of Seneca's tragedies, collating two manuscripts. Mussato composed the first post-classical secular tragedy, *Ecerinis* (*c.* 1314–15), depicting the blood-soaked career of the local warlord Ezzelino da Romano (d. 1259), portrayed in the play as literally the devil's spawn. It was during this initial moment of the Renaissance that the first great classical textual discovery was made—that of Catullus's elegant and licentious love poetry, which survived through the Middle Ages in a single manuscript. This surfaced in Verona at some time in the late thirteenth or early fourteenth century, discovered 'under a bushel', or basket, according to a Latin epigram of the time.[3]

One remarkable feature of this first dawn of humanism in Italy is that it occurred so early. Mussato (1261–1329) is an almost exact contemporary of the Florentine poet Dante Alighieri (1265–1321), whose works represent the pinnacle of medieval poetic and intellectual culture in Italy. Lovati was born around a quarter of a century before Dante; his dates are *c.* 1240–1309. This serves as a reminder that the term 'Renaissance' is understood here as designating a cultural movement rather than a chronological period. It can also act as a reminder of the importance of geography in understanding Italian culture at this time. Where the Paduans Lovati and Mussato wrote exclusively in Latin, the Florentine Dante wrote principally in the vernacular. His few Latin works date from the time of his exile from Florence, after a long stay in Verona, close to Padua and another important centre for early humanism. Dante's relationship with the classics is also quite different from that of his northern contemporaries. Vivid as his response was to those classical authors he knew well, especially Virgil and Ovid, he seems to have been content with what was essentially the school 'grammar' (i.e. literature) curriculum. He shows little of the impulse we see in Lovati and Mussato to seek out more arcane and less visited texts. As much as by the classics, Dante's intellectual horizons were shaped by contemporary, scholastic university culture, especially theology, while his literary style mingles classical influences with the powerful legacy of medieval vernacular verse.

Dante's, and Mussato's, great successors, Francesco Petrarca and Giovanni Boccaccio, born in the opening decades of the fourteenth century, were the heirs to both of these traditions, the medieval and the Renaissance. Petrarch produced the crowning work of the medieval tradition of love lyric in his *Rerum vulgarium fragmenta* (*Vernacular Fragments*), also often referred to as the *Canzoniere*, or *Songbook*, while Boccaccio produced the first great prose masterpiece of Italian, the *Decameron*, drawing on the medieval tradition of *novelle* or *fabliaux*. Both writers also showed a zeal for classical culture reminiscent of the circles of Lovati and Mussato—Petrarch from the beginning of his career, Boccaccio especially during the second half of his. Both writers did important work in compiling and popularizing classical knowledge. Petrarch wrote a compilation of classical and biblical biographies, *On Famous Men*, which Boccaccio later complemented with his *On Famous Women*. Boccaccio also compiled a guide to classical mythology, *The Genealogy of the Pagan Gods*, prefacing the work with a powerful defence of the moral legitimacy of reading pagan poetry, despite its appearance, to a Christian, of being made up of 'lies'. Petrarch was responsible for reviving several classical literary genres, such as the personal letter, the dialogue (*On the Secret Cares of My Soul*), and the historical epic (*Africa*). This last-mentioned text is one of the earliest neo-classical works to deal with a classical subject-matter (the Punic Wars between Rome and Carthage)—a distinctly 'Renaissance' project, and one that helps underline the profound cultural gulf that separated Petrarch from Dante.[4]

Petrarch was similarly a precursor of the mature Renaissance in the range of his classical interests. Like Lovati's circle, he was not content with the relatively thin diet of classic writings that survived in the medieval educational curriculum, and he devoted much energy to seeking out little-known texts. In 1333 in Lièges, he discovered Cicero's oration *Pro Archia*, with its impassioned praise of the civilizing role of poetry and literature. A decade later in Verona, he came across a manuscript containing Cicero's letters to Atticus—the work that inspired him to embark on his own vast and fascinating epistolary corpus, his most original and influential Latin work. While these are his chief 'finds', Petrarch also succeeded in laying his hands on numerous other rare classical works, exploiting his extensive network of friends in Italy, France, and Germany. He was an early reader of Catullus, of Propertius, and of Quintilian (in a *mutilus* version), and he painstakingly assembled the most complete manuscript of Livy's *History of Rome* known in his day. Boccaccio followed his lead in this regard, seeking out rarities such as Tacitus's *Annals*, Varro's *On the Latin Language*, and Apuleius's *Metamorphoses* (or *Golden Ass*).

In addition to their Latin scholarship, Petrarch and Boccaccio also played an important role in the early history of the study of Greek in the West. Both were keenly aware of the impossibility of understanding classical culture in any depth without direct knowledge of the Greek language. Petrarch made a first attempt to study Greek in Avignon in the 1340s with Barlaam (Bernardo Massari), an Italian-Greek scholar and theologian from Calabria, in southern Italy, where a strong tradition of Byzantine monasticism was found. Petrarch's studies with Barlaam were not sufficient, however, to allow him to read a manuscript of Homer sent to him by a Byzantine diplomat, Nicholas Sigeros, in 1353; in his letter of thanks, Petrarch poignantly speaks of the manuscript remaining mute to him—or he deaf to it—even if he derives pleasure merely from gazing at the text.[5] In the late 1350s and 1360s, a breakthrough seemed possible when Petrarch and Boccaccio made contact with another Greek-speaking Calabrian, Leontius Pilatus, and persuaded him to translate the *Iliad* and *Odyssey* and write commentaries on them. The results were uninspiring. Pilatus's Latin was weak and his translation so literal that Petrarch confessed that beginning to read it had almost made him lose interest in Homer. Before the end of the fourteenth century, the northern humanist Antonio Loschi had offered to recast Pilatus's prose crib in a more ornate Latin verse.[6]

The next important moment in the history of Greek study, more transformative in its effects, occurred in 1397, when the chancellor of Florence, Coluccio Salutati, invited the Byzantine scholar and diplomat Manuel Chrysoloras to teach Greek to the circle of young intellectuals who had gathered in Florence under Salutati's aegis. Pilatus had already attempted to teach Greek in Florence in the 1360s, at Boccaccio's instigation, but little had come of the initiative. Chrysoloras's teaching, by contrast, had the effect of a lit fuse. Through his three years' teaching in Florence, and his later teaching in Pavia and Venice, he produced a talented generation of Greek-literate scholars—the first in the West outside the residual Greek-speaking regions of southern Italy—who set themselves to translating, commenting, and imitating Greek texts. One of Chrysoloras's most brilliant pupils, Leonardo Bruni, who eventually followed Salutati into the role of chancellor of Florence, translated Greek works by Plato, Aristotle, Plutarch, and Demosthenes and wrote historical compendia based on Polybius, Procopius, and Xenophon. Bruni also drew extensively on Greek sources in his independent literary works, perhaps most famously in his *Panegyric of the City of Florence* (*c.* 1403–4), based on an encomium of Athens by the second-century sophist Aelius Aristides: one of the earliest Renaissance speeches composed in classicizing Latin and following classical rhetorical rules.

Bruni's interest in classical oratory hints at the new direction the humanist movement would take in the fifteenth century. Throughout the whole of the previous century, even as it gained in momentum, the classicizing movement in Italy had remained a private, scholarly interest. Public documents and speeches continued to be written in medieval Latin, and according to formal rules drawn up in the *ars dictaminis* ('art of letter writing'), a stripped-down version of classical rhetoric, laying much emphasis on rhythm (*cursus*). Salutati wrote his personal letters in an approximation to classical Latin, but his powerful public voice as Florentine chancellor differs little in style from that of his great thirteenth-century predecessor in the post, Dante's mentor, Brunetto Latini. The classicizing interests of the humanists had not widely inflected school curricula, either, up to this point. Although we know of fourteenth-century university professors who were important conduits for humanism—such as the evocatively nicknamed 'Virgil John' (Giovanni del Virgilio) and 'Rhetoric Peter' (Pietro da Moglio, or Pietro della Retorica)—formal education, both at school and university level, remained largely medieval in character. Cicero's rhetorical theory was taught at the University of Bologna, but as a complement to *ars dictaminis* teaching, and without any intent to encourage students to cultivate a classicizing style.

All this began to change in the very late fourteenth century and the early fifteenth, with the key generation being made up of men born in the 1370s, the first with the opportunity to learn Greek. Besides Bruni and Poggio Bracciolini, humanists of this generation included Pierpaolo Vergerio from Capodistria (now Koper, in Slovenia), the author of the first humanist educational treatise, *On the Noble Manners and Liberal Studies fitted for Adolescents* (1400–1402); the northern Italian scholars and educators Guarino of Verona and Vittorino da Feltre; and the Sicilian Giovanni Aurispa, who studied Greek in Byzantium, bringing back to Italy a remarkable collection of manuscripts, including the sole copy of two of Aeschylus's plays to survive into the modern world. None of these men manifest the same dissonance between their private and public writings that we find with Salutati. Bruni, appointed chancellor of Florence in the 1420s, used his elegant classical Latin for public documents, as well as private letters, and was commissioned by the Florentine government to compose a classicizing *History of Florence*. Vergerio elaborated his educational views while working as tutor to the lord of Padua, and Guarino and Vittorino were invited, respectively, to Ferrara and Mantua, where they established rival schools. Aurispa also taught at Ferrara. Poggio, though a layman, spent his life in the service of the papacy, which was in these years reinventing itself in an ever more classicizing guise.

By 1450, from the amateur pursuit it had been a century earlier, humanism had become the establishment language of the Italian states: a means of triumphantly proclaiming continuity with the glories of the classical, and especially the ancient Roman, past. While not all humanist scholars were from elite backgrounds themselves—Poggio was the son of an apothecary, Guarino, the son of a blacksmith—it was the movement's appeal to the peninsula's wealthy elites that ensured its remarkable success. Roman history was seductive for Italian rulers because an archetype could be found for each and every modern regime. Republics like Florence, Venice, and Siena could mirror themselves in the great Roman republic described by Livy and extolled by Sallust and Cicero. Meanwhile, princes and popes could look to later periods of Roman history and imagine themselves a new Caesar or a new Augustus or Constantine or Trajan. Noblewomen, too, could find fresh and alluring archetypes within the ancient world. Bruni's elegant humanist educational manifesto *On Studies and Letters* of the 1420s was addressed to Battista da Montefeltro, the educated and politically astute wife of the lord of Pesaro, on the Adriatic coast below Venice. The opening lines of the work airily sketch in classical precedents for the new cultural type of the learned and eloquent laywoman, mentioning Sappho, the Greek philosopher Aspasia, and Cornelia, the daughter of Scipio Africanus.[7]

HUMANISM AND SCHOLASTICISM

Key to the dissemination of Renaissance learning was the radical educational reform introduced in this period by humanist teachers such as Guarino and Vittorino. The educational curriculum that the humanists introduced was based on the ancient Roman one, with rhetoric as its core subject—hence the excitement at Poggio's rediscovery of Quintilian's *Education of the Orator*. The model of education humanists distilled from their classical sources privileged what became known in this period as the *studia humanitatis*, or 'studies of humanity', a phrase of Cicero's first picked up and used by Coluccio Salutati. These consisted of grammar (essentially, the study of the classical languages), rhetoric, history, poetry, and moral philosophy, the origin of the modern 'humanities'. The *studia humanitatis* were conceived, with high earnestness, as a means of shaping the pupil as a self-conscious moral agent, possessed of a supple, historically informed understanding of human nature and affects, an advanced mastery of the Latin language, and the eloquence necessary to argue a case and to influence those around him for the good. Whether humanist education attained its moral ends may be disputed, but it certainly helped produce a distinctive cultural style in its pupils, characterized by rhetorical dexterity, a keen sense of history, and a profound reverence for the classical world.

It is from the notion of the *studia humanitatis* that the modern scholarly notion of 'humanism', current in academic discourse since the 1960s, takes its cue. The term *humanista*—non-existent in classical Latin—developed in the Renaissance as university slang for a teacher of the humanities. Academics today use the term more broadly, to designate Renaissance intellectuals engaged with the *studia humanitatis*, either as teachers or as scholars; or, still more broadly, to designate all those invested in the study and imitation of classical antiquity.[8] Recently, it has been suggested that the term humanist be extended still further, to incorporate not merely those intellectuals possessed of the full linguistic and scholarly toolkit traditionally associated with humanism, but also those whose primary encounter with the new classical learning came about through secondary means such as translation.[9]

'Humanism' is often found in discussions of this period paired with or contrasted with 'scholasticism', and it is useful to have a grasp of both terms in understanding the cultural dynamics of the Renaissance. The term scholasticism is used to designate an intellectual movement that developed in the early universities of Europe, which began to be founded from the late eleventh and twelfth centuries.[10] Like 'humanism', the term does not indicate a shared body of doctrine so much as an educational system and a critical approach to learning—in the case of scholasticism, one based on formal logic and disputation, tending to the abstract, and geared to the production of universal, general truths. As Aristotle's logic, metaphysics, and natural philosophy began to become accessible in the West in Latin translation, via Arabic sources, the vast, collective endeavour began of assimilating this powerful body of thought to Christianity. In a theological context, the term scholasticism generally refers to the product of this assimilation: a strongly Aristotelian-inflected version of Christian thinking, especially associated with the figure of Thomas Aquinas (1225–74).

In considering the development of Renaissance humanism as an intellectual movement, it is important to recall that it grew up at a time when university culture was dominated by scholasticism. As humanism developed and gained confidence as a movement, polemics became common between these two very different intellectual styles or traditions, beginning with Petrarch's amusingly irate diatribes of the 1360s, such as *On His Own Ignorance and That of Many Others*. Scholastics accused humanists of a lack of logical rigour, and sometimes (as in Petrarch's case) of ignorance. Humanists responded by deploring university philosophers' use of jargon, their logic-chopping, their indifference to classical learning, their radically unclassical Latin. In addition to these essentially stylistic issues, Petrarch accuses scholastic philosophers of an inattention to core ethical questions he found better tackled by pagan moralists like Cicero and Seneca, and a failure to recognize the importance of eloquence in reaching and affecting readers' hearts and minds.[11] Lorenzo Valla, in the mid-fifteenth century, was still more trenchant on this score, arguing that scholastic philosophers came close to sacrilege or heresy in their reliance on rational means to probe the mysteries of God. Valla instead advocated a return to the rhetorical theology of patristic writers such as Lactantius and Jerome.[12]

Neither side 'won' this dispute. Although humanism established a foothold in the universities from the mid-fifteenth century, it did not replace Aristotelian scholasticism, which continued as a strong presence throughout the sixteenth century, with many thinkers influenced by both. If humanism did not triumph in its polemics with scholasticism, however, it certainly emerged from them strengthened. The challenge of constituting itself as an alternative to a very different, and institutionally entrenched, cultural and educational system forced humanism to interrogate itself and articulate its values. It was this, in large part, that gave humanism the character of a conscious 'movement', rather than simply a consonance of classicizing tastes.

THE MATERIAL RENAISSANCE

It was not only texts that the Italian Renaissance unearthed in its quest for a closer knowledge of Graeco-Roman antiquity. The classical concerns of humanism brought with them a new interest in the surviving material artefacts of the ancient world—architectural fragments, statues, sarcophagi, vases, coins, inscriptions, of the sort that could be turned up with ease in many parts of Italy as foundations were laid for new buildings. That was in addition to remnants of antiquity still standing and visible—the Pantheon, for example, and the temple of Hercules Victor near the Tiber in Rome, both converted into churches in the early Middle Ages, or the abandoned Colosseum, where the sculptor Benvenuto Cellini talks of retiring one memorable evening for a terrifying exercise in black magic conducted by a renegade Sicilian priest.[13]

Interest in the material remains of classical antiquity is apparent from the dawn of the humanist movement in Italy. A late-antique sarcophagus uncovered in Padua some time before 1260 was revered as the tomb of the Trojan Antenor, the legendary founder of Roman Padua, or Patavinum. Around the turn of the fourteenth century, a Roman inscription came to light in the same city, seemingly referring to Patavinum's most distinguished son, the historian Livy. Both these artefacts aroused keen interest within the classicizing circles of Lovati and Mussato. An arched stone structure that had been erected over the sarcophagus was restored in 1283, with a Latin inscription by Lovati, echoing Livy's and Virgil's allusions to the Trojan hero. Lovati also left instructions for his own burial alongside the Antenor shrine.[14] The Livy inscription, meanwhile, was affixed to the walls of the Basilica of Santa Giustina and became a site of cultural pilgrimage. Petrarch presents his letter to Livy—one of an evocative series of 'letters to the underworld' he addressed to ancient authors—as written 'in the vestibule of the Temple of Justina Virgo, and in view of your very tombstone'.[15]

Neither the Tomb of Antenor episode nor the Livian inscription episode says a great deal for early humanism's historical and philological expertise. The Trojan foundation myth was, precisely, a myth, while to read the inscription as relating to the historian Livy involved a degree of wishful reading (the 'T. Livius' it refers to is a freedman named Titus Livius Halys, as the inscription clearly states). What is evocative in these early anecdotes is the impulse to 'relicization' apparent in the treatment of both finds, and the strong civic-patriotic impulse that inspired it. Padua was a city of considerable Christian charisma, housing the bones of the thirteenth-century Franciscan saint, Anthony of Padua, canonized in 1232, and those of the early Christian martyr, Justina. The lay veneration of Livy and Antenor evinced by the reverent treatment of their 'relics' conscripts them to the same logic of privileged memorialization enjoyed by these saints. Although the echoes of Virgil and Livy in Lovati's epitaph for Antenor speak to a nascent classicizing sensibility, the cult of a semi-sanctified civic founder was near-ubiquitous in thirteenth- and fourteenth-century Italy, speaking to the powerful connection the early Italian city-states felt to their classical roots. Perugia feted as its founder the Trojan prince 'Eulistes', who appears in a statue on the magnificent thirteenth-century fountain in the main city square, the Fontana Maggiore.[16] Genoa went one better, claiming a Roman god as its founder: the two-faced Janus, god of gateways, with one face set to the future, one to the past.[17]

Traces of this same, patriotic response to Roman antiquity—though on a much grander, national scale—are apparent in an interesting anecdote that Petrarch tells of himself in a letter of 1355, recounting a diplomatic mission to Mantua in which he encountered the Holy Roman Emperor Charles IV. Petrarch self-flatteringly recounts that Charles expressed an interest in his moral compendium of ancient history, *On Famous Men*, but that he was unable to gratify him with a copy of the work, since it was still unfinished. As a kind of proxy, he gave Charles 'some gold and silver effigies of our princes inscribed with tiny, ancient letters, which were dear to me'—that is, coins depicting the ancient Roman emperors— 'among which was an image of Augustus that seemed to breathe'.[18] Petrarch presents his gift to the emperor as didactic in intent, and reports that he accompanied it with an exhortation: 'Behold, Caesar, those you have succeeded; behold those you should strive to imitate and admire'.[19]

Setting the political context aside (many Italians were unhappy at Charles's refusal to engage in the political tensions of the peninsula, despite his nominal position as overlord of northern Italy), this story is fascinating from the perspective of Petrarch's attitude to antiquity and, more particularly, to classical art. Collecting ancient coins was not a common pastime at the time, as it would become by the fifteenth century. Petrarch may have cultivated his interest in Roman coins in imitation of Augustus, whose biography by Suetonius was an important source for his own self-fashioning (Suetonius tells us that among the gifts Augustus distributed at the feast of Saturnalia were 'old coins of the kings', probably the striking portrait coins struck by some Hellenistic kings).[20] As his description of his gift to Charles shows, two aspects that interested Petrarch in these miniature artefacts were the style of their lettering—quite different from the Lombard and Gothic scripts common in his day—and the vividness of their portraiture, which must indeed have looked remarkable within a culture in which a tradition of realistic, individualized portraiture barely existed. Also interesting is Petrarch's alertness to material portraiture as a potential vehicle for moral discourse; the coin-portraits here are credited with the same potential exhortatory efficacy as the missing verbal rhetoric of *On Famous Men*. It is noteworthy in light of this that the earliest recorded fresco-cycle of famous classical heroes, dating from the late 1360s or 1370s, was commissioned by Francesco I Carrara, lord of Padua, to whom Petrarch had been close in his last years.[21]

Petrarch's interest in the look and feel of classical antiquity was taken up and amplified by his successors. Handwriting offers an interesting example. Petrarch was keenly aware of the different styles of writing found in modern, Gothic script, sometimes known as 'blackletter', and in the older scripts he encountered, in Roman inscriptions and coins, and in classical manuscripts dating from the Carolingian era. In a scathing letter, he criticized the modern script for its 'luxuriance' and decorative flourishes, arguing that script should be restrained (*castigata*), clear, and easy to read.[22] Early fifteenth-century humanists put this into practice, developing an exquisite, neo-Carolingian script that they believed accurately reflected the handwriting of the ancients. The key innovators here were Poggio Bracciolini, who perfected the style now known as 'humanist minuscule', later adopted by printers as the basis for what we still call 'Roman' type (Fig. 3), and Niccolò Niccoli, who evolved a swifter, cursive style that is the basis of our modern 'Italic'. These handwriting innovations were adopted first for classical and humanistic texts, while scholastic works continued to be written using the earlier, Gothic script, lending a visual dimension to the 'two cultures' division as the fifteenth century progressed (Fig. 4). The visual clarity and restraint of humanistic handwriting had a particular rhetorical force, since humanists characteristically thought of the difference between their language and that of the medieval scholastics in terms of 'purity' or 'cleanliness'. Medieval Latin, for the humanists, was a language encrusted with ugly accretions, which it was the mission of the humanists to castigate or purge.

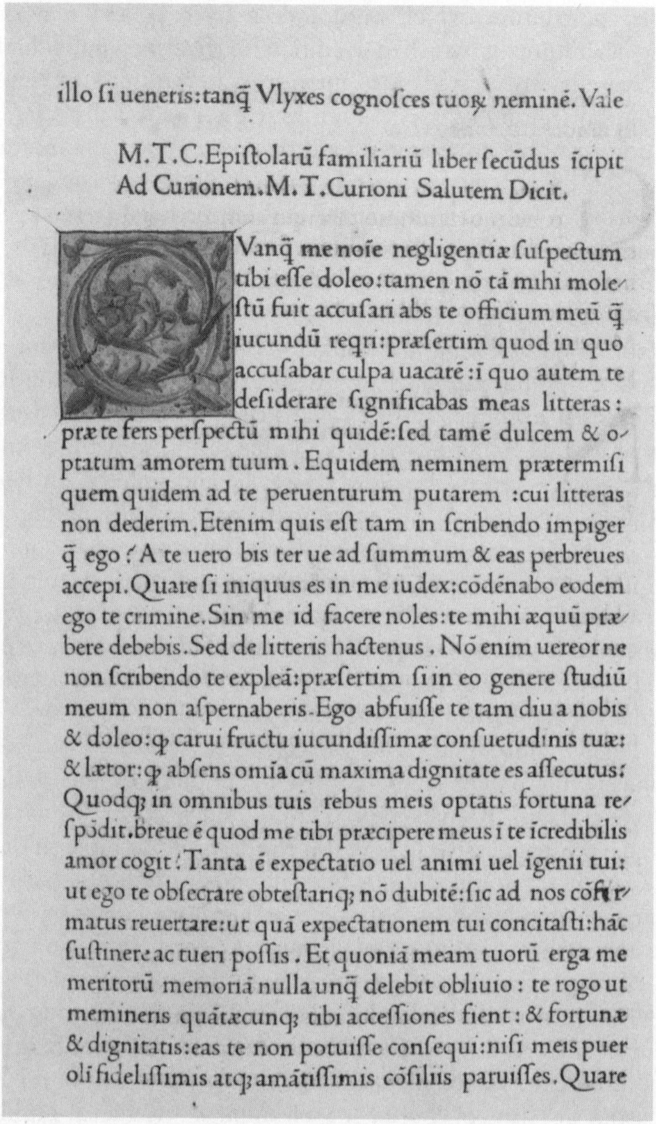

illo ſi ueneris: tanq̄ Vlyxes cognoſces tuoꝝ neminē. Vale

M.T.C.Epiſtolarū familiariū liber ſecūdus īcipit
Ad Curionem.M.T.Curioni Salutem Dicit.

QVanq̄ me noīe negligentiæ ſuſpectum tibi eſſe doleo: tamen nō tā mihi moleſtū fuit accuſari abs te officium meū q̄ iucundū reqri: præſertim quod in quo accuſabar culpa uacarē: ī quo autem te deſiderare ſignificabas meas litteras: præ te fers perſpectū mihi quidē: ſed tamē dulcem & optatum amorem tuum. Equidem neminem prætermiſi quem quidem ad te peruenturum putarem: cui litteras non dederim. Etenim quis eſt tam in ſcribendo impiger q̄ ego? A te uero bis ter ue ad ſummum & eas perbreues accepi. Quare ſi iniquus es in me iudex: cōdēnabo eodem ego te crimine. Sin me id facere noles: te mihi æquū præbere debebis. Sed de litteris hactenus. Nō enim uereor ne non ſcribendo te expleā: præſertim ſi in eo genere ſtudiū meum non aſpernaberis. Ego abfuiſſe te tam diu a nobis & doleo: ꝙ carui fructu iucundiſſimæ conſuetudinis tuæ: & lætor: ꝙ abſens omīa cū maxima dignitate es aſſecutus: Quodq; in omnibus tuis rebus meis optatis fortuna reſpōdit. breue ē quod me tibi præcipere meus ī te īcredibilis amor cogit. Tanta ē expectatio uel animi uel īgenii tui: ut ego te obſecrare obteſtariq; nō dubitē: ſic ad nos cōfirmatus reuertare: ut quā expectationem tui concitaſti: hāc ſuſtinere ac tueri poſſis. Et quoniā meam tuorū erga me meritorū memoriā nulla unq̄ delebit obliuio: te rogo ut memineris quātæcunq; tibi acceſſiones fient: & fortunæ & dignitatis: eas te non potuiſſe conſequi: niſi meis pueroli fideliſſimis atq; amātiſſimis cōſiliis paruiſſes. Quare

Fig. 3: Example of Roman typeface. Marcus Tullius Cicero, *Letters* (*Epistolae ad familiares*) (Venice: Nicolaus Jenson, 1471), 15r.

criminalis questio preiudicat ciuili: aliquando ciuilis criminali. unde in libro tertio codicis ti. de ordine iudiciorum legitur. Iulii questione intermissa sepe fit ut prius de crimine iudicetur: quod utpote maius minori merito prefertur. Item. li. viiij. codice qui ac. non poss. l. i.

Prius est ut tu respondeas criminibus cedis atque uulnerum que tibi ut grauiora crimina ab aduersario tuo obiiciuntur: et tunc ex euentu cause iudex extimabit: an tibi permittendum sit eundem accusare: tamesi prior inscriptionem deposuisti. Aliquando ciuilis preiudicat ciuili: aliquando criminali. sicut enim in. vij. ti. de ordine cognitionum legitur. Si de hereditate et libertate controuersia est: prius debet agi causa libertatis. Item. Si crimen aliquod inferatur ei: qui ingenuus esse dicitur: libertatis causa suo ordine ante debet agi cognitionem suam presidente prebente: quoniam si delictum probatum fuerit: antea scire necesse est: utrum in liberum et ingenuum: an in seruum constitui oporteat. Item. Qui confitetur se pati controuersiam status: frustra postulat sibi dari potestatem accusandi eum: qui se suum dominum esse fatetur. Causa uero libertatis terminata: si seruus pronunciatus fuerit: dominum suum accusare non poterit. Codice. li. ix. ti. i. Si quis enim ex familiaribus uel seruis cuiuslibet domus cuiuscumque criminis delator atque accusator emerserit: eius extimationem caput et fortunas petiturus: cuius familiaritati inheserit uel dominio ante exhibitionem testium ante examinationem iudicii in ipsa expositione criminum et accusationis exordio ultore gladio feriatur. uocem enim funestam interdici oportet potius quam audiri. Maiestatis autem crimen excipimus. Similiter et si liberti accusatores manumissorum heredumue esse presumpserint: eodem quoque ut serui supplicio tenebuntur luituri penas ante prohibite delationis exordium.

Quidam uir in excommunicatione constitutus episcopum accusare disposuit. adolescentem infra. xiiij. etatis sue annum ad assertionem sue cause adducit. prohibitus ab accusatione adolescentem accusatorem et se testem facit. adolescens personam accusatoris et testis gerere cupit. die statuta ad iudicium electorum iudicum ueniunt. episcopus minime occurrit. a communione suspenditur. tandem renouato iudicio accusator culpabilis in accusatione inuenitur. demum ad assertionem proprie cause procedit. Hic primum queritur: an in excommunicatione constitutus alium accusare ualeat. Secundo: an infra. xiiij. annum in criminali causa testari quis possit. Tertio: an ab accusatione prohibitus personam testificantis possit assumere. Quarto: an idem possit esse accusator et testis. Quinto: an die constituta non occurrens a communione sit remouendus. Sexto: si in episcoporum iudicio accusatoris persona culpabilis inuenta fuerit: an ad assertionem proprie cause de cetero sit admittenda.

De prima questione sic statutum legitur in concilio chartaginensi. vij. cui interfuit faustinus romane ecclesie legatus.

Fig. 4: Example of Gothic typeface. Gratianus's twelfth-century law textbook, the *Decretum*, with the commentary of Bartolomeo da Brescia (Venice: Nicolaus Jenson, 1474), 141r.

THE ARTISTIC RENAISSANCE

By the time the new classicizing style of handwriting was beginning to become disseminated in the early fifteenth century, an artistic revolution was taking place in Italy that would transform the languages of architecture, painting, and sculpture in profound and lasting ways. This artistic *renovatio* may be compared to the intellectual and literary transformation wrought by humanism, and the two shifts demand to be considered together. Although the history of Renaissance art cannot be told as a pure narrative of classical rediscovery, the influence of classical artistic culture was certainly fundamental in this period. Artists increasingly looked to classical models for their formal inspiration, and patrons showed an increasing taste for classicizing artistic decorum, and even classical subject matter. Meanwhile, humanist intellectuals exhumed classical writings on Greek and Roman art and architecture, such as Pliny's extensive discussion of classical art in his *Natural History*, and Vitruvius's *On Architecture*. Inspired by these works, a new humanistic tradition of writings on art history and art theory began to appear.

The history of Renaissance art is a complex one, but there seems little reason to question the traditional narrative that locates the key turning-point in that history to Florence in the early decades of the fifteenth century and to the remarkable group of artists who flourished here. Foremost among these were the architect Filippo Brunelleschi and the sculptors Donatello and Lorenzo Ghiberti, all born in the 1370s–80s, and the painter Masaccio, born around 1401. The remarkable decade of the 1420s, when all these artists were active, saw the introduction of a new, classicizing style of architecture in Florence epitomized by Brunelleschi's work for the Foundling Hospital building (*Ospedale degli Innocenti*), begun in 1419, with its round arches, precise use of the orders—Corinthian in this case—and its careful observation of geometrical proportion. In sculpture and painting, the most remarkable development of these years was the beginning of the use of perspective, apparent both in Masaccio's paintings and in sculptural reliefs by Ghiberti and Donatello, such as the former's second set of doors for the Florentine baptistery. By the 1430s, when the humanist Leon Battista Alberti—Florentine by descent, though born in exile—visited the city of his ancestors, he was able to marvel that the classical arts he had once thought dead were now flourishing anew. Alberti underlines the suddenness of this resurgence with wonder, positing it as more remarkable than anything the ancient world witnessed. Where ancient artists and architects had built on a long tradition, learning their art organically through imitation of existing models, the artists of his age had 'no teachers, no examples'; they had created their new art from scratch.[23]

This last statement of Alberti's is, of course, a hyperbole, and it is perfectly possible to trace a more gradualist version of the artistic Renaissance. The late thirteenth and early fourteenth centuries in Italy had seen an earlier artistic revolution, with the painting of Cimabue, Pietro Cavallini, and Giotto, and the sculpture of Nicola and Giovanni Pisano, Arnolfo del Cambio, and Tino da Camaino. Some of these artists, especially the sculptors, show marked classical influences, and may be seen as anticipating fifteenth-century developments; Nicola Pisano's pulpit for the baptistery of Pisa Cathedral (*c.* 1260), for example, contains a remarkable classicizing nude figure, based on representations of Hercules. In certain respects, fifteenth-century Florentine art may be seen as reaching back to this century-old 'first Renaissance', beyond Italian art's more recent immersion in Gothic influences from northern Europe. This is especially the case with Masaccio, whose realism may be seen in part as an inspired re-visitation and updating of Giotto's pictorial language, building on Giotto's fundamental move towards an exploration of depth and mass in painting, his use of chiaroscuro for modelling, and his remarkable ability to express human affect through physical gesture and stance (Figs 5 and 6).

Another useful caveat to bear in mind when approaching Renaissance art is that the new classicism of the Renaissance did not in any sense simply displace or take over from Gothic, any more than humanism displaced scholasticism. The stylized elegance and decorativeness of the Gothic style had an enduring appeal for Renaissance Italians, competing with the more austere and intellectual, neo-Giottesque style pioneered by Masaccio. In the same decade when Masaccio began work on the Brancacci Chapel, the 1420s, the banker Palla Strozzi paid out the significant sum of 150 florins for Gentile da Fabriano's lavishly gilded, richly ornate *Adoration of the Magi*, now in the Uffizi. More than 30

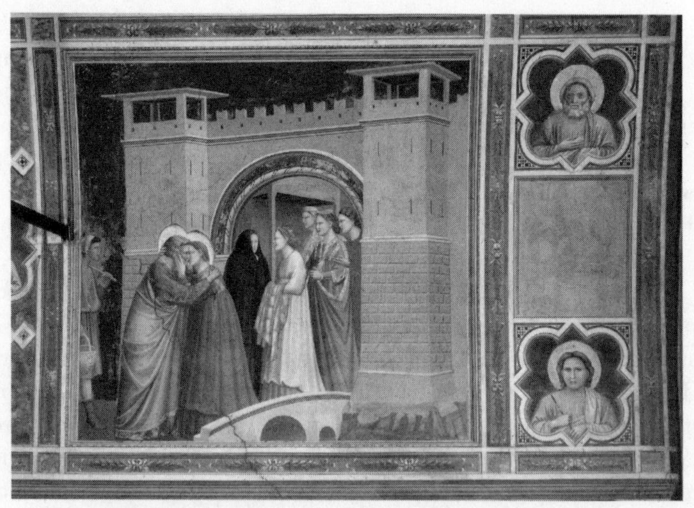

Fig. 5: Giotto di Bondone, *The Meeting of Joachim and Anne at the Golden Gate*, *c.* 1305. Scrovegni Chapel, Padua.

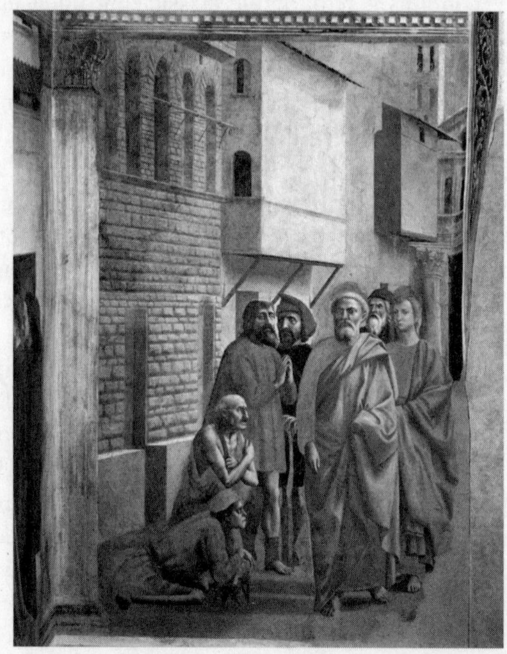

Fig. 6: Masaccio (Maso di San Giovanni), *St. Peter Healing the Sick with his Shadow*, *c.* 1426. Brancacci Chapel, Santa Maria del Carmine, Florence.

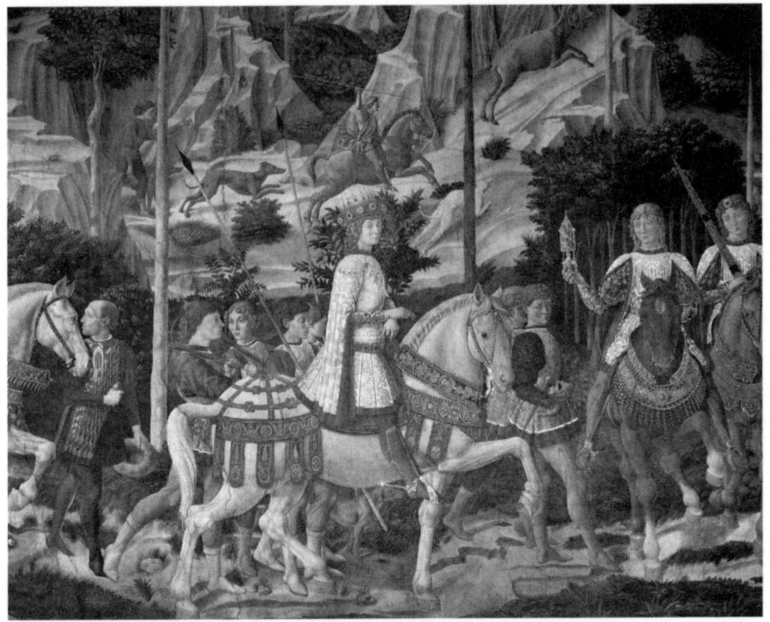

Fig. 7: Benozzo Gozzoli, *Procession of the Magi*, *c.* 1459–63 (detail). Palazzo Medici Riccardi, Florence.

years later, Benozzo Gozzoli completed his fairy-tale image of the *Procession of the Magi* for Piero di Cosimo de' Medici, the effective ruler of Florence (Fig. 7). These are instances of works that may be unproblematically qualified as Gothic, but it is not difficult, either, to identify iconic Renaissance works that mingle classical and Gothic influences. One is Donatello's *David*, of the 1430s, sculpted for Cosimo de' Medici—the first freestanding bronze nude since antiquity (Fig. 8). The conception of the statue is classicizing, especially in its choice to portray the hero nude, and there are *all'antica* details in the sculpture such as the vanquished Goliath's helmet, decorated with a frieze of Cupid and Psyche. David's girlish, gracefully posed figure, with its decorative hat, however, owes as much to Gothic aesthetics as to classical. Later in the century, Sandro Botticelli's *Primavera*, discussed below, although classical in its subject matter, shows Gothic influences in its frieze-like composition and in its privileging of delicacy and sinuousness of line over the evocation of volume and spatial depth.

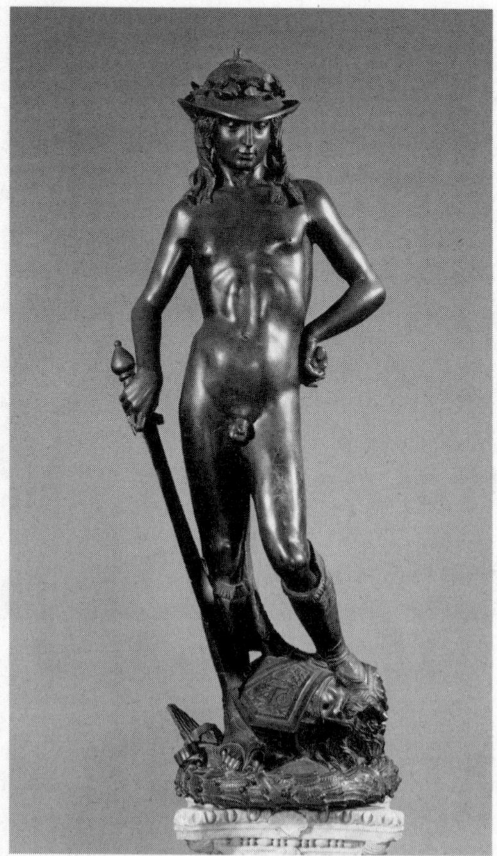

Fig. 8: Donatello (Donato di Niccolò di Betto Bardi), *David*, 1428–32.

These examples are all from Florence, but the story of the Renaissance in art is not purely a Florentine one, even in the fifteenth century, let alone the sixteenth. A major Renaissance development such as the revival of the classical genre of the portrait medal, from the late 1430s onwards, was mainly the work of artists like the Pisan Antonio di Puccio ('Pisanello') and the Veronese Matteo de' Pasti, working for northern and central Italian lords such as Leonello d'Este of Ferrara and Sigismondo Malatesta of Rimini. Sigismondo Malatesta was also responsible for commissioning one of the most remarkable early Renaissance buildings, the so-called *Tempio Malatestiano*

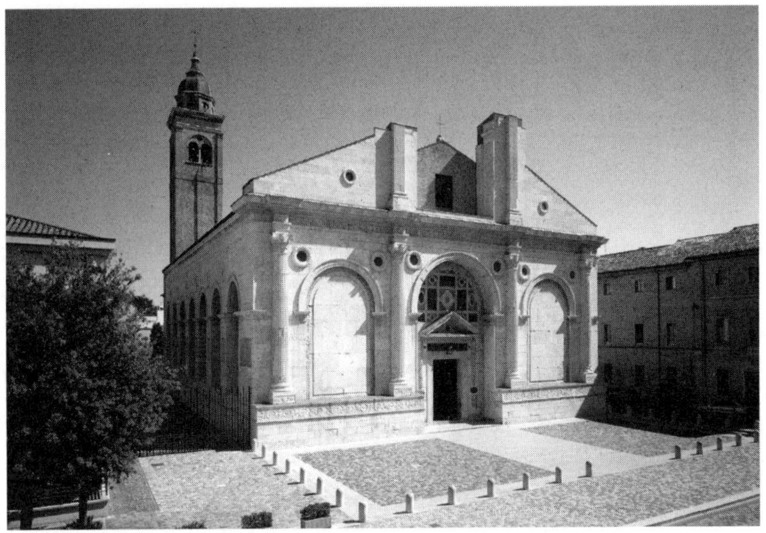

Fig. 9: Tempio Malatestiano, Rimini,
built to a design of Leon Battista Alberti; begun *c.* 1450.

('Malatestine Temple') in Rimini, begun around 1450 (Fig. 9): a classical remodelling of a Gothic Franciscan church, with a façade by Leon Battista Alberti based on the proportions of the Roman Arch of Augustus in the same city, and incorporating the first post-classical inscription based accurately on ancient prototypes in terms of its lettering and style.[24] Other important Renaissance buildings outside Florence in the second half of the Quattrocento include the remarkable classical arch added to the medieval fortress of Castel Nuovo in Naples, with its sculptural friezes based on Roman triumphal arches (Fig. 10); the Colleoni Chapel in Bergamo, north of Milan, incorporating scenes of the labours of Hercules into its façade, along with biblical episodes; and the superb palace of Urbino, designed for the humanist prince Federico da Montefeltro, probably by the Dalmatian architect Luciano Laurana. By the end of the century, even Venice, which had long clung to the Gothic style of architecture, was acquiring its first Renaissance churches, such as San Michele in Isola and San Zaccaria, both by the Bergamasque architect Mauro Codussi. In the 1490s, the duke of Ferrara, Ercole d'Este, embarked on what was probably the most ambitious urban planning project to be realized in the fifteenth

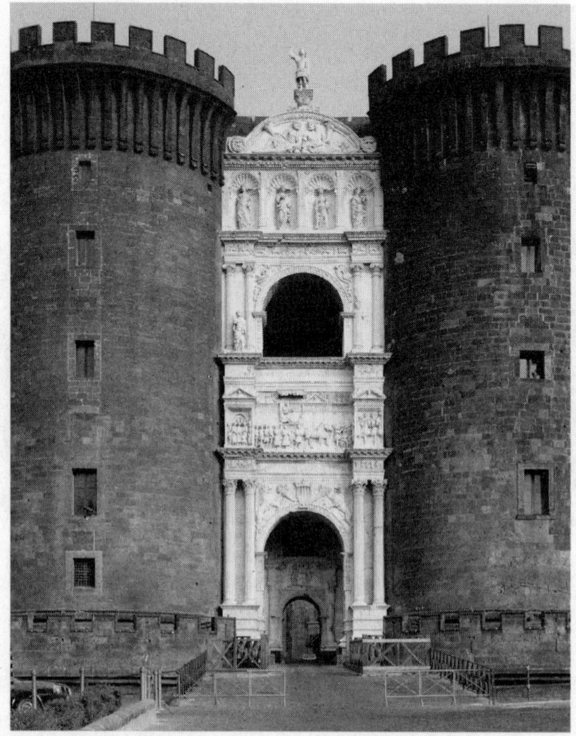

Fig. 10: Triumphal arch of Alfonso I, Castel Nuovo, Naples, sometimes attributed to Francesco Laurana [Frane Vranjanin], 1453–68.

century: the vast extension to his city known after its patron as the Addizione Erculea (the 'Herculean Extension'), with its wide, straight streets and monumental architecture. This includes the great 'Diamond Palace' (Palazzo dei Diamanti), designed by the Ferrarese architect Biagio Rossetti, with its light-reflecting façade made up of more than 8,000 diamond-cut marble blocks.

By the time of the Addizione Erculea, classicizing architectural styles were becoming virtually the norm across Italy for large public and private buildings, such as churches and palaces. What was inside these buildings was also increasingly classicizing—in the case of secular buildings, not merely in form, but also in subject-matter. As the humanistic educational curriculum became widely adopted by the elites across this period, illuminated classical manuscripts began to be in demand among

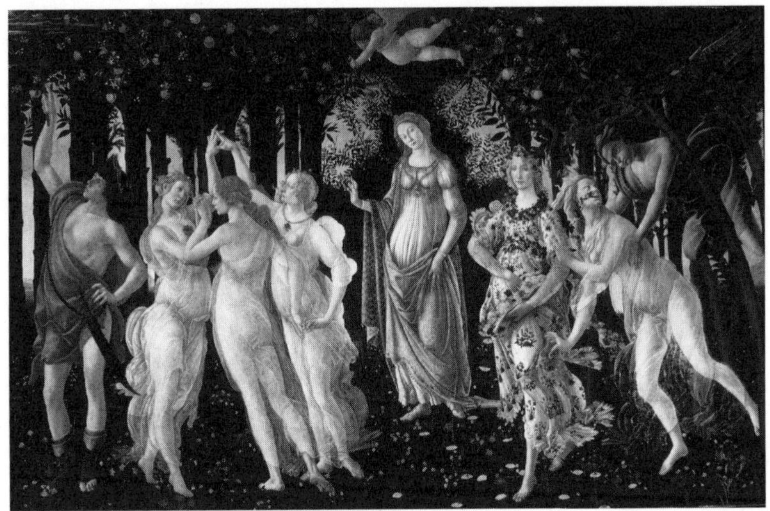

Fig. 11: Sandro Botticelli [Alessandro di Mariano di Vanni Filipepi], *Spring* [*Primavera*], *c.* 1477.

wealthy patrons, and painters became more conversant with secular and classicizing subjects. Classically themed panel paintings, too, began to emerge as a recognizable sub-tradition, especially after the vogue for the showpiece study spaces known as *studioli* evolved in princely circles from around the mid-century.[25] From this time onwards, we begin to see the kind of close collaboration between humanists and artists that would later characterize the sixteenth century, producing works that would consciously seek to emulate the complexity and layeredness of classical literature in paint or stone.

A good early example of this tradition of classically themed art is Sandro Botticelli's famous *Primavera*, painted in the 1470s for a junior branch of the Medici family (Fig. 11). The image draws on writings by Ovid, Horace, Seneca, and Lucretius, in a learned evocation of the Roman mythology surrounding the coming of spring. The 'fable' of the painting is so subtle and erudite—and so poetic—that it has been plausibly conjectured that the great humanist, poet, and Medici client Angelo Poliziano was involved in its elaboration.[26] On the viewer's right, Zephyr, the wind god, abducts the nymph Cloris and she transforms into the flower goddess Flora. On the left, Mercury, associated with spring in the ancient Roman calendar, ushers the season in, accompanied by the dancing Graces. In the centre, the love gods Venus and Cupid preside over all.

Although it is now reverently displayed in a museum as an independent work, evidence from inventories suggests that Botticelli's *Primavera*, like many Renaissance works, was originally intended as a piece of site-specific room décor. It was intended to hang above a *lettuccio*—a day-bed, or settle, already presumably adorned with a carved back-piece or *spalliera*. The popularity of classical scenes for such elite domestic art from the mid-fifteenth century onwards is highly suggestive of the extent to which humanist interests had become diffused by this point. Scenes from Roman myth and history rivalled biblical and chivalric narratives as choices of subject-matter for the painted and sculpted furniture with which wealthy families furnished their homes, which, besides *spalliere*, included *cassoni* (marriage chests) and *deschi da parto* ('birth trays', used to bring sweets and gifts to women recovering from childbirth).[27] The classical scenes on these furnishings were typically painted in a lively Gothic-influenced style with the figures dressed in contemporary garments (the Victoria and Albert Museum's 1460s *cassone* by Apollonio di Giovanni featuring the 'Continence of Scipio' offers an excellent example, as do Biagio d'Antonio's *cassone* or *spalliera* panels illustrating the myth of Jason and the Argonauts in the Metropolitan Museum [Fig. 12]). Late in the century, however, it is also possible to find more formally classicizing works, such as a *cassone* of the 1480s or 1490s in the Metropolitan Museum with a gesso frieze representing the myth of Ceres and Proserpina. This looks forward to the sixteenth century, when carved friezes imitating ancient sarcophagi displaced painting as the norm of *cassone* design.

This shift in the direction of a stricter classicism is a notable trend in the later fifteenth century, and reflects Renaissance Italy's ever deeper and more precise knowledge of the classical world. New archeological-artistic discoveries assisted this classicism. Around 1480, the first extensive and well-preserved example of Roman wall-painting was discovered, in the form of a wing of Nero's buried Domus Aurea (Golden House) complex, excavated on the Esquiline Hill. Arduously exploring its cramped underground passages, scholars and artists imbibed the style of late imperial room decoration, with its fanciful 'grotesques', or *grotteschi* as they came to be known (literally 'cave-paintings', from the Domus's cave-like rooms). Again

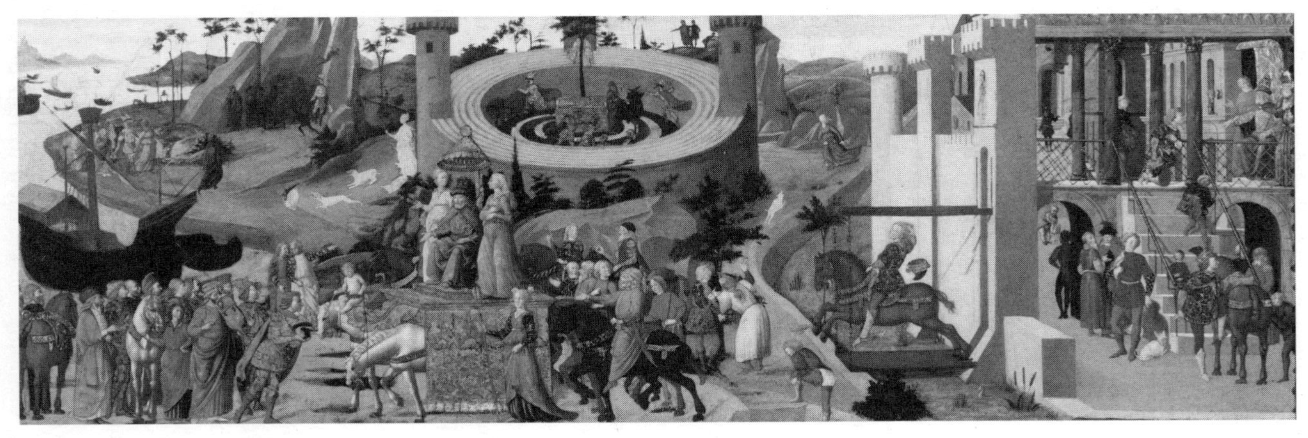

Fig. 12: Biagio di Antonio, *Scenes from the Story of the Argonauts*, *c.* 1465.

probably in the 1480s, the Apollo Belvedere was unearthed: one of the greatest marble sculptures to survive from classical antiquity, and the first of a series of remarkable sculptural finds of the late fifteenth and early sixteenth centuries. These included fragments of a colossal, eight times life-size statue of Constantine, found in 1487, and the dramatic, writhing group of the priest Laocoön and his sons attacked by snakes, uncovered in 1506. While artists of the earlier Renaissance had drawn largely on relief sculpture and smaller free-standing bronzes for their knowledge of classical art, from this point they had direct access to the heroic tradition of marble statuary of which Pliny speaks in his *Natural History*. Michelangelo's *David*, of 1501–4, the first colossal nude statue of the Renaissance, speaks to the potency of this new inspiration, as do his statues for the proposed tomb of Julius II, the Moses and Slaves of 1513–19.

Prior to the final triumph of classicism in early sixteenth-century Rome, a monument to the dream of reborn antiquity in Renaissance art is Andrea Mantegna's remarkable nine-canvas *Triumphs of Caesar*, probably painted between around 1486 and 1506 for the Gonzaga family in Mantua. Mantegna's image of the Gallic triumph of Julius Caesar in 46 B.C. draws on accounts of this extravagant triumphal parade in Plutarch, Appian, and Suetonius, probably via the humanist Biondo Flavio's treatise *Rome Triumphant* (1459), with its vivid descriptions of such rites. These textual sources were supplemented by the surviving representations of Roman triumphs on the Arches of Titus and Constantine in Rome. Mantegna synthesizes these sources into a dazzling profusion of detail, with Roman weapons, chariots, vases, trumpets, banners, garlanded sacrificial bulls, all portrayed in a plausibly 'antique' style. The result is a compelling imaginative evocation of Rome's power and otherness, as well as an implicit celebration of the rising glories of the Italian courts (Fig. 13).

This classicizing trend in art found its apotheosis in Rome during the pontificates of Julius II (Giuliano della Rovere) and Leo X (Giovanni de' Medici), two of the greatest patrons of humanistic culture of the entire Italian Renaissance. Julius's and Leo's exalted vision of Rome's destiny as the resurgent capital of Christendom is expressed in the boldness of their artistic and architectural commissions. Julius was responsible for the commission of Michelangelo's Sistine ceiling and Raphael's Vatican stanzas, together with audacious schemes of urban planning, including the decision to tear down the venerable

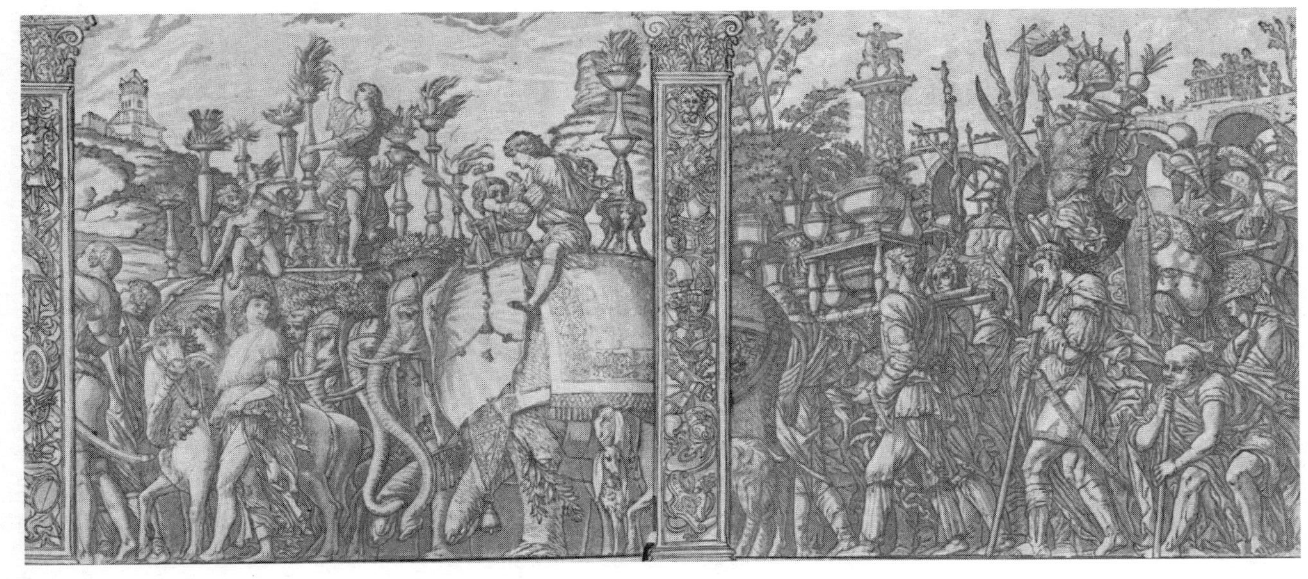

Fig. 13: Andrea Andreani, with Bernardo Malpi, *Elephants and a Man Lighting a Candelabrum*, 1599; print after Andrea Mantegna, *The Triumphs of Caesar*, 1486–1506.

fourth-century Basilica of St Peter's and to replace it with a modern design. Leo sponsored the continuation of Raphael's decorative scheme in the Vatican, and commissioned the same artist to devise cartoons for ten great tapestries to hang in the Sistine Chapel below Michelangelo's ceiling. Woven in Brussels, and incorporating lavish quantities of silver and gold thread, these were one of the most costly art commissions of the age. Less well known as a project of these years, but speaking richly of the classicizing bent of Roman culture, was an initiative Raphael was engaged on at the time of his tragically early death at the age of thirty-seven in 1520: a plan for a complete survey of the surviving monuments of ancient Rome, conducted according to the latest methods of architectural drawing and urban cartography. In true humanistic style, this was intended to serve both as an historical record of the greatness of antiquity, and as inspiration for new, Renaissance architecture to come.

HUMANISM AND CHRISTIANITY

By the early decades of the sixteenth century, it was possible for a humanistically educated Italian aristocrat to classicize his lifestyle to a notable extent. He might live in a decent approximation of a Roman villa; he might speak and write in a passable reconstruction of Cicero's Latin; he might plant classical statues of Greek gods in his courtyard, and attend performances of classical plays. It was even feasible by this period to conduct one's sex life in a self-consciously classicizing manner. One of the most intriguing cultural novelties of early sixteenth-century Rome, discussed in Chapter 6, is the reappearance of the figure of the educated courtesan on the model of the ancient Athenian *hetaira*. We also find quite numerous references in humanistic writings to the kind of pederastic homoerotic relationships that Plato idealized as the perfect form of love: a case of an existing and widespread social practice, well documented in the judicial archives of Italian cities, being given a degree of cultural legitimation through the existence of a prestigious classical pedigree.[28]

A question that naturally arises when we consider this ongoing classicization of Italian elite culture is the extent to which it implies a dilution of, or departure from, Christian values and Christian beliefs. To scholars of the nineteenth century and much of the twentieth, the

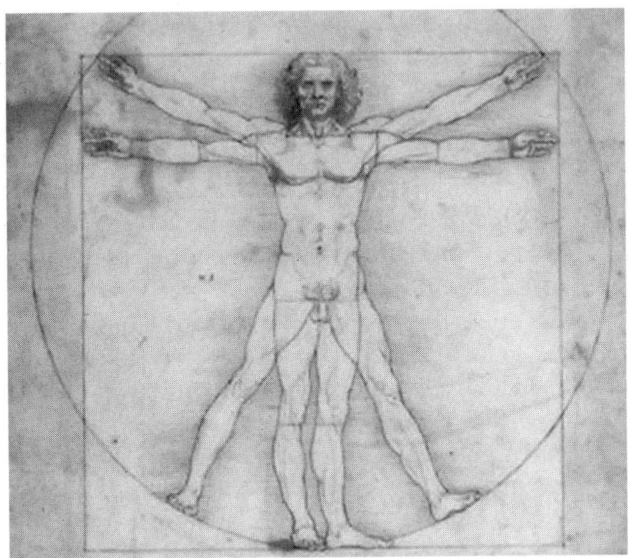

Fig. 14: Leonardo da Vinci, *Proportions of the Human Body according to Vitruvius*, *c.* 1490.

notion of a 'paganizing' Renaissance seemed obvious and intuitive. The Italian Renaissance's embrace of the classics seemed indicative of a shift in world-view from a medieval, religious, ascetic paradigm to something more worldly and materialistic. Changes in attitudes to the body appeared symptomatic of this. Where a familiar medieval religious stance conceived of the body as a corrupt and rotting 'prison' for the immortal soul, Renaissance art, like classical art, often glorifies the human body, seeing its proportions as reflecting the secret geometry underlying artistic and cosmic harmony and beauty. A famous expression of this is a drawing by Leonardo da Vinci of around 1490 exploring the relationship between the ideal human form and the 'perfect shapes' of the square and the circle (Fig. 14). The idea derives from Vitruvius's architectural theory, which sees the human form as the model on which architectural proportion should be based.

The question of the degree to which the Italian Renaissance represented a decisive shift towards a secular, world-embracing model of culture is a complex one. One thing that can hardly be denied is that the entire period from the twelfth and thirteenth centuries in Italy saw a general secularizing cultural tendency, resulting from urbanization and economic development. This continued during the period of the Renaissance. The development of national and international trade; the growth of a banking and financial industry; the expansion of consumerism—all these led to a progressive acceptance of secular and materialistic values, such as the legitimacy of wealth acquisition and of conspicuous expenditure (or magnificence, in the language of the day). It is misleading, however, to represent this advance of secularism and materialism as locked into a zero-sum, agonistic relationship with the Church or with Christian values, even if the more ascetic strains in Christian thought condemned attachment to material possessions as sinful. The Church benefited very considerably from the growing wealth of the Italian cities and proved adept at devising means for servicing the consciences of the merchants and bankers who drove the urban economy. Much of the great religious art we admire in Italian churches and galleries was financed by men and women who had profited from trade and finance, and who wished to speed their passage through Purgatory by investing in spiritual goods such as prayer, charity, the saying of masses, and the endowment and beautification of places of worship.

One reason why it has been easy in the past to tell the story of the Italian Renaissance as one of progressive secularization is that studies of this period have often been selective in their emphases, giving particular salience to those figures who meet the secularization hypothesis best. A major focus of English-language scholarship on the Italian Renaissance in the second half of the twentieth century was the tradition of thought generally referred to as 'civic humanism'—a tradition particularly centred in Florence, republican in character, and having as its chief figures politically engaged intellectuals such as Coluccio Salutati, Leonardo Bruni, and Niccolò Machiavelli. The modernity of this tradition was seen as lying in its positive embrace of the active political life (*vita activa civilis*)—seen as equal or superior to the 'contemplative life' that had constituted the medieval monastic ideal. The writings of Bruni were celebrated as especially influential in articulating this new, secular and 'active' perspective. In a famous article of 1938, for example, the historian Hans Baron, key in formulating the notion of civic humanism, drew a sharp contrast between Bruni's enthusiastic championing of Cicero as a Roman patriot and statesmen with medieval views of Cicero that cast him as a contemplative, world-denying sage.[29]

Interesting though the civic humanist tradition foregrounded by Baron and others undoubtedly is, to see this as representative of Italian humanism in general is misleading. As proof, we only need to compare Bruni's career and intellectual production with that of his younger contemporary Ambrogio Traversari (1386–1439), born in Forlì, near the Adriatic coast, but resident in Florence for much of his adult life. Traversari, like Bruni, was one of the first humanists with a good knowledge of Greek, and he was deeply involved in the study of Greek and Latin antiquity. He wrote in Ciceronian Latin, and he moved in distinguished humanist circles; he was a close friend of Niccolò Niccoli, owner of the finest classical library in early fifteenth-century Florence, and of the important humanist patron Cosimo de' Medici, for whom he translated Diogenes Laertius's *Lives of the Philosophers*. Traversari even played a role in the Florentine artistic Renaissance in the 1420s, when he collaborated with Cosimo de' Medici and his brother Lorenzo to commission a sculpture from Lorenzo Ghiberti.

While Traversari's credentials as a humanist may hardly be doubted, he was very far from the model of lay state bureaucrat embodied by Bruni. He was a Benedictine monk, of the Camaldolese order, and his intellectual energies as a humanist were mainly taken up with work on the early Church fathers. Traversari translated numerous Greek patristic texts into Latin, most notably by St John Chrysostom, known as 'golden-mouthed' on account of his eloquence. Some patristic texts he even rediscovered, in monastic book-hunting expeditions reminiscent of Poggio Bracciolini's. The work of Ghiberti's that Traversari was involved in commissioning was a classicizing bronze reliquary in the form of an ancient sarcophagus, sculpted to house the remains of three third-century Christian martyrs. The casket stood in Traversari's convent of Santa Maria degli Angeli, which, under his guidance, became an important locus for the confluence of humanism and spirituality sometimes referred to by the formula of *docta pietas* ('learned piety').[30]

Looking at Bruni and Traversari together, it seems arbitrary and anachronistic to speak of one as more 'Renaissance' than the other. Certainly, it would be distinctly odd to label a figure like Traversari 'medieval' simply because his intellectual interests were predominantly theological and devotional in character—just as we would not label Ghiberti's reliquary as artistically 'medieval' simply because it was constructed to house the relics of saints. Traversari's cultural profile, as a cleric committed to the *studia humanitatis*, was as novel in the fifteenth century as Bruni's—indeed, more so, as fourteenth-century humanists had tended to be laymen, or at most in minor orders, like Petrarch. The rise of clerical humanism in the fifteenth century is one of the great signs of the success of the classicizing movement—an indication that the Church could not do without the intellectual technology humanism supplied. From the mid-fifteenth century, with Nicholas V and Pius II, Christendom had its first humanist popes.

One advantage of prising the story of the humanist movement away from the narrative of the rise of secularism is that it can help to account for the fact that 'medieval', other-worldly Christian values seem not only to have maintained themselves robustly throughout the entire period of the Renaissance, as traditionally understood, but also to have experienced a full-scale revival in the later sixteenth century, with the Counter-Reformation. The way in which this uncomfortable fact is conventionally dealt with is to portray the Counter-Reformation as a reactionary movement, which put an abrupt end to the Renaissance advance towards modernity (see Chapter 1). Once the relation between humanism and Christianity is understood in a more historically accurate manner, however, it becomes apparent that the Counter-Reformation was less a termination of the Renaissance than a continuation, albeit with changes of emphasis. The 'two humanisms' just detected, in Bruni and Traversari, were in equilibrium for much of the fifteenth and early sixteenth centuries, while, in the later sixteenth century, the Christian model took ascendance throughout most of Italy, with the partial exception of Venice. The impulse that prompted a Counter-Reformation proto-archeologist like Antonio Bosio (*c.* 1576–1629) to spend his life scouring the catacombs in Rome for evidence of Paleochristian remains was not so different from that which inspired Traversari to hunt down forgotten patristic texts. There is no reason why we should not see this story as part of the Italian Renaissance in the same way as that of the discovery of Nero's Golden House.

STRATEGIES OF CONCILIATION: ALLEGORY AND SYNCRETISM

A useful notion in understanding Italian Renaissance intellectuals' attitude to pagan antiquity is the linguistic concept of code-switching, used to describe the way in which bilingual or multilingual speakers move between languages in the course of a single conversation. We see much literal code-switching between Latin and the vernacular in sixteenth-century writings, most educated men being fluent in both. More than this, however, Renaissance Italians were adept at metaphorical, conceptual code-switching between Christian and classical culture, with their very different beliefs and values. If seriously interrogated on their beliefs, Renaissance Christians would happily have agreed that the Olympian gods did not exist, nor the Muses; that nymphs and dryads did not haunt the woods; that the world was not governed by the volatile and vindictive goddess Fortune, but by divine providence. For the purposes of art and literature, however, these strictures could be suspended. Renaissance Italians showed a marked ability to code-switch between the 'true' world of Christianity, and the 'false' one of paganism, moving between the two more or less seamlessly and drawing inspiration from both.

Nor was the true/false binary rigid. The argument that Graeco-Roman mythology, even if false on a literal level, could encompass allegorical truths had already been made by Boccaccio in the fourteenth century, but philosophical developments in the following century gave this claim a more robust grounding. One of the bodies of Greek philosophy that found its way to the West in the fifteenth century was the late, Hellenistic school of Platonic philosophy known as Neoplatonism—a version of Platonism that tended strongly towards the mystical and that is compatible with Christian monotheism in its positing at the centre of its metaphysics a supreme, transcendent One, identifiable with Good and Beauty. Ancient Neoplatonism was influential on early Christian theology, and Western Christians' re-encounter with it in the fifteenth century had a powerful impact precisely because of its strange mixture of familiarity and exoticism. Here was Christian theology, or something very like it, but voiced in a seductively arcane manner, accessible only to an intellectual elite.

Drawing on this consonance, the Florentine philosopher and priest Marsilio Ficino, a client of the Medici, evolved a modern, Christianized version of ancient Neoplatonism in his influential *Platonic Theology*. Ficino also translated and commented on the works of Plato, Plotinus, and other Platonic philosophers. Ficino argued for a direct relationship between pagan and Christian wisdom, both of which were the product of divine revelation. God simultaneously transmitted his truth to the Hebrew prophets of the Old Testament and the ancient Egyptian sage Hermes Trismegisthus, whom late Platonists claimed as the philosophical ancestor of Pythagoras and ultimately Plato. Both the prophets and Hermes communicated this truth 'darkly' (or 'hermetically'), in fables and riddles, and only with the coming of Christ was the truth adumbrated in these mysterious early writings made plain.

The model of philosophical syncretism practised by Ficino was not without roots within medieval Christian culture; Plato and Aristotle feature among the sages foretelling the birth of Christ on the late thirteenth-century façade of Siena Cathedral, and myth had long told that the classical prophetesses known as Sibyls had predicted the birth of Christ. Within Ficinian Neoplatonism, however, these mysterious hints became a system, and one that proved flexible enough to encompass other languages of dark truth. In addition to the supposed teachings of Hermes Trismegisthus, translated into Latin by Ficino as the *Corpus hermeticum*, other texts that fed into Ficino's tradition of *prisca theologia* (ancient theology) were the so-called *Chaldean Oracles*, thought to contain the wisdom of the Persian sage Zoroaster; Jewish Kabalistic writings (a special interest of Ficino's disciple, Giovanni Pico della Mirandola); and a treatise on hieroglyphs attributed to a mysterious ancient Egyptian author, Horapollo. These 'scriptures', thought by Renaissance Neoplatonists to date from the remotest antiquity, were in fact mainly products of mystic philosophical traditions of the first to the fifth centuries C.E. A fascinating visual document of Neoplatonic religious syncretism is found in the suite of rooms in the Vatican decorated for the notorious Borgia pope, Alexander VI, by the Sienese artist Bernardino di Betto, known as Pinturicchio ('the little painter'). The ceiling of one room contains representations of the ancient Egyptian gods Isis and Osiris, and the bull god Apis, a reincarnation of Osiris: a convenient way to unite the hermetic expression of sacred truths with glorification of the Borgia dynasty, whose heraldic emblem was a bull.

One convenient aspect of this Neoplatonic interpretive strategy was that it helped Renaissance Italians to domesticate some of those aspects of Roman religious mythology most disturbing to Christian morality, such as the so-called 'loves of Jove', more accurately termed serial episodes of rape and abduction, or Apollo's macabre flaying of the satyr Marsyas, who had the temerity to challenge him to a musical

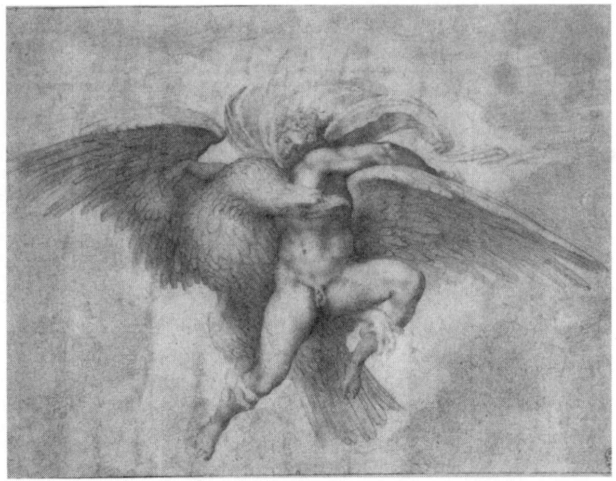

Fig. 15: Giulio Clovio, copy after a lost drawing by Michelangelo Buonarroti, *The Rape of Ganymede*, 1532.

duel. Seen through a Neoplatonic lens, these disturbing, violent myths became allegorical prefigurations of Christian truth. Jove's abduction of the shepherd-boy Ganymede, whom he carried off to Olympus in the form of an eagle, became an allegory of the Christian soul, rapt to heaven by God. Apollo's flaying of Marsyas had a similar meaning, illustrating graphically how union with the divine involved a shedding of the mortal self, figured in Marsyas's flayed skin. The possibility of a Christian meaning of this kind allowed Renaissance artists and poets to explore subject matter that would have been difficult to justify in its pure literal meaning. A classic example is Michelangelo's startlingly sexual drawing of Jove's abduction of Ganymede, which he sent in 1532 to the young Roman aristocrat Tommaso de' Cavalieri, with whom he was erotically obsessed (Fig. 15).

The Renaissance urge to conciliate ancient and Christian traditions of wisdom finds memorable artistic expression in Raphael's decoration of the Stanza della Segnatura in the Vatican (1508–11). The room was designed to house Pope Julius II's private library, and Raphael's frescoes for it allude to the contents of an ideal papal library, embracing theology, philosophy, law, and poetry. One shows Mount Parnassus, crowned by Apollo and Muses, surrounded by the greatest classical and Christian poets; another, law, in the paired figures of the Emperor

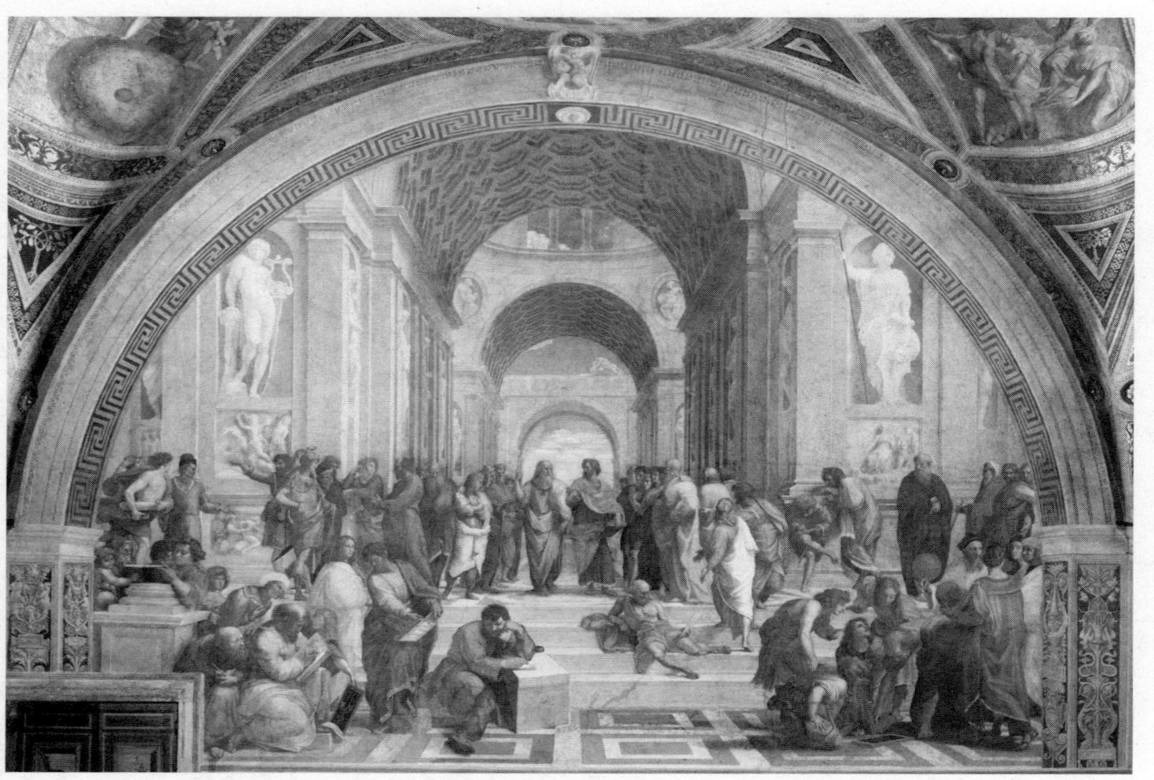

Fig. 16: Raphael [Raffaello Sanzio], *The School of Athens*, *c.* 1510–12. Stanza della Segnatura, Vatican Palace.

Justianian and Pope Gregory IX, the latter shown with the features of Julius himself. The two long walls figure Theology and Philosophy. The first, the so-called *Disputation on the Sacrament*, shows Christ in glory with the Virgin and the apostles, and below them an altar with the host, surrounded by Christian thinkers of all ages debating on the mystery of transubstantiation. Opposite this stands the most famous of all Raphael's paintings, known as the *School of Athens*, representing an animated throng of pagan philosophers engaged in disputation, with Plato and Aristotle at their centre, in a vast, imposing classical architectural space (Fig. 16). The scheme of the room translates into visual terms a favoured rhetorical theme of Julius II's papacy, of his Rome as a 'new Athens', embracing both ancient poetry and philosophy and Christian, revealed wisdom, reconciled in a harmonious whole.

STRATEGIES OF CONCILIATION: DOUBLE TRUTH

Raphael's luminous vision in the *School of Athens* is, of course, highly idealized. The reality of the relationship of Christian and pagan thought was considerably less harmonious, especially where the key figure of Aristotle is concerned. Despite the efforts of scholastics to Christianize Aristotle's philosophy in the first, medieval phase of its reception in the West, there was much in Aristotle's thought that was problematic for Christian thinkers. Most notably, Aristotle conceived of the universe as having existed from all eternity, rather than having been created, as was taught in Christian doctrine, and his *De anima* (*On the Soul*) is unclear on the crucial question of whether the soul is immortal. Aristotle's commentators differed on this point, with the influential twelfth-century Spanish-Muslim commentator Averroes (Ibn-Rushd) contending that only a collective 'possible intellect' enjoyed immortality, while the souls of individual human beings perished with their bodies. Debate on this subject, which had begun in the thirteenth century, was reinvigorated in the fifteenth century by humanism, as Aristotle's texts began to be studied in the original, and the works of early Greek commentators such as Themistius and Alexander of Aphrodisias began to be known.[31]

The danger of speculative Aristotelianism was one to which the Church was particularly sensitive, given the centrality of Aristotle within the university curriculum. In 1513, Julius II's successor Leo X felt the need to reaffirm that belief in the immortality of the soul was Christian dogma, and to stipulate that philosophers teaching texts that explored contrary hypotheses should make it clear to their pupils that these ideas contradicted revealed truth. The Paduan university professor Pietro Pomponazzi, one of the most original thinkers of the age, supplied a first test for Leo's bull with his treatise *On the Immortality of the Soul* (1516), which put the case for the 'mortalist' position quite robustly before concluding that reason is insufficient to resolve the dilemma, and that the Church's truth should be preferred. Pomponazzi's treatise proved predictably controversial—copies were even burned in Venice—but *On the Immortality of the Soul* was never banned. Even during the Counter-Reformation, Aristotelian philosophers continued to explore potentially heretical notions speculatively while protecting themselves by some variant of 'double truth' theory—the notion that the truths the Church teaches, attained through Christian revelation, may differ from the rational truths unaided human reason might reach.

Aristotelianism was not the only pagan philosophy that had the potential to trouble Christian belief systems. Others were Pyrrhonian scepticism, which taught that nothing could be known or rationally believed; and Epicureanism, which taught that the universe had come into being by chance, that the gods did not concern themselves with mortal affairs, and that the soul, like the body, was made up of material particles ('atoms') and hence that it perished on death. Both these philosophical schools became known for the first time in the fifteenth century, through texts such as Diogenes Laertius's *Lives of the Philosophers*, which summarized the thought of ancient philosophers as well as recounting their biographies, and Lucretius's compelling Epicurean philosophical poem *On the Nature of Things*, which was rediscovered by Poggio Bracciolini in 1417.

As was the case with Aristotelianism, we should not assume that the availability of ancient texts that contradicted Christian dogma was in itself sufficient to undermine the Christian belief system. Most Renaissance thinkers were too heavily invested in Christianity at a social, emotional, and intellectual level for their faith to be easily shaken; and a long tradition taught humanists to combine boundless admiration for classical culture with a conviction of its fundamental inadequacy, as the product of human reason operating alone without the aid of divine revelation. Humanists proved adept at incorporating elements of Epicureanism and scepticism into their thinking without feeling the need to respect the integrity of these philosophical systems in their original form. In his dialogue *On Pleasure*, Lorenzo Valla ingeniously misappropriated Epicurus's doctrine that pleasure was the highest human end, using it in a profoundly un-Epicurean manner to argue for Christian heavenly beatitude as the true end of human life. Still more improbably, Giovanni Francesco Pico della Mirandola, a disciple of the fundamentalist preacher Girolamo Savonarola, drew on the ancient sceptic philosopher Sextus Empiricus to advance a Savonarolan religious agenda, arguing that the erroneousness of all philosophy and of human reason in general underlined the importance of the Scriptures as the only valid source of truth.[32]

PANDORA'S JAR: THE DANGERS OF 'ANCIENT THINGS'

Despite the conciliatory and syncretistic tendencies of most Renaissance thinkers, it would be mistaken to speak of Christianity as having survived its prolonged encounter with the religious 'Other' of pagan antiquity entirely unscathed. New genies were let out of the bottle in this period, and older ones, like Averroism, gained new life and impetus. Awkward questions were raised, which it later proved difficult to suppress. An example of such challenging thinking was Pietro Pomponazzi's *On Incantations*, left prudently unpublished during his lifetime, but brought out posthumously in Basel in 1556. This treatise supplied natural explanations for elements of contemporary Christian belief such as the existence of angels, demons, and miracles, while at the same time rehearsing a historical interpretation of the rise and fall of religions that comes close to concluding that Christianity, like previous such 'laws', will naturally wane over time. *On Incantations* was placed on the Index of Prohibited Books, yet this ban did not prevent it from being taken up by seventeenth-century libertine thinkers, such as Giulio Cesare Vanini, who was executed for heresy in Toulouse in 1619. In a work purporting to condemn atheism, but generally considered to condone it, Vanini revisited Pomponazzi's thought, and that of other controversial sixteenth-century authors such as Niccolò Machiavelli, representing them as atheists who regarded religion either as a pure political imposture, or as a collective fiction constructed on the basis of 'miraculous' phenomena that in fact stemmed from natural causes.[33]

Vanini's citing of Machiavelli as an atheist was not without precedent in the sixteenth century. Already in the 1530s, well before

Innocent Gentillet's much-published *Anti-Machiavel* (1576), which popularized the notion of Machiavelli as devilish unbeliever, the English cardinal Reginald Pole was characterizing his works as having been 'written by the finger of Satan'. Most modern commentators rightly regard this imputation of atheism as a distortion, emphasizing that Machiavelli is careful to disassociate himself from questions of dogma, and to address himself purely to the role of religion within social and political life. Nonetheless, it is not difficult to see why Machiavelli's political writings caused such outrage as they first began to circulate in print, five years after his death in 1527 (interestingly, evidence of their initial, manuscript reception within the political circles of his native Florence suggests that they had occasioned relatively little controversy there).[34] A chapter in Machiavelli's *Discourses on Livy* (2.2) offers a coolly objective assessment of the respective virtues of the Christian and the ancient Graeco-Roman religions as ideological support-structures for political and military prowess, remarking that the pagan religion was superior in this regard, in that it glorified not 'humble and contemplative men'—the saints—but great warriors and leaders of men. More troubling still was Machiavelli's advice in *The Prince* that a ruler should systematically affect piety and moral virtue, while being prepared to act 'contrary to faith, contrary to humanity, contrary to charity, contrary to religion' when political circumstances demand.[35]

In the dedicatory letter of *The Prince*, Machiavelli identifies two contributory components in his thinking: his 'long experience of modern things' and his 'continual reading of ancient ones'.[36] When gauging the sources of his restlessly exploratory thinking, we must be careful to give due weight to both elements. As second chancellor of the Florentine republic between 1498 and 1512, Machiavelli was at the forefront of politics and diplomacy during a dramatic and volatile period in the Wars of Italy (see Chapter 3), and he observed the brutal, strongarm politics of the Borgia era from a front-row seat. At the same time, however, Machiavelli engaged deeply throughout his life in the study of classical history and thought, and we should not underestimate the role that his dialogue with the ancients played in the evolution of his thought. His engagement with Epicureanism, in the form of Lucretius, is documented by a manuscript copy he made of *The Nature of Things* in the 1490s; and there is evidence, too, for his engagement with the Greek historian Polybius, whose analysis of religion as an instrument of social discipline finds echoes in some of Machiavelli's views.[37] Even classical rhetoric, an indispensible tool for Renaissance political bureaucrats such as Machiavelli, offered models for a 'realist' analysis of political decision-making, setting moral considerations to one side to pursue the question of the material interest of the state.[38]

CONCLUSION

The extraordinarily protracted and intense experience of immersion in classical culture that lies at the root of what we call the Italian Renaissance left a powerful imprint on all aspects of elite cultural production, not only in Italy but throughout Europe. The classical world fascinated both for its similarity to modernity and for its intriguing and troubling otherness. It was both a mirror to the modern world and a fantasy parallel universe: an imaginative space in which thoughts that Christian doctrine would label as false and desires and imaginings that Christian social mores would condemn as deviant might be safely pursued under the guise of philosophical speculation, literature, and art.

This did not amount to anything that may be properly called 'paganism' or a rejection of Christianity; and the myth of a 'pagan Renaissance' is one of the many tendentious claims of nineteenth-century Renaissance historiography that modern scholarship has thoroughly laid to rest. Nonetheless, it seems undeniable that Renaissance thinkers and writers, through their prolonged double life in the pagan and Christian worlds, acquired a richly articulated, historically sedimented, contradictory and complex understanding of the world, founded on a kind of cultural 'bilingualism', to pursue my earlier linguistic metaphor of code-switching. While this did not weaken Christianity at any obvious level, it may certainly be seen within a longer historical perspective as having laid a conceptual basis for forms of relativistic thinking that would become more common in centuries to come.

3

THE RENAISSANCE AND THE MODERN

THE PAST REINVENTED

At the beginning of the second book of his treatise *On Painting*, written in the mid-1430s, the Florentine humanist Leon Battista Alberti gives a stirring account of the reverence in which the visual arts were held in ancient Rome. After pillaging Pliny's *Natural History* for a few anecdotes concerning regard for individual artworks (Demetrius I of Macedon supposedly refused to burn the city of Rhodes because a famous painting by Protogenes was housed there), Alberti goes on to speak of the social cachet attaching to artistic practice in the Roman world.

> The most noble citizens, philosophers and quite a few kings not only enjoyed painted things but also painted with their own hands. Lucius Manilius, Roman citizen, and Fabius, a most noble man, were painters. Turpilius, a Roman knight, painted at Verona. Sitedius, praetor and proconsul, acquired renown as a painter. Pacuvius, tragic poet and nephew of the poet Ennius, painted Hercules in the Roman forum.[1]

Alberti has a clear personal agenda here, as a man of elite ancestry who practised painting and sculpture as an amateur (he is responsible for what is probably the first independent artist's self-portrait, a bronze relief plaque showing him in Roman dress). More generally, however, Alberti's concern is with the broader societal status of painting, still to a large extent regarded as a 'mechanical art', or craft, the equivalent of carpentry or weaving, and hence below the purview of the elite. By emphasizing the exalted status the profession of artist enjoyed in the Roman world, Alberti seeks to persuade his contemporaries that it deserves the same status in present-day Italy.

The irony here is that, unlike their Greek cultural forebears, the ancient Romans had *not* accorded any special honour or status to artists. Most Roman artists were slaves or freedmen, and the profession was regarded as distinctly 'mechanical'. The passage in Pliny which is Alberti's main source here states that after Pacuvius, painting was no longer practised by 'respectable hands'. The obscure knightly Turpilius is cited as a rare exception, not by any means as a rule.[2] In Alberti's Italy, by contrast, the status of painters was already beginning the upward trajectory that would leave the leading painters of the sixteenth century adored cultural icons. Already in the fourteenth century the remarkable figure of Giotto had been honoured by the Florentine civic authorities and lauded by poets and humanists such as Dante, Petrarch, and Boccaccio. The most famous Tuscan painter of Alberti's own day, Masaccio, was the son of a notary, a distinctly 'respectable' profession. The fourteenth-century shift in artists' status is captured in Cennino Cennini's *Book of Art*, written around 1390, the first manual on art composed by a practising painter. Cennini concedes that some painters are drawn to the art by financial 'necessity' and 'gain', but notes that others choose art through an innate love of painting, seen as a sign of a 'noble spirit' (*animo gentile*).[3]

This passage in Alberti illustrates an interesting and relatively little-observed feature of Renaissance humanist culture—its tendency to craft convenient caricatures of antiquity to suit modern rhetorical ends. The classical world had the status of an unassailable paradigm in humanistic culture, and appeals to ancient precedent could offer powerful rhetorical ballast for recent and still precarious cultural trends. Another good example of this dynamic is found in the vision Italian humanists fabricated of women's social and cultural role in ancient Greek and Roman culture. By the later fifteenth century treatises and letters making the case that women's abilities fitted them for a wider range of activities than they were traditionally permitted were becoming commonplace, and, by the sixteenth, they exploded into a fashionable genre. Such treatises generally featured impressive lists of classical names of 'famous women', the product of humanists' sedulous trawling of classical texts. These included historically certifiable figures such as the philosopher Hypatia, the poets Sappho and Corinna, and the Syrian warrior queen Zenobia, but they were augmented by many figures of dubious historicity, such as the legendary Assyrian queen Semiramis, the Amazons, and Diotima, the mystic philosopher of Plato's *Symposium*. Some especially obscure figures turn out to be misreadings, such as 'Pythagoras's sister', sometimes found listed as a philosopher in humanist texts; this has been traced to a text linking Pythagoras to Delphi (the Greek word for sister is *adelphe*).[4]

The humanists' vision of a classical world filled with high-achieving women offered a powerful argument for reconsidering women's modern-day potential. This notion was, however, no more historically accurate than Alberti's account of ancient Rome's fabled tradition of high-born painters. As in the case of Alberti and painting, the humanists who advocated a broader vision of women's capacities were projecting back modern-day concerns onto their reading of antiquity. For reasons that will be examined in Chapter 6, women of the Italian elites in this period were beginning to attain a new cultural and political visibility, and the dominant feminine stereotype of the 'chaste, silent, and obedient' matron was proving inadequate to their self-image. The list of classical heroines crafted by Renaissance humanists supplied an ideal 'ancestry' for the modern court lady, freighted with the normative value and cultural capital that any allusion to antiquity possessed.

A CHANGING WORLD

Renaissance Italy's relationship with the classical past was inventive and adaptive because that relationship was functional, rather than purely scholarly or antiquarian. Humanism plundered the rich resources of antiquity the better to understand and explain and, where necessary, to retool or repackage contemporary Italian culture. Comparisons and analogies between ancient and modern were a fundamental cultural strategy of the period: great artists were 'the new Apelles' or 'the new Praxiteles'; great rulers 'the new Augustus'; great writers 'the new Virgil'—or, as women emerged as poets, 'the new Sappho'.

Despite this, however, Renaissance Italy was a very different place from its classical dream twin, and it was getting more different by the moment. In the course of the fifteenth century, three changes took place that revolutionized the West's experience of warfare, communications, and navigation. Gunpowder, which had already migrated to the West from China by the thirteenth century, began to become fundamental in warfare from around the mid-fifteenth century, following technological improvements. Moveable-type printing developed in Germany in the 1430s, spreading to Italy by the 1460s. Finally, this was the great age of world-expanding exploration. In 1492, the Genoese mariner Cristoforo Colombo, or Columbus, under the patronage of the Spanish monarchs Ferdinand and Isabella, became the first European explorer certifiably to cross the Atlantic and 'discover'—from a Eurocentric perspective—the New World.

None of these developments affected Italy exclusively, of course, but all three impacted immensely on Italian culture. A man born in 1460 who lived out his full 'three score years and ten', dying in 1530, would leave a world radically different in many ways than that into which he was born. In addition to printing, artillery, and the discovery of the New World, he would have witnessed the advent of the new medical scourge of syphilis, which arrived in Europe in the 1490s, probably as a legacy of the New World. He would also have seen the beginning of what proved the definitive schism of medieval Western Christendom in the form of the Protestant Reformation. Luther broke definitively with the Catholic Church in the early 1520s. By 1530, several German states had broken with Rome, as had a number of cities in Switzerland. England, Sweden, and Denmark followed suit over the next decade.

Italy also underwent very radical political change over this same period. In 1494, the French king Charles VIII crossed the Alps with an army, seeking to enforce a hereditary claim to the Kingdom of Naples. This was the first of a relentless series of foreign invasions, as the most powerful of the emerging nation-states of Europe, France and Spain, fought for possession of the Italian peninsula's rich spoils. Italy's political disunity served it ill in this period. In Machiavelli's withering analysis in *The Prince*, Italian rulers themselves conspired to bring about the peninsula's 'servitude' to foreign powers by actively inviting these powers to invade Italian soil, with the hope of using them in their own, parochial power-struggles against other Italian states. In 1559, when the Wars of Italy finally concluded with the Treaty of Cateau-Cambrésis, they left Spain the dominant power in Italy, ruling Milan and Naples, together with the whole of southern Italy, directly, and exercising hegemonic power over large parts of central and northern Italy. This sealed what had been the reality on the ground since the late 1490s, where the south and Milan were concerned. The first half of the sixteenth century hence proved a key turning-point historically for the Italian peninsula. Large swathes of northern Italy and the whole of the south would remain in foreign hands until the Risorgimento in the mid-nineteenth century.

Unsurprisingly, living in this volatile material and political environment, Renaissance Italians developed an acute sense of changeability as the fundamental condition of human life. Their classical erudition gave them a ready-made conceptual and discursive framework for managing this intuition, in the form of the notion of fortune, figured by the Romans as a goddess, Fortuna (the Roman equivalent of the Greek Tyche). Fortuna was traditionally conceived of as capricious and changeable, equipped with a turning wheel on which mortals were carried up or dashed down. Arbitrariness was an important feature of a Fortune-governed world. Although the Romans flirted with the notion that Fortune favoured the bold, more pessimistic versions of Fortune represented her as favouring no one consistently, or even perversely tending to favour the least deserving, in order better to demonstrate her power. The difference was very sharp from the Christian, providential version of historical causality, whereby the events of the world were determined by God, and hence could be assumed to have some benign or just meaning, even if this was not immediately apparent to human observers.

The Christian world-view, of course, had no place for goddesses, and a literal belief in Fortuna in the Roman sense would have been heretical. Renaissance humanists' capacity for conceptual code-switching was sufficient, however, to allow them to appropriate the notion of Fortune metaphorically without concerning themselves with its theological implications. Even when theological sensitivities around this subject grew with the Counter-Reformation, publishers could avoid censorship simply by appending a disclaimer to works that spoke of Fortune, noting that the term was not meant as a literal reference to an independent causal force. The metaphor of Fortune could be used, in practice—as it was by political thinkers like Machiavelli—to call attention to the complexity and unpredictability of the external forces determining human outcomes, and to emphasize the flexibility of response political actors should cultivate, in order to attain success in changing times. One of Machiavelli's key insights, writing at the time when the Italian Wars had dramatically demonstrated the powers of 'Fortune', was that to adhere to a single policy—or even a single, inflexible moral code—was potentially disastrous. Changeability was human beings' natural habitat, and they should evolve to accommodate that fact.[5]

If the new centrality accorded to the notion of Fortune was one consequence of the rapidly changing material landscape of early sixteenth-century Italy, an emerging notion of cultural progress was another. The two were complementary—where negative experiences such as the Wars of Italy tended to prompt gloom-ridden reflection on the arbitrariness of human existence, positive developments such as technological and cultural advances fostered a more optimistic view of society as evolving along a coherent trajectory. Our notional Renaissance everyman—born in 1460, dying in 1530—could hardly escape feeling that he had lived through an exceptional age, assuming he was culturally literate and engaged. In addition to the introduction and development of printing, and the discovery of the New World, he had lived through one of the most remarkable periods in the history of Western art, encapsulating the entire productive careers of Leonardo and Raphael, and a significant part of the careers of Michelangelo and Titian. He had also witnessed the rebirth of Italian vernacular literature, after a long period in the early fifteenth century in which Latin absorbed the majority of Italian humanists' literary energies. The opening decades of the sixteenth century saw the creation of one of the greatest narrative poems in the European tradition, Lodovico Ariosto's *Orlando furioso*, as well as the political writings of Machiavelli and Baldassare Castiglione's *Book of the Courtier*, the last vastly influential in shaping the ethos of 'Renaissance man' throughout Europe.

One intuition we find expressed increasingly in the course of the sixteenth century was that modern Italian culture had now reached the point where it rivalled or even surpassed the cultures of classical antiquity. This could be controversial where subjective literary or artistic judgments were concerned; when Ariosto's enthusiasts proclaimed his poem the equal of Virgil's *Aeneid*, this provoked a debate that continued for most of the sixteenth century.[6] Where material advances were concerned, however, there could be little room for doubt that the modern world had in some ways surpassed its classical role model. The ancients had not known the art of printing, nor the mechanical reproduction of images through engraving. They had fought with military means that seemed primitive to armies equipped with cannons and with increasingly portable and effective handguns. They did not know of the existence of the New World.

The combination of these two perceptions—of cultural progress, on the one hand; of the mutability of the human environment, on the other—gives sixteenth-century thought much of its peculiar air of modernity. Although we should be careful not to exaggerate the exceptionality of sixteenth-century Italians' sense of their age as one of accelerated change (few people in history can ever have seen their own era as static and changeless), it seems safe to generalize that a factor we have in common with observers in this period is precisely this sense of living in a rapidly changing world, with all the anxiety and exhilaration that brings.

Aside from the epochal discoveries of the age, and its dramatic political and religious history, change imposed itself on Italian sixteenth-century consciousness in less weighty respects. In dress, for example, this was the period when the modern notion began to consolidate that constantly changing fashions were an intrinsic feature of the elite sartorial system. This crowned a long-term trend towards an acceleration of changes of dress style dating back to the thirteenth and fourteenth centuries, when a consumer culture began to emerge within Italy's wealthy urban centres.[7] In a world in which the poor possessed few clothes over the course of their lifetime, and those mainly pre-worn, rapid changes of fashion were a way in which the elites and the aspirational 'middling sort' might mark their wealth, along with the use of luxury fabrics and complex tailoring. The result was a fashion culture sufficiently mobile to allow dress historians to date portraits to the decade in some cases. While the modern Italian term for fashion, *moda*, did not come into use until the seventeenth century, the term *foggia* conveyed the same meaning. John Florio's 1611 Italian–English dictionary translates it as 'any kind of fashion, guise, manner, forme, or new invention, namely in clothes and apparell', and conveys such associated, short-lived coinages as *foggiare* ('to follow fashions') and *foggiatore* ('an inventor or follower of new fashions'). Similarly, from the early sixteenth century, we begin to find the phrase *all'usanza* employed to mean what would later be called *alla moda*, to indicate a mode of dress in keeping with usage, or the time.[8]

One index of the Renaissance fascination with modernity and change was the fashion for books of inventions, such as Polidoro

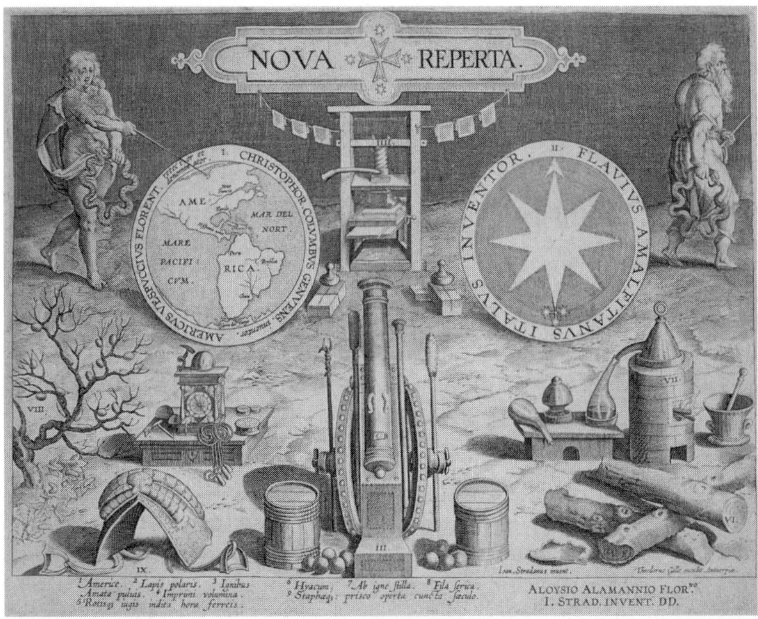

Fig. 17: Print by Jan Collaert after Giovanni Stradano [Jan van der Straet]. Title page to *Nova reperta* (*Modern Discoveries*), *c.* 1591.

Virgilio's vastly popular and much-translated 1499 compendium *On the Inventors of Things*.[9] Polidoro's book incorporates both ancient and modern inventions, but some treatments of the inventions theme are focused exclusively on modernity, such as the series of 20 engravings that the Florence-based Flemish artist Giovanni Stradano, or Jan van der Straat, made for the Florentine erudite Luigi Alamanni in the late 1580s.[10] Stradano's *Modern Discoveries* (*Nova reperta*) enticingly mix the geographical discoveries of Columbus and Magellan and technical innovations unknown to the ancient world, such as spectacles, stirrups, water mills, the printing press, the magnetic compass, clocks, gunpowder, the practice of polishing weapons, the art of engraving itself (Fig. 17). Less happily, syphilis also features, along with *guaiacum*, a New World drug used for its treatment. At the end of the Renaissance, Stradano's *Discoveries* allowed Florentines a dazzling vista back over an age of innovation, inviting them to measure how much the world they inhabited differed from the ancient world. The distance is extreme from the kind of humanistic worship of the superiority of antiquity that we see Leonardo Bruni portraying, and perhaps satirizing, in the figure of Niccolò Niccoli in his *Dialogues* of 1405, who represents modern culture in purely negative terms, as a squalid ruination of the splendours of the classical past.

THE 'DISCOVERY OF THE WORLD AND OF MAN'

Central to the conception of the Italian Renaissance as it emerged in nineteenth-century Europe was the notion that this age saw a new curiosity about the physical and human world, sharply contrasted with the medieval, otherworldly worldview. This vision is encapsulated in a phrase of Jules Michelet, later picked up and developed by Burckhardt, 'the discovery of the world and of man'.[11]

Although the starkness of Burckhardt's contrast between medieval and Renaissance is undoubtedly exaggerated, there remains an element of truth to it. The quantity and quality of the attention Renaissance Italians directed to the study of nature and society was impressive and innovative in many ways. The world was more thoroughly 'mapped' in 1600 than it had been in 1400, and not simply as a result of the expanding geographical reach of the 'age of discovery'. Important work was done in mathematics, in astronomy and cosmology, in anatomy, and in the various branches of natural history (botany, zoology, mineralogy, gemology). Engineering, surveying, navigation, and cartography profited from the development of new or improved instruments of measurement. Geography, history, and travel writing flourished, as did novel forms of ethnographic mapping such as Cesare Vecellio's remarkable costume books of the 1590s, illustrating the dress of men and women of different classes and social groups throughout Italy, Europe, Africa, Asia, and the New World, and ranging back from the present day to ancient Rome.[12]

Striking as an example of the protoscientific culture of the later Renaissance is the extraordinary natural history collection assembled by the Bolognese patrician Ulisse Aldrovandi, which he evocatively described as a 'microcosm' and a 'theatre of nature', as well as a museum.[13] In the year of his death, in 1605, Aldrovandi enumerated his collection as comprising more than 18,000 specimens of the 'diverse things of nature', including 7,000 dried plants in 15 volumes. In addition to material specimens, Aldrovandi's microcosm contained a vast collection of manuscript notes, drawings, and woodcuts intended to assist in the dissemination of his researches in print. Four volumes of his *Natural History*, classifying birds and insects, appeared during his lifetime, and a further nine were published posthumously by his students, covering molluscs and crustaceans, fish, mammals, serpents and dragons, monsters, minerals and mining, and dendrology.

The presence of a volume on monsters within Aldrovandi's natural-historical *microcosmus* serves as a useful reminder that the Renaissance culture of 'discovery of the world' did not fully map onto that of modern science, even if it presages it in some ways. Renaissance thinkers approached the study of the natural world with different methods, different assumptions, and a different perspective than later scientists. In Michel Foucault's influential formula in *The Order of Things* (1966), they operated according to a different 'episteme', or fundamental configuration of knowledge: a more mystical understanding of the universe, privileging the notion of resemblances between the cosmic, the natural, and the human spheres.[14] Renaissance thinkers also allowed more weight in their methodology to cultural and textual traditions, which supplemented and demanded to be integrated with empirical observation. The analytic headings Aldrovandi uses to organize his descriptions include such 'unscientific' categories as *mystica*, *moralia*, *hieroglyphica*, *emblemata*, so that his chapter on peacocks, for example, includes not only a physical description of the bird and a description of its diet and reproductive habits, but also a detailed discussion of the complex and contradictory moral and symbolic meanings that have attached to it within a long tradition of bestiary lore, religious allegory, and literary representation.[15]

The story of the Renaissance investigation of the natural and human world offers a vivid illustration of the ways in which humanism's rediscovery of classical culture interacted with often practically driven impulses to empirical exploration and experimentation. It also allows us to see in action the sense of progression, advancement, and modernity that is such a defining characteristic of the sixteenth century, in particular. Two fields well suited to this kind of analysis are physical and cultural geography, and the study of the human body through anatomy. The next two segments of this chapter will examine these two important areas of Renaissance intellectual and practical culture in turn.

MAPPING THE WORLD: GEOGRAPHY AND CARTOGRAPHY

The impulse towards a fuller description and mapping of the physical world in the Renaissance may be seen as stemming initially less from any intellectual or humanistic source than from the pragmatic culture of merchant shipping, an essential element in the infrastructure of late-medieval commerce. At some point in the twelfth or thirteenth century, in an important development in the history of navigation and cartography, nautical charts of the type sometimes known as 'portolan maps' began to appear, mapping coasts frequently sailed by merchant mariners with unprecedented precision. The origin of these maps is unsure, but it seems likely that they reflect a confluence of Byzantine and Islamic mapping traditions. Italian maps of this kind, such as the famous Carta Pisana, show the Mediterranean in great detail, together with a sketchier representation of coasts farther afield. The accuracy of portolan charts is remarkable by comparison with the contemporary world maps known as *mappae mundi*, which feature a symbolic, radically unrealistic treatment of space, intended to narrate the world and to convey cultural and especially religious information, rather than to assist materially in orientation and travel (Figs 18 and 19).

The development of portolan charts was dependent on a prior technological development: the introduction of the compass as a navigational instrument. The use of 'wet compasses' for navigation—magnetic needles suspended in water—is first recorded in Europe in the twelfth century (having previously developed in China). Its successor, the 'dry compass', evolved in the thirteenth. In addition to the traditional, coast-hugging navigation reflected in the portolan maps, the availability of compasses facilitated oceanic navigation, and the late thirteenth century saw the first, failed attempt to find a route across the Atlantic from Spain to India, on the part of the Genoese brothers Ugolino and Guido, or Vadino, Vivaldi (1291). The expedition vanished without trace, perhaps inspiring the fate that Dante, in his *Inferno*, imagines for the Greek hero Ulysses. Dante's Ulysses does not return to Ithaca after the Trojan War like Homer's; instead, gripped by an unholy desire for knowledge, he sails beyond the 'Pillars of Hercules' that God positioned at the straits of Gibraltar as the proper limit of human knowledge, continuing his 'mad flight' until his ship is sucked into a vortex and the waters close above his head. Ironically, the stirring oration Dante has Ulysses give to his

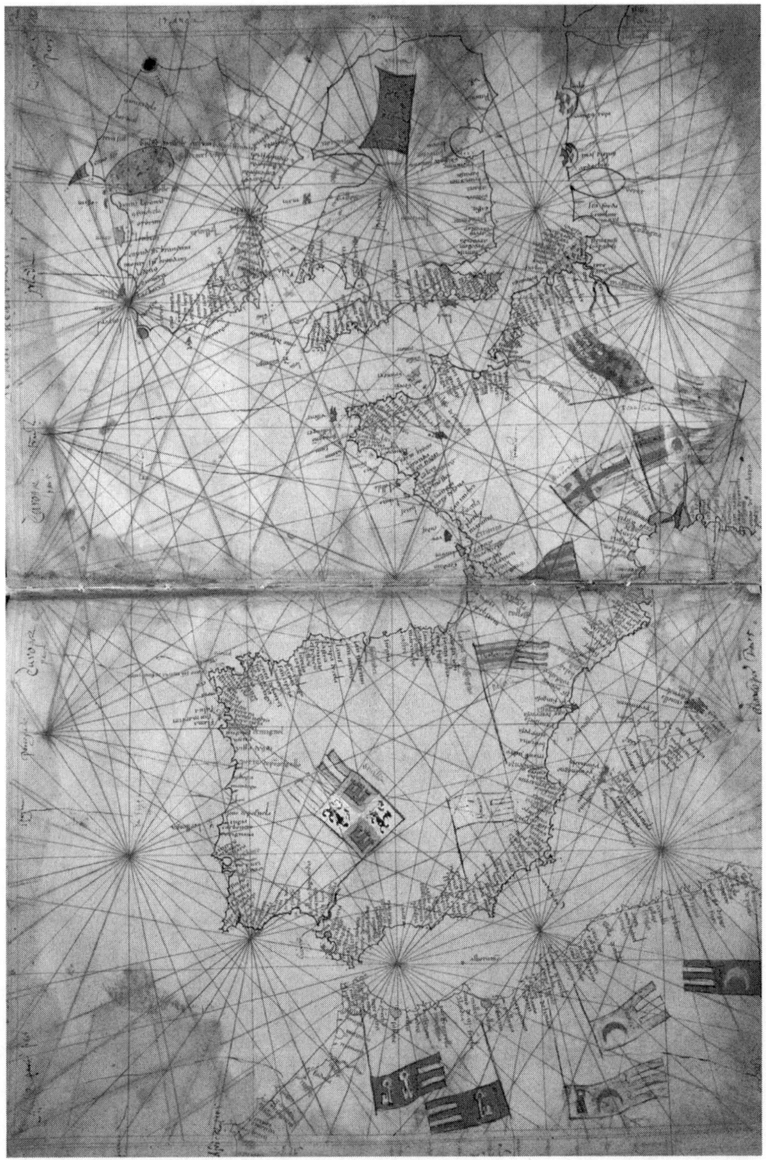

Fig. 18: Pietro Vesconte, Map of the Atlantic coast of Europe in the style of a portolan chart, showing north Africa, Spain, France, and the British Isles, from a manuscript of Marin Sanudo the Elder, *Liber secretorum fidelium crucis*, Venice, *c.* 1320–25.

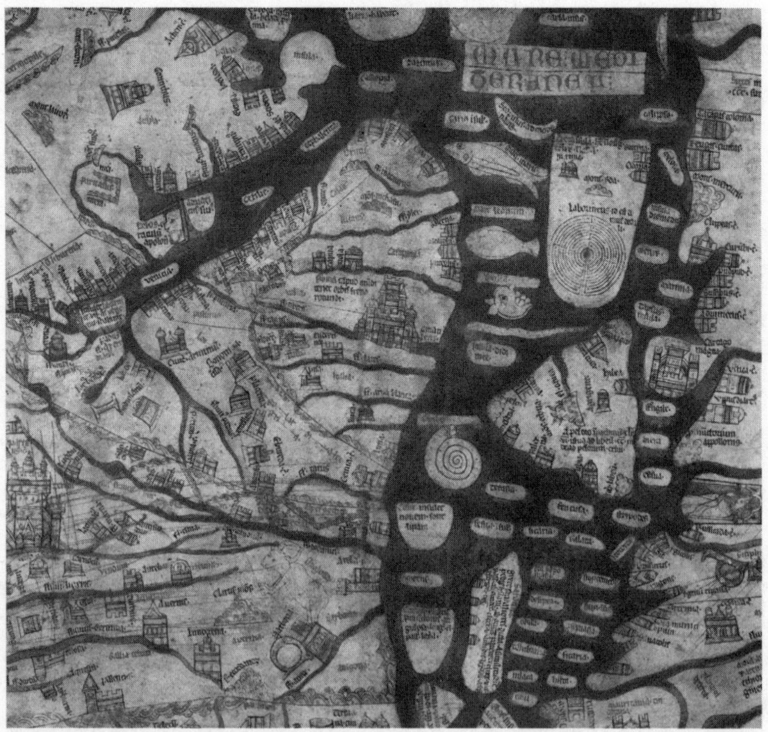

Fig. 19: Richard de Bello, detail depicting Italy from the *Hereford Mappa Mundi*, *c.* 1280. (The orientation of the map is approximately south–north, with the Greek mainland top left, the Italian peninsula in the centre, dominated by Rome, and Crete, with its labyrinth, and Sicily to the right.)

men—the speech that earns him his condemnation to Hell for 'false counsel'—is one of the earliest and most evocative anthems of the dawning age of exploration, speaking eloquently of the forbidden lure of experiencing 'the unpeopled world behind the sun'.[16]

Despite Dante's admonition, exploration beyond the Pillars of Hercules continued, with a probable voyage to the Canaries prior to 1339 by the shadowy figure of the Genoese Lanzarotto Malocelli, for whom Lanzarote is named, followed by a better-documented Italian-led, Portuguese-sponsored expedition of 1341, which mapped the entire archipelago of the Canary Islands for the first time. The thirteenth and early fourteenth centuries were also a period in which travel to India, Central Asia, and China was newly possible, in consequence of the so-called Pax Mongolica, the period of stability ushered in by Genghis

Khan's establishment of the Mongol Empire. Travellers to the East in this era include the Franciscans Giovanni da Pian del Carpine (*c.* 1180–1252), the author of an important *History of the Mongols*; Giovanni da Montecorvino (1247–1328), who established the first Catholic missions in China; and, more famously, the Venetian merchant Marco Polo (1254–1324), who, with his father and uncle, spent more than 20 years in China at the court of the legendary Mongol ruler Kublai Khan. Polo's memoir of his travels, ghost-written by Rustichello da Pisa, rapidly established itself as a classic of early travel writing and survives in around 150 manuscripts.

It is within this context of expanding horizons and cartographic experimentation that we need to locate the interest in geography manifested by Petrarch and Boccaccio, although a further impulse to this study undoubtedly derived from their encounters with classical texts. The principal works of ancient geography available to these authors were Pomponius Mela's *Chorography*, which Petrarch discovered in Avignon in 1335, and Pliny's *Natural History*, which he acquired in Mantua in 1350. The keenness of Petrarch's geographical interests is well illustrated by his annotations to the geographical sections of Pliny; he developed a system of marks highlighting the topographical features Pliny describes, distinguishing between mountains, rivers, and cities. Part of the impulse behind these labours lay in the frustration Petrarch felt in reading classical texts without adequate annotation. A long note in his manuscript of Virgil's *Aeneid*, at the point describing Aeneas's first sighting of Italy in Book 3, vividly illustrates the difficulty in Petrarch's day of spatially locating classical narratives and histories.

> Many things cause errors concerning the identification of places, including the following: the remoteness of some regions, inaccessible to men of the present day; the changes in names; the difficulties in locating some authors' works, and their obscurity; and sometimes the inconsistencies that exist among them; but above all the intellectual inertia of those who care for nothing they do not see before their eyes.[17]

Petrarch goes on to note that his own researches permit him to identify the site of Aeneas's first landfall as lying at Castrum Minervae, or Castro, in Puglia, speaking of his sources as 'not only the works of the *auctores*, especially the cosmographers, but also descriptions of the world and certain very ancient maps [presumably, portolan charts] that have come into our hands'.[18]

Boccaccio's intellectual commitment to geography was still more marked than Petrarch's, to the extent that he wrote two Latin works on the subject. One was a dictionary of classical topography, systematizing the kind of identification work Petrarch had begun in his annotations to Pliny (*On Mountains, Forests, Springs, Lakes, Rivers, Swamps or Marshes, and on the Different Names of the Sea*). Boccaccio worked on this for around a quarter of a century, from 1350 to his death in 1374. His other geographical work, more contemporary in its focus, was *On the Canaries and the Other Islands Newly Found in the Sea Beyond Spain*, a Latin account of the 1341 expedition to the Canary Islands drawing on an eyewitness vernacular letter by one of its lead mariners, Nicoloso da Recco. Boccaccio's fascination with travel and topography is also apparent in his narrative masterpiece, the *Decameron*, whose stories have the reach of a portolan map, spanning the Mediterranean from Acre and Alexandria to Majorca and Marseilles.

The fifteenth century, with the beginnings of Greek study, saw a remarkable expansion of geographical erudition, as the sophisticated learning of the Hellenistic world became available for the first time. Among the earliest Greek texts to be translated into Latin was the *Geography* of Ptolemy of Alexandria, translated in the first decade of the century by Jacopo Angeli da Scarperia, a student of Manuel Chrysoloras. Ptolemy's text exemplified a mathematical approach to geography, using geometrical coordinates, or latitudes and longitudes, to map the world. This transformed the practice of mapmaking, inspiring cartographic feats such as the extraordinary sets of manuscript maps produced in the late 1440s–1450s by the traveller and Camaldolese friar Fra Mauro, in collaboration with the mariner and cartographer Andrea Bianco (Fig. 20), or the series of maps made by the German-born monk, Nicholas Germanus, to accompany a deluxe printed edition of Ptolemy in 1470.[19] Building on the earlier innovations of the fourteenth-century Genoese cartographer Pietro Vesconte, these mapmakers began to reconfigure the world map in the realist idiom of the earlier portolan charts. While drawing richly on Ptolemy, later fifteenth-century maps also incorporated material deriving from post-classical sources, some very contemporary. Besides Marco Polo and Muhammed Al Idrisi (1099–c. 1165), the sources for Fra Mauro's map include Alvise da Mosto, or Cadamosto (1432–83), who had compiled a detailed record of his exploration of the west coast of Africa in the 1450s in the service of the Portuguese.

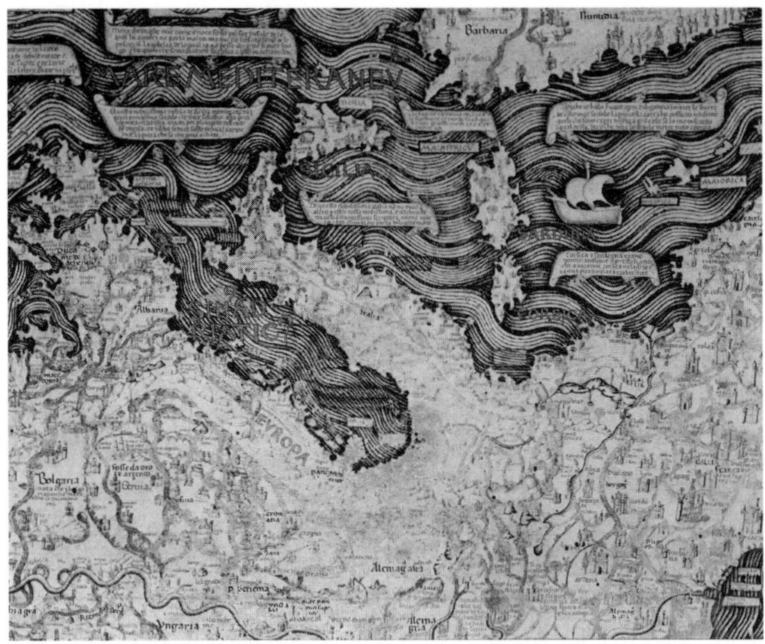

Fig. 20: Detail of Italy and the Mediterranean Basin, from the only extant copy of the world map of Fra Mauro (*c.* 1450), in the Biblioteca Marciana, Venice. (The map is oriented south–north, with the coast of Africa top right.)

If Ptolemy's mathematical approach to geography inspired a new school of cartography, another Hellenistic rediscovery of the fifteenth century, Strabo's *Geography*, launched a new humanistic tradition of geographical works of a more cultural-historical, 'human geography' kind. The founding text of this tradition is Biondo Flavio's *Italy Illuminated* of the 1450s, a detailed geographical-historical account of the various regions of Italy, notable for its precocious sense of Italy as a unified territory. Following Flavio, Enea Silvio Piccolomini, the future pope Pius II, wrote descriptions of Bohemia and Germany, as well as a universal history, which sets out to compare and synthesize the findings of ancient and modern geography. A copy of the first printed edition of Piccolomini's text held by the Biblioteca Colombina in Seville was owned and annotated by Christopher Columbus: an evocative record of the intersection between the humanistic and the practical traditions of geographic exploration. The importance geography had assumed in humanistic culture by the early sixteenth century is well illustrated in Raphael's *School of Athens*, discussed in Chapter 2. Ptolemy and Strabo are given a prominent place in the lower right hand corner of the painting, grouped with artists and flanked by geometers, as the 'philosophers' most invested in mapping the physical world.

By the time Raphael painted this image, of course, the discovery of the New World had lent a new excitement to the discipline of geography. The year before he started work on it, 1508, saw the first printed edition of Ptolemy to be updated with a map of the new land mass beginning blurrily to take shape across the ocean. Print technology allowed written accounts of the expeditions to be disseminated rapidly and widely. Columbus's letter describing his first 1492 voyage was first printed in Italy, in a Latin translation, in May 1493, two months after his arrival back in Spain. By June, a versified version was available in the Italian vernacular (Giuliano Dati, *The New Islands Found by the King of Spain*). It has been estimated that around 3,000 copies of the letter were printed in Europe between 1493 and 1500, half of them in Italy.[20] Amerigo Vespucci's letters, too, circulated widely, as did the various editions of the first formal history of the voyages of discovery, Pietro Martire d'Angheria's *Decades on the New World*, published between 1516 and 1530. Such was the demand for exploration literature that older works found their way into print at this time, alongside burningly current ones. A collection of 1507, *New-Found Lands and New Worlds*, includes Alvise da Mosto's 1450s narrative of his explorations of west Africa, as well as the more recent exploits of Vasco da Gama, who pioneered a new sea route to India via the Cape of Good Hope, and of Pedro Alvarez Cabral, who discovered Brazil.

It was not solely through textual accounts that the New World entered Italy. From the earliest voyages onwards, explorers brought with them plants, animals, birds, and rare woods. Other such *mirabilia* (marvels) arrived from the Far East, newly opened up to European travel since da Gama's voyage in 1498, and from the coastal regions of Africa, increasingly frequented at this time. It has been estimated that more than 20 times as many new species of plants entered Europe in the course of the sixteenth century than in the previous 2,000 years.[21] Already in 1515–18, when Giovanni da Udine painted his exuberant—and uncannily accurate—festoons of fruits, vegetables, and flowers in Agostino Chigi's riverside villa in Rome (now known as the Farnesina), he included three New World

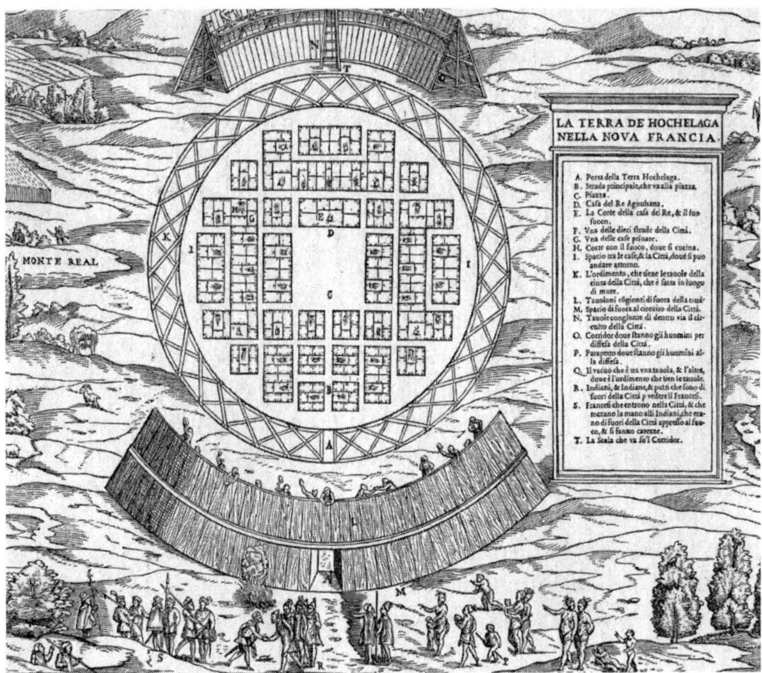

Fig. 21: Giacomo Gastaldi, Iroquois Village in Hochelaga, Canada, from the third volume of Giovanni Battista Ramusio, *Delle navigationi et viaggi* (Venice: heirs of Luc'Antonio Giunti, 1566).

plants among the 170 species portrayed there, including the first European image of maize.[22] The arrival of such novelties intersected with humanism to promote new research and inquiry, exactly as in the parallel case of geography. In 1545, the first botanical garden in Europe was founded, in Padua—first, nominally, as a medicinal resource, but soon for more disinterested botanical study. A year earlier, the Sienese doctor and naturalist Pier Andrea Mattioli had published his commentaries on the Greek herbalist Dioscorides, naming a hundred species unknown to his classical predecessor, including the tomato, described here for the first time.

The greatest textual monument to the Renaissance interest in travel, first published between 1550 and 1559, was the Venetian Giovanni Battista Ramusio's remarkable three-volume anthology, *Navigations and Voyages*, containing accounts of voyages to the Near and Far East, to Africa, and to the New World (Fig. 21). Ramusio's collection has a distinctly Italian, and Venetian, take on the age of discovery: the first volume opens with a parallel between Marco Polo and Columbus, as the great pioneers of land exploration eastwards and sea exploration to the West. A point of interest in Ramusio's collection, and of sixteenth-century travel writing more generally, is the confidence it evinces at points concerning the superiority of modern geographical knowledge to ancient. Introducing the illustrative maps in the second edition of Volume 1 of his *Navigations and Voyages*, Ramusio notes that they illuminate the world in such a way that 'there will be little need henceforth to weary oneself over the tables of Ptolemy'. Amerigo Vespucci says of the New World's fauna, 'Pliny did not touch upon a thousandth part on the species of parrots and other birds, and animals, too, which exist in those same regions'.[23] Most emphatically of all, Ramusio prefaces his translation of a text attributed to the ancient Greek writer Arrian with an exasperated comment on the inconsistency of the revered geographical authorities of antiquity, concluding that 'men who delight in knowing the places of the earth should give infinite thanks to the Lord for ensuring that they were born in the present day'.[24]

MAPPING MAN: DISSECTION AND ANATOMY

The discovery of the inner 'geography' of the human body through dissection followed a trajectory similar in some ways to that of the exploration of the external physical world, in terms of the interaction of humanistic study and practical, empirical exploration. A major difference, however, is the status of the disciplines. While geography as a field of study was essentially a humanistic rediscovery, conducted by interested individuals outside the context of the universities, medicine was a recognized academic discipline long before the advent of humanism. Salerno, south of Naples, had an internationally famous medical school, which attained its peak of influence between the tenth and thirteenth centuries. By the second half of the thirteenth century, the study of medicine had been institutionalized at the University of Bologna, where it was taught in close conjunction with the arts and with Aristotelian natural philosophy. The principal ancient authorities on medicine, Galen and Hippocrates, were known in this period, in Latin translations from the Greek via the Arabic, and

Latin translations were also available of the principal authorities of the medieval Arabic tradition, notably the eleventh-century Persian polymath Avicenna.

It is at the University of Bologna in the early fourteenth century that we first find evidence of the use of human dissection in university medical education, as a practical adjunct to the study of Galen's anatomical writings (animal dissections had already been practised at Salerno). An outstanding document of this early phase in the history of anatomical study is represented by the 1316 dissection manual and anatomy treatise of the Bolognese professor Mondino de' Liuzzi, *Anathomia*: an immensely influential text that continued to be published and used in university teaching for the next two hundred years. Although Mondino's are the first recorded dissections for teaching purposes, it seems likely that the practice was introduced by his predecessor Taddeo Alderotti in the late thirteenth century, which is the time when we begin to find the earliest recorded instances in Italy of autopsies carried out for public health and forensic reasons. From these Bolognese beginnings, the practices of autopsy and pedagogical dissection spread to other centres in Italy across the course of the fourteenth century.[25]

The reintroduction of dissection as a routine practice within medical teaching was historically momentous; this was the first time dissection had been practised systematically since the early third century BCE, when it was briefly adopted by the Alexandrian medical school under Herophilos of Chalcedon and Erasistratus. Dissection of human bodies was banned in ancient Rome on religious grounds, with the result that Galen was limited to practising dissection on animals anatomically close to humans, such as pigs and Barbary apes. Thus we see that, ironically, one of the most 'medieval' aspects of Christianity, its disdain for the corruptible and mortal physical body, in this case enabled a distinctly 'Renaissance' practice, which would eventually contribute significantly to man's understanding of the physical world. That there was no medieval taboo on dissection of the body is strikingly illustrated by the fact that post-mortem autopsies were conducted on men and women of outstanding holiness in search of the secrets of their sanctity (images of the cross and the other instruments of the Passion were found in the heart of St Chiara of Montefalco when she was cut open in 1308; three stones bearing holy images in that of the Blessed Margherita of Città di Castello in 1320).[26] Medical dissection, in which the form of the body and face were destroyed, was regarded with greater distaste, and it was generally conducted on executed criminals; yet it was not regarded as a sacrilege. Pope Sixtus IV gave official sanction to the practice in 1482, as long as it was conducted with the approval of the ecclesiastical authorities, and was followed by Christian burial of the remains.[27]

Partly because the medieval scholastic tradition of medical teaching was so firmly entrenched in the fourteenth- and fifteenth-century Italian universities, the impact of humanism on the discipline was relatively belated, although humanist interest in medicine was stirred by the discovery of the Roman writer Aulus Cornelius Celsus's elegant and accessible compendium *On Medicine* in 1426. In the second half of the fifteenth century, we find the humanist Niccolò Leoniceno calling for a reformed and classicizing model of medical study, based on the original Greek texts of Galen, Hippocrates, and Aristotle, and on their early Greek commentary tradition. Significantly, Leoniceno taught not at the long-established scholastic powerhouses of Bologna or Padua, but rather at a far more recent institution, the University of Ferrara, founded in 1391 under the aegis of the d'Este family, noted for their interest in humanist culture. A cultured bibliophile, close to the court, he may be seen as a prototype for the new model of humanist doctor who would become a familiar figure in the cultural landscape of the sixteenth century. More broadly, Leoniceno exemplifies the rise of scientific humanism in general in the later fifteenth and early sixteenth centuries, initially primarily in Latin, but, from the 1520s and 1530s, increasingly also in Greek.[28]

A further important development in the history of dissection in this period was a growing interest in the practice on the part of artists. As realism in the rendition of the human body became an imperative in art, and as the influence of antiquity reintroduced the nude into artists' repertoire, a close knowledge of anatomy became an ever more crucial qualification for artists to acquire. From the later fifteenth century, we begin to find the first indications of artists taking an interest in *notomie* (literally 'anatomies'), as dissections were called. The sixteenth-century painter and art historian Giorgio Vasari credits the Florentine Antonio Pollaiuolo with priority on this score.[29] Although art historians dispute whether Pollaiuolo observed

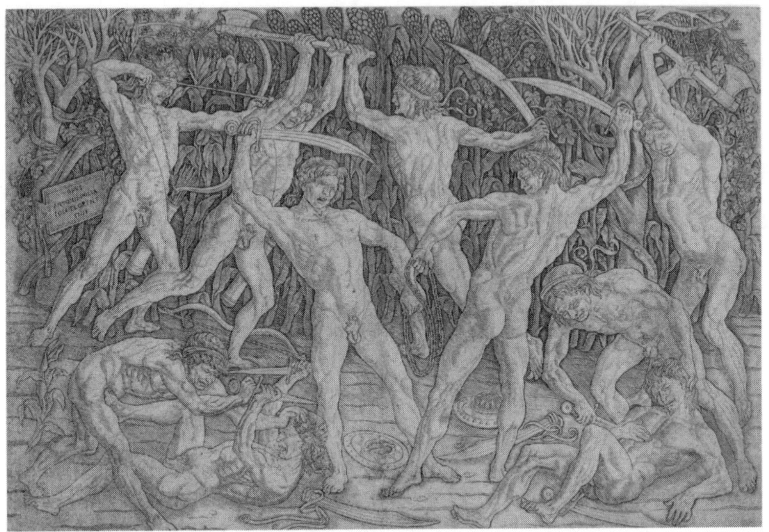

Fig. 22: Antonio Pollaiuolo, *Battle of Nude Men*, *c.* 1470–74, engraving.

notomie himself, or whether he limited himself to a close scrutiny of surface anatomy, his *Battle of Nude Men* (*c.* 1465) certainly broke new ground in the explicitness and detail of its representation of human musculature (Fig. 22).[30]

The most famous instance of an artist's involvement in dissection is, of course, that of Leonardo da Vinci, who combined artistic and scientific-philosophical interests more fully than any other figure of his day. Leonardo first seems to have developed a systematic interest in anatomy in the 1480s, when he was employed at the court of Milan. There, precisely on 2 April 1489, he commenced what he later described as a 'book entitled *The Human Figure*', initiated with a series of remarkable studies of skulls, employing techniques developed by architects and engineers to reproduce three-dimensional effects within a two-dimensional medium like drawing (Fig. 23).[31] Leonardo's interest in the subject grew in the first decade of the sixteenth century, and he gained first-hand experience of 'anatomizing' (his first recorded dissection, in 1507, was famously of a man claiming to be 100 years old and who died peacefully 'without any movement or sign of any other mishap'; Leonardo speaks of dissecting him to discover the secret of 'so sweet a death').[32]

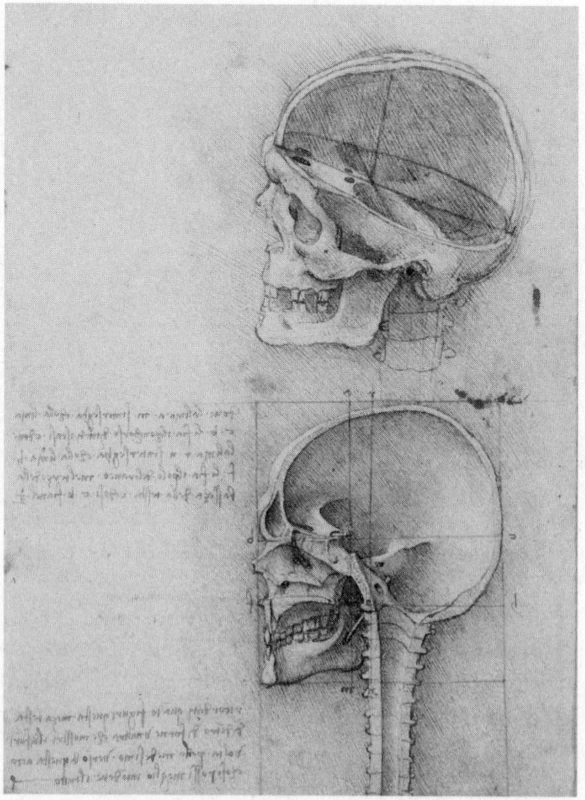

Fig. 23: Leonardo da Vinci, two drawings of skulls seen from the left, 1489. Royal Collection, Windsor [RCIN 919057].

According to Vasari, in 1510–11, Leonardo collaborated with the medic Marcantonio della Torre, a professor at the University of Pavia, with the intention of publishing a work on anatomy, although the plan was interrupted by della Torre's early death.[33] Whatever the truth of this, the legacy of anatomical drawings Leonardo left is striking both for its level of scientific insight and the clarity and finesse of its artistic rendition. In some cases, Leonardo's drawings record details of human anatomy that academic medicine did not register for centuries afterwards.[34] Although he never published his drawings, certain of Leonardo's representational techniques appear to have become known to his fellow artists, and the early sixteenth

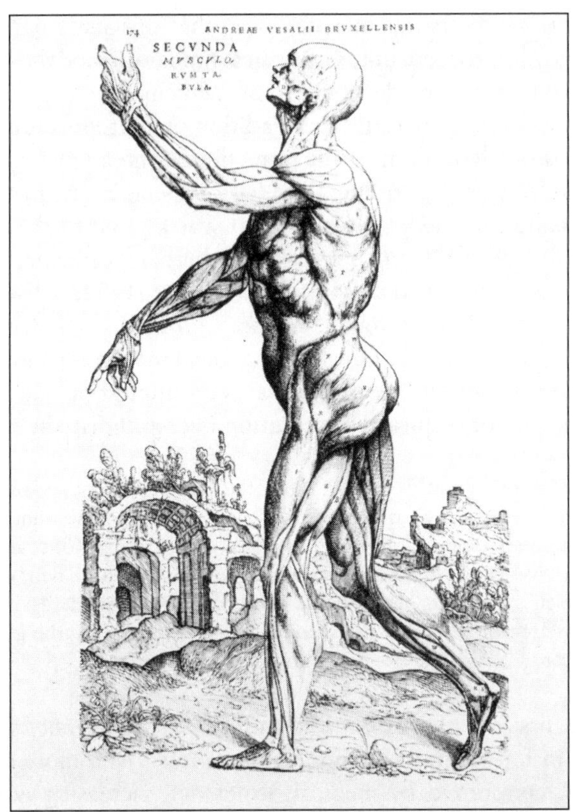

Fig. 24: Second plate of the muscles, from Andreas Vesalius, *On the Fabric of the Human Body* (*De humani corporis fabrica*) (Basel: Johannes Oporinus, 1543).

century saw the art of anatomical drawing generally advancing to a remarkable degree of accuracy (Fig. 24).

Leonardo was unusual for his day in his investigative attitude to dissection, as a means of gaining new knowledge about the structure and functioning of the human body. Within university culture, dissection had traditionally been relegated to a pedagogical and illustrative role, providing visual evidence of a textually inscribed and implicitly unimprovable body of knowledge. Standard university practice was for technicians such as barber-surgeons to conduct dissections while the *praelector* in charge read and commented on Mondino's work. By the early sixteenth century, however, attitudes were beginning to change in such a way that this static paradigm of knowledge came to seem obtuse. Medical humanism and the discovery of Celsus's text had made scholars of medicine more aware of the ancient Alexandrian investigative tradition of anatomy embodied by Herophilos of Chalcedon. At the same time, contemporary advances in geography were spreading the idea that empirical investigation might expand knowledge beyond what was known to the ancients. Already in the field of botany and herbal medicine, Niccolò Leoniceno had published a provocative treatise (1492; revised 1509), pointing out numerous errors in Pliny's *Natural History*, arising both from Pliny's confusion of Greek terms for plants and his insufficient observation. Leoniceno's work contains an interesting statement on the importance of empirical observation over authority in science:

> Why did nature grant us eyes and the other senses, if not that we might see and investigate the truth with our own resources? We should not deprive ourselves and, following always in others' steps, notice nothing for ourselves: this would be to see with others' eyes, hear with others' ears, smell with others' noses, understand with others' minds, and decree that we are nothing more than stones, if we commit everything to the judgment of others and decide on nothing ourselves.[35]

By the first decades of the sixteenth century, university studies of anatomy in Italy were beginning to move towards a more empirical paradigm, epitomized by medical professors' increasing willingness to dirty their hands in the practice of dissection. An anatomy treatise by Jacopo Berengario da Carpi, published posthumously in 1535, dissents from Galen on a number of points, rooting its arguments in the author's experience of dissection.[36] More famously, in 1543, the great Flemish-born anatomist Andreas Vesalius (Andries van Wezel) published his influential treatise *On the Fabric of the Human Body*, based on dissections he conducted in Padua, and including an illustration of Vesalius himself in the act of dissecting an arm. Vesalius's treatise is notable for its numerous corrections to Galen's anatomical writings and its trenchant assertion that Galen's errors derived from the fact that his knowledge of the interior of the human body was based on the dissection of animals, rather than humans.[37] Although Vesalius, in humanist fashion, represented his modern practice as a return to antiquity, and specifically to the pre-Galenic, Alexandrian tradition of dissection-based anatomy, his correction of Galen met with some sharp opposition. Vesalius's Paris-based former teacher Jacobus Sylvius (Jacques Dubois) punningly branded him Vaesanus (meaning a madman) and claimed that, rather than Galen being incorrect, we should rather assume that human anatomy had changed since Roman times.[38] Despite such resistance, however, Vesalius's empirical tradition flourished in later sixteenth-century Italy. Further advances in anatomical knowledge were made by Matteo Realdo Colombo, who collaborated with Michelangelo in the 1540s; by Gabriele Falloppio, famous for his discovery of the Fallopian tubes, though also the author of breakthroughs in the understanding of the anatomy of the head and ear; and by the embryologist Girolamo Fabrici d'Acquapendente, whose pupils included William Harvey, discoverer of the circulation of the blood.

GIORGIO VASARI AND THE PROGRESS OF ART

The histories of geography and of anatomy illustrate areas of Italian Renaissance culture in which the study of ancient texts combined with empirical observation to produce knowledge that might clearly be represented as an advance on that of the ancients. The nature of these fields made such judgments relatively easy. It was difficult by 1550 to deny that the moderns knew of lands of which the ancients had been ignorant; and it was equally difficult by 1600 to deny that modern anatomists knew the human body more accurately in certain respects than did Galen. By the later sixteenth century, Falloppio could compliment Herophilos's greatness by describing him as the Vesalius of antiquity: a telling reversal of the long-established humanist commonplace that flattered modern thinkers or writers by describing them as the Socrates or the Virgil of their day.[39]

Within fields such as art and literature, the notion of progress was clearly more problematic, since it inevitably had to rest on subjective judgments of aesthetic value. This, however, did not impede the Tuscan artist and writer Giorgio Vasari, chief artistic advisor to the Medici court in the mid-sixteenth century, from elaborating a narrative of artistic progress sufficiently compelling and confident to shape the nascent disciplines of art history and criticism in ways that may still be felt today. Vasari's *Lives of the Artists*, first published in 1550 and then in a revised version in 1568, tells how Italian art emerged from crude beginnings in the thirteenth century to a point where it equalled the great achievements of the ancients. Still more stirringly, Vasari claimed that his contemporary Michelangelo Buonarroti reached beyond the highest achievements of antiquity. Equally titanic in his accomplishments as painter, sculptor, and architect, Michelangelo had left the legendary Greek artists lauded by Pliny far behind.

Vasari's *Lives of the Artists* is one of the great books of the Italian Renaissance: formidable in its research and vast in its scope and ambition. It is also highly original in its conception, having no obvious classical or humanistic model. Collections of biographies of men prominent in particular fields were a popular genre, stemming back to works such as Diogenes Laertius's *Lives of the Philosophers* and the *Lives of the Ten Attic Orators* long attributed to Plutarch. A Renaissance example, crafted in the form of a dialogue, is Lilio Gregorio Giraldi's 1545 *On the Poets of our Times*.[40] Vasari combines this biographical model with an ambitious cultural-historical narration of the evolution of the arts over time, structured as a process of growth and maturation. There are some parallels for this in Cicero's account of the development of Roman oratory in his dialogue *Brutus*, in Pliny's narration of the evolution of Greek and Roman art in the thirty-fifth book of his *Natural History*, and in Vitruvius's history of the development of Doric, Ionic, and Corinthian orders in the fourth book of his *On Architecture*, but none of these classical texts matches Vasari in the structural centrality they accord to the notion of progress.[41] In a way that profoundly shaped the subsequent tradition of art history, Vasari narrated the story of Italian art between the thirteenth and the sixteenth centuries as one of maturation, with each age improving on the previous one. He organizes his artistic biographies into three broad chronological-stylistic eras and prefaces his discussion of the artists of each era with a general discussion of the characteristics of that age. The first era runs from Cimabue in the mid-thirteenth century down to the end of the following century, while the second encompasses the majority of the fifteenth century, from the heroic generation of Masaccio, Donatello, and Brunelleschi down to the time of Botticelli, and the third focuses on artists of the early sixteenth century (extending to the mid-sixteenth century in the expanded second edition). The divisions between the eras are not solely chronological. Botticelli, Luca Signorelli, and Pietro Perugino, all born in 1445 or 1446, are regarded as part of the second age, while Leonardo da Vinci, born only seven years later, ushers in the third and greatest age.

In a manner already established in evolutionary accounts of the arts in antiquity, Vasari represents the ascent of modern art partly in terms of advances in realism. After the initial quantum leap effected by Giotto, by comparison with his Byzantine ancestors (whom Vasari amalgamated into a single 'Greek painter'), the fifteenth century saw a further stride forward with the development of linear perspective. By the later fifteenth century, painters could reproduce nature with an accuracy of which no previous age could have dreamed. The third age, however, pressed beyond this achievement, creating paintings and sculptures more beautiful than anything in nature. Vasari here echoes Neoplatonic thinking about art, which saw its vocation as that of capturing the essence or 'Idea' of an object, rather than the imperfect appearances of the material world.

Taken on its own terms, Vasari's narrative of artistic development mimics the process of human development from childhood to adolescence to adulthood. The thirteenth-century emergence of art from its medieval doldrums is seen, however, not merely as a birth but a 'rebirth' or renaissance, so that the growth of Italian art is also a recapturing of an ancient maturity and formal perfection now lost. This was already an established humanistic model of cultural historiography, seen, for example, in Leonardo Bruni's *Life of Petrarch* (1436), with respect to literary and intellectual culture. Where Bruni only appeared to envisage the moderns eventually equalling the attainments of antiquity, however, Vasari went further, confidently stating that the classical tradition had been superseded by the art of his own day. In this audacious cultural leap, Vasari was assisted by the fact that so much of classical visual culture had perished—including the Greek tradition of painting almost in its entirety—making direct comparisons between ancient and modern achievements less easy to make than in the case of literary culture. Even so, we should not underestimate the significance of Vasari's assertion that modern art had come to equal that of antiquity, not as a piece of passing rhetorical hyperbole, but as a sober statement of fact.

It is interesting to consider the extent to which Vasari's triumphalist modernism in the *Lives* is indebted to the influence of contemporary developments such as Vesalius's correction of Galen and the growing sense among geographers and natural historians of the superiority of modern knowledge to ancient. It seems certain that he was aware of both, given the professional involvement of artists with the worlds of cartography and anatomy. At the time of the revision of the *Lives* for their second edition, Vasari was involved in an ambitious cartographic scheme for his patron, Cosimo I de' Medici, intended to decorate the *Guardaroba* of the Palazzo Vecchio in Florence. The project was effectively a 'microcosm', inspired by the same impulse to a theatricalization of knowledge as Aldrovandi's museum, containing more than 50 maps, representing the entire known world, together with cabinets of natural specimens and artworks from the various continents, and celestial and terrestrial globes.[42] Vasari's description of the maps, which were planned in collaboration with the cosmographer and polymath Egnazio Danti, emphasizes their extraordinary precision and modernity. All are 'measured with perfect accuracy and corrected after the most recent authorities', including Ramusio. As Vasari confidently states, in the whole history of cartography, 'no greater or more perfect' scheme has ever been realized.[43]

CULTURE AND TECHNOLOGY: THE IMPACT OF PRINT

By the later sixteenth century, the notion that antiquity represented an insuperable peak of cultural excellence that modernity could only strive to imitate had given way in several fields and disciplines to a more confident sense of the possibility of progress. In addition to the examples discussed here, others might easily have been selected—warfare, military architecture, surveying, cryptography, plastic surgery. This is not to mention astronomy, where the work of Copernicus and Tycho Brahe had begun to call into question the understanding of the structure of the universe that had prevailed since Aristotle's and Ptolemy's day.

The field in which it was most difficult for a sense of progress to take root was Renaissance humanism's original territory of literature, where the dazzling legacy of classical antiquity constituted a daunting obstacle. How could a modern writer equal the achievements of Homer, of Virgil, of Ovid, of Horace, of Cicero, especially when these figures came surrounded with the aura created by a millennium and a half of reverend commentary and citation? The problem was compounded by the fact that those modern writers who had the highest claim to rival the ancients—Dante, Petrarch in his lyric poetry, Lodovico Ariosto—were difficult to compare directly with their classical predecessors. This problem was especially marked in the cases of Dante and of Ariosto, in that they seemed to flout the rules of classical literature as Aristotle prescribed them and as theorists inferred them from classical practice. Dante came under fire for his lack of decorum, and his mingling of 'low' and high' styles in a single poem; Ariosto for the digressive structure of his poem, which derived from medieval traditions. Some apologists of Ariosto, such as Giovanni Battista Giraldi Cinzio, argued innovatively for a flexible and historically relativistic standard of literary excellence, so that Ariosto's *Orlando furioso* should not be judged by the standards of classical epic but considered on its own terms, as a representative of a new genre, romance.[44] This argument, however, struggled to make headway at a time when the Aristotelian ideal of unity of plot, articulated in the *Poetics*, was the object of new theoretical enthusiasm. It was not until Torquato Tasso, writing in the 1570s, produced his more classically regular *Jerusalem Delivered* that Italian critics could begin confidently to congratulate their culture on having produced the first true modern epic worthy of the name.

In two respects only could observers of Italian literary culture in the sixteenth century speak confidently of progress with respect to antiquity. One was a traditional one—that, for all its sophistication, classical literature was flawed on grounds of the intrinsic falseness of the religious beliefs that informed it, and that Christian literature was superior since it could serve as a direct vehicle for truth. This belief came to enjoy a new ascendancy in the Counter-Reformation era, as religious subject-matter became increasingly fashionable. New and assertive models of sacred literature evolved in this period, combining Christian subject-matter with humanistic and classicizing form: the sacred tragedy (a Jesuit specialism), the sacred epic, the sacred lyric—even, more unexpectedly, the sacred comedy.[45] This new Christian literature was quite explicit in its claims to superiority over pagan literary production. A popular commonplace of Counter-Reformation literature, echoing the opening of Tasso's *Jerusalem Delivered*, unfavourably contrasted the muses of classical antiquity, their laurels now withered, with the new Christian muse, located in heaven, not on Mount Helicon.

The second respect in which modern literary culture might be seen as having progressed with respect to antiquity—and to the pre-Renaissance past in general—was technological. The late fifteenth and sixteenth centuries saw a communications revolution on a scale to rival the emergence of digital and internet culture in the late twentieth and early twenty-first centuries. The accompanying cultural and social changes were similarly radical, and, to an extent, also similar in kind. The principal technological advances that drove the Renaissance communications revolution were, in chronological order, the development of woodcut printing for images, from around 1400; the development of copper-plate engraving, from around the 1430s; and the development of moveable-type metal printing for text, from around 1450. (These dates are for the European emergence of these technologies; all were available much earlier in Asia.) All three technologies are first recorded, within Europe, in Germany, but they spread very swiftly to Italy. Venice had by 1500 established itself as the chief publishing centre in Europe. A prior technological development, almost equally momentous for book history, was the introduction of paper in the late Middle Ages as a cheaper alternative to parchment and vellum. This spread northward from Muslim Spain and Sicily in the twelfth and thirteenth centuries. Fabriano, in the Marches, one of the most important Italian paper-making centres, is recorded as having two paper mills in operation already in 1283.

The impact of these technologies on Italian culture was vast. Most immediately, they served to disseminate written material far more widely than had ever before been possible and to reach far wider swathes of the population. Already in the 1460s, it has been calculated that the cost per page of printed books was around an eighth that of manuscripts, and the price of books came down consistently across the course of the following century and a half, as a result of technical advances, while at the same time wages and the cost of living generally rose through inflation. Where the earliest Italian printers in the 1460s asked six *lire* for 200 pages in quarto format, in 1592, a single *lira* would buy 150 pages in the same format.[46] This was comfortably within a day's wages for a craftsman or even a labourer. A master builder in Venice in the early 1590s earned more than 2 *lire* a day, up from a *lira* and a half in 1565. Over the same period, the wage of a semi-skilled worker in the same trade had increased from a *lira* to a *lira* and a half.[47]

As a result of these changes, books migrated from the status of luxuries to that of everyday possessions, even for people of relatively humble status. The Friulian miller Menocchio Scandella, whose 1599 trial for heresy was examined by Carlo Ginzburg in his classic 1976 study *The Cheese and the Worms*, showed knowledge in his depositions of around a dozen books, including the Bible in the vernacular, saints' lives, popular history, Boccaccio's *Decameron*, a translation of the fourteenth-century exotic travel narrative of 'Sir John Mandeville', and an Italian translation of the Koran.[48] Higher up the social elite, we have evidence of intellectuals owning libraries vastly more extensive than anything even princes and popes had been able to assemble a century before. Niccolò d'Este, Marquis of Ferrara, is recorded as owning 279 manuscripts in 1436. The library of the great Greek scholar Basilios Bessarion (d. 1472) amounted to around 800 manuscripts; that of Federico da Montefeltro, duke of Urbino (d. 1482) around 1,100. By contrast, in the later sixteenth century, the humanist and bibliophile Gian Vincenzo Pinelli (1535–1601)—a private citizen, if a wealthy one—amassed a library in his house in Padua that amounted to more than 7,000 manuscripts and books.[49]

Together with written texts, mechanically reproduced visual images circulated widely in late fifteenth- and sixteenth-century Italy, at both an elite and a popular level. At the higher end of the market, the arts of engraving and woodcut became media of remarkable sophistication and beauty, capable of attracting the most talented artists of the day. Raphael collaborated with the engraver Marcantonio Raimondi to create reproductions of his own paintings, but also original works designed for the new medium. Titian did the same with both woodcuts and engravings, while Dürer and Parmigianino were both involved in the development of the fascinating sub-genre of the chiaroscuro woodcut, the first colour reproduction technology in the West. At the lower end of the social spectrum, woodcuts supplied cheap prints for domestic use, especially in devotion. An early example of this is the oldest surviving Italian woodcut, the so-called 'Fire Madonna' (*Madonna del Fuoco*), a hand-coloured xylograph depicting the Virgin and Child surrounded by saints, that was posted on the wall of a school in Forlì in the 1420s and 'miraculously' survived a fire there in 1428.

In addition to its importance for the history of literature and thought, the introduction of printing is important for the history of communication and the dissemination of news. Cheap print broadsheets and pamphlets served from the late fifteenth century to spread news of discoveries, battles, and portents, and to disseminate comments on current affairs. By the mid-sixteenth century, governments were utilizing print technology extensively for communicating with their citizens, where once they would have used oral means such as itinerant town criers. The new technology early proved its worth for ideological and propagandistic purposes, playing a key role, for example, in the religious controversies surrounding the Protestant Reformation. It has been alleged with some truth that the reason why the Reformation succeeded where previous reform movements had been successfully suppressed by the Church was that Luther's texts circulated in print.[50]

Although print must take the starring role in the history of this period's communications innovations, another novelty of the sixteenth century deserves mention here: the development of a robust and established system of circulating manuscript news sheets (*avvisi*), originating especially in Venice and Rome. These *avvisi* developed from the earlier system of merchant communications, of which documentary traces remain from the thirteenth century onwards. By the late sixteenth century, professionals known as *novellanti* or *menanti* dedicated themselves to the gathering and dissemination of news. Their reputation is evocatively conjured in a warning a dialogue of 1598 proffers to cardinals' secretaries not to have anything to do with such men, who are capable of 'taking the egg out of a chicken's body, let alone a secret out of a youth's mouth'.[51] The availability of protojournalistic instruments such as *avvisi* contributed to the emergence of what might be called a protojournalistic public. In 1596, a proposal was made to the Bolognese Senate for a public reading room where *avvisi* would be available to read, and where they would be read aloud for the benefit of the illiterate. The public envisaged was 'men of letters, gentlemen, citizens, and others who wish to hear and understand what is happening each day in various parts of the world'.[52]

The magnitude of these changes in culture and communications did not escape contemporary observers. Not all were happy to see this cultural transformation. Print introduced new protagonists into book culture, beyond the traditional manuscript culture figures of author, scribe, reader, patron—editors, printers, publishing entrepreneurs. It also introduced a market dynamic into the production of literature, paving the way for the emergence of professional authors who could support themselves through their pens. The taint of commerce concerned some aristocratic authors, who preferred to circulate their works by manuscript well into the print era. Talk of printers as mercenary and sloppy and of editors as ignorant became popular commonplaces among writers and intellectuals. Fifteenth-century scholars lamented that printers' greed and carelessness had introduced hundreds of new errors into classical texts.[53]

More momentously, as the social reach of written culture expanded, the political and religious authorities became increasingly preoccupied with the potentially subversive effects of print technology and its role in disseminating unorthodox and critical ideas. Censorship practices began to be introduced in Italy from the early sixteenth century, at first on a local and relatively *ad hoc* basis; then, in an increasingly systematic and centralized manner. The first Index of Prohibited Books (a particularly severe one, later mitigated) was issued by Pope Paul IV in 1559. By the later sixteenth century, printers were required to submit their forthcoming books for pre-publication scrutiny by local ecclesiastical censors, who assessed them for religious unorthodoxy, and, to a secondary extent, for moral indecency. This undoubtedly had the effect of inhibiting some of the bolder and more controversial strains within Renaissance culture. Machiavelli's works, for example, were officially banned after 1559, although they remained available under papal licence for those who could claim a legitimate need to consult them, notably rulers and military leaders.[54]

The rise of journalism in the later sixteenth century aroused the suspicions of the authorities as much as printed books—perhaps more, as it was less easily controlled. A bull issued in 1572 by Pope Gregory XIII complains that not only is humanity suffering from its customary vices, but new ones are arising by the day, unknown to previous eras. Among these new threats to the moral order is:

> [a] sect of improperly curious men, who propose, receive, and scribble down everything concerning public and private affairs that comes to their notice, or that they themselves wilfully invent, concerning both domestic and foreign affairs, mingling together in complete disorder the true, the false, and the uncertain, so that one may say a new art has been instituted.[55]

Gregory's bull introduced new punitive measures against *menanti*, reinforced by his draconian successor Sixtus V.

Despite these institutional attempts to curb the freedom of the press and to discipline its power, the impact of the new technology was still transformational. The market dynamic of the publishing industry encouraged literary and editorial innovation, as printers sought to enhance their trade by spiking the interest of readers. Humanists, following the example of Petrarch, had put together and circulated collections of their letters already in the fifteenth century, but the gossipy vernacular *Lettere* of Pietro Aretino, published in six volumes between 1538 and 1557, launched a new and seemingly inexhaustible vogue for works in this genre. Similarly, collections of poetry by various authors already circulated in manuscript in medieval Europe, but the lyric anthologies published by the dynamic and inventive Venetian publishing house of Gabriele Giolito from 1545 again proved wildly popular and spawned numerous imitations. Giolito is generally credited with the invention of the series of books, still known in Italian as a *collana*, a necklace, after the first instance of it, the *Collana storica*: a series of classical and modern historical writings that Giolito began to publish in 1563 with his editor Tommaso Porcacchi. Popular print genres in the mid- to late sixteenth century included richly illustrated emblem books, costume books, and books of lace patterns, along with collections and anthologies of all kinds: of speeches, jokes, games, cosmetic and culinary recipes, political axioms, medical 'secrets'. Even the advent of the Counter-Reformation, which repressed some sectors of the printing industry, provided opportunities for enterprising publishers, who evolved attractive new religious products for their vernacular readership, such as rosary-themed books; anthologies of sacred dramas, lyrics, or saints' lives; and meditations and 'books of tears' (*lagrime*), intended to structure readers' personal spiritual experience.[56]

One especially evocative and characteristic late-Renaissance print genre is the *selva*, or 'forest'—a kind of popular encyclopedia of general knowledge, pulling together a vast, often seemingly arbitrary mass of historical, scientific, and cultural information.[57] These derived from classical models such as Valerius Maximus's hugely popular *Memorable Sayings and Deeds*, which went through more than 70 editions in the Italian sixteenth century in Latin and the vernacular. An example is Luigi Contarini's 1586 *Charming and Delightful*

Garden, in Which There May Be Found the Unhappy Ends of Many Famous Men; Diverse and Remarkable Examples of Virtue and Vice; the Deeds and Deaths of Prophets; the Names and Works of the Ten Sibyls; the Discourse of the Muses; the Origins and Campaigns of the Amazons; Marvelous Examples of Women; the Inventors of All Sciences and Arts; the Origins of Religions and Chivalric Orders; the Excellence and Virtues of Many Natural Cures; Some Injunctions of Popes ... and the Seven Wonders of the World. Works such as these placed in vernacular circulation bodies of knowledge that, a century earlier, would have been available only to the learned. Together with translations of classical works, they enabled those with no Latin some second-hand access to the world of classical erudition, establishing a shared patrimony of secular 'common knowledge' that helped bridge the gulf between elite and popular culture.

As books became more available across the course of the sixteenth century and translations and divulgative works flourished, we begin to find a few authors commenting in interesting ways on the democratizing effects of print. A 1564 work by the 'empiric' doctor, popular medical writer, and pioneer of plastic surgery Leonardo Fioravanti, notes that, in the field of medicine, it was possible in the past for learned doctors to convince their patients of anything they wished:

> ... because there was a great shortage of books, and whenever anyone could discourse even a little in *bus* or *bas* [i.e. speak Latin], he was revered as a prophet and whatever he said was believed. But ever since the blessed printing press came into being, books have multiplied so that anyone can study, especially since the majority are published in our mother tongue.[58]

By making books available at a low cost, the blessed press has 'awakened the world, which was sleeping in ignorance'.[59] Where once only the wealthy could study, now 'almost everyone can read, both men and women', so that a day can be envisaged when 'we will all be learned [*dottori*] together'.[60] Fioravanti's rhetoric of reawakening is markedly Burckhardtian, yet he locates the moment of revival at the moment of dissemination, not discovery. In his striking metaphor, the age of print marked the moment when 'the kittens opened their eyes'.[61]

4

IDENTITY AND THE SELF

One of the central intuitions of Jacob Burckhardt's *The Civilization of the Renaissance in Italy* is that 'Renaissance man' differed in fundamental respects from his medieval forebears. As Burckhardt expresses it,

> In the Middle Ages, both sides of human consciousness—that which was turned within as that which was turned without—lay dreaming or half awake under a common veil ... Man was conscious of himself only as a member of a race, people, party, family, or corporation—only through some general category. In Italy this veil first melted into air ... Man became a spiritual *individual* [and] recognized himself as such. (p. 98)

Conceiving of human, worldly life as an arena in which glory could be sought, rather than as a vale of tears, Renaissance man sought to excel, developing his innate physical, intellectual, and creative powers to the maximum. In the process, he proudly differentiated himself from his fellows, becoming a 'phoenix', a species unto himself—a popular rhetorical compliment of the time.

Burckhardt's notion of 'Renaissance man' as defined by individualism has not fared well in recent scholarship. Modern historians have emphasized that the collective identity frames which Burckhardt portrayed as having 'melted' with the advent of the Renaissance in fact remained firmly in place throughout the entire period. Family and lineage remained crucial to men's and women's social identities in this period, especially within the moneyed elites, where family identities were reinforced through such vehicles as genealogies, heraldry, ancestral portraiture, family chapels, and family tombs. Other collective identity frames were offered by religious institutions such as religious orders and lay confraternities; by professional and trade institutions such as guilds; and by cultural associations such as the literary academies that flourished in every Italian city and town in the later sixteenth century. Neighbourhood identities within cities were also often strong, and reinforced by civic rituals and sporting events, such as the horse race known as the Palio still fiercely contested by the city wards, or *contrade*, of Siena. Less official neighbourhood-trade groupings included the Venetian gangs or civic factions of the Castellani (mainly dockyard workers), and the Nicolotti (mainly fishermen).[1] These met annually in the autumn for bloody fist fights on bridges. Although notionally illegal, these were in practice one of the highlights of the Venetian social calendar, attracting sponsorship from local patricians and gambling interest from all social ranks.

Overarching all these more local and parochial identity constituents was civic identity, which had immense force in the period. This was reinforced throughout the year through rituals and had a strong religious component that endowed state institutions with a quasi-sacred aura. Venice, perhaps the Italian city with the richest array of civic rituals, celebrated the fifth-century foundation of the city on 25 March, coinciding with the Feast of the Annunciation, in a way that aligned the birth of the city with the spiritual redemption of mankind. Every city had a patron saint—many more than one—and many could muster a miraculous icon that might be paraded in supplicatory processions in case of drought or plague or war. Bologna had an image of the Virgin purportedly painted by St Luke; Lucca, a crucifix said to have been carved by Nicodemus, eye-witness to the crucifixion; Turin, the famous shroud, supposedly imprinted with the face of Christ, that is still an object of pilgrimage today. Grandest of all, Rome and Venice could boast the bones of two apostles, respectively Peter and Mark (the latter stolen from Alexandria in the ninth century by a party of pious Venetian merchants and transported out in a barrel of pork). The possession of relics and shared sacred legends served to bond civic communities, as did memorialization of past military victories and political accords. Florence celebrated St Barnabas's day on 11 June with a horse race and fireworks, to commemorate the Battle of Campaldino in 1289, when Florentine government forces had defeated a powerful party of political exiles. Venice's famous Ascension Day ceremony of the Marriage of the Sea, in which the Doge 'wedded' the sea with a ring on behalf of the city, commemorated both Venice's conquest of Dalmatia at the turn of the tenth century and a twelfth-century Venetian-brokered peace accord between the papacy and the Holy Roman Empire.[2]

Once we consider these multiple, overlapping collective identities, it becomes clear that it is simplistic to consider Renaissance identities purely in terms of individualism—just as it would be similarly simplistic today. Modern social psychology distinguishes between an 'individual self' (comprising those aspects of a person's self-conception that differentiate him or her from others); a 'relational self' (comprising those aspects of self-conception formed through interpersonal interaction within defined social roles); and a 'collective self', 'achieved by inclusion in large social groups and contrasting the group to which one belongs (the in-group) with relevant out-groups'.[3] The same analysis may be usefully applied to the period we are looking at here, although most scholars would agree that the relational and collective components of self-conception and identity were far more dominant in Renaissance culture than they are today, at least in the West. Contemporary cultural neuroscience has dramatically exposed the profundity with which cultural differences shape individuals' self-conception, so that Chinese experimental subjects show a different cognitive style of self-representation than Western subjects, emphasizing interdependence and relationality over psychic autonomy.[4] It seems licit to speculate that a time-travelling cultural neuroscientist projected back into Renaissance Italy would find comparable differences between Renaissance and modern-day Western minds.

The notion of the relational self is especially useful within a society such as that of Renaissance Italy, in which family and kinship ties were a more powerful force than they are today, and in which much of professional, social, and political life was conducted on a patronage-clientelage basis. Men of social standing poured vast energies into cultivating relationships with those more powerful than themselves, and gaining social capital through the public allegiance of less powerful men. The discussion of 'friendship' (*amicitia*) in the fourth book of Leon Battista Alberti's 1430s dialogue *On the*

Family, one of the most insightful analyses of Renaissance social dynamics of the period, is largely devoted to a speaker's account of his techniques for winning the patronage of princes and popes.[5] The skills of positioning oneself accurately within a hierarchical network and behaving accordingly were fundamental in this society, and they were inculcated young. Earlier in Alberti's dialogue, in a discussion of the upbringing of children—or, more precisely, of boys—a speaker emphasizes with great insistence the undesirability of allowing young boys to play alone, or to spend too much time in the company of their mothers. Instead, they must be brought into adult male company early, and taught to 'show themselves reverent' to their elders.[6]

We find similar concerns expressed in practice in a letter of Baldassare Castiglione, the author of the Italian Renaissance's most famous conduct manual, *The Book of the Courtier*. Castiglione wrote to his mother in 1524, expressing pleasure at a letter he had received from his four-year-old son Camillo, who was being brought up by his grandmother after the tragically young death of his mother, while Castiglione's professional commitments kept him from home. Castiglione asks that Camillo be instructed henceforth to sign his letters to his father 'your respectful son and servant'.[7] Although, to modern eyes, this instruction may seem pompous and cold, the reason Castiglione gives is revealing: not that he is concerned for his own dignity, but that he wishes Camillo to 'make a start on learning to be *humano*'.[8] The term might be translated as 'civilized' or 'mannerly', but literally, of course, it means 'human'. To be fully human in Renaissance Italy was to be socialized to a relational culture in which each quasi-instinctively knew his place.

RENAISSANCE INDIVIDUALISM REVISITED

Although it is certainly important justly to weigh the importance of the relational and collective elements in Renaissance selfhood, Burckhardt's thesis of the Renaissance as the birthplace of individualism does not need to be completely discarded. The modern Western notion of the individual self did not spring into life fully formed in the Renaissance, as Burckhardt suggests, but nor did it emerge only later, from the Enlightenment or Romanticism.

Rather, it was the product of a long evolution, in which the period in which we are interested here forms an important chapter. In investigating Renaissance individualism, we do not need to embrace Burckhardt's particular, heroic, self-sufficient model of the individual. Individualism may be conceptualized more neutrally, as a set of practices and discourses geared to articulating and memorializing what are perceived as the distinctive physical and moral traits of particular people. Understood in this sense, it seems indisputable that the Italian Renaissance saw individualism on the rise.

The most dramatic sign of this is the re-emergence in this period of a tradition of realist portraiture, intended to preserve the physical appearance of particular individuals. Throughout the long centuries of the Middle Ages, the impulse to such distinctive physical memorializing does not appear to have been keenly felt. Kings, queens, popes, powerful barons were content to be recorded through generic images, evocative of rank and majesty, but not the *haecceitas* ('thisness') of the individual person (to quote a revealing scholastic concept, first formulated in the thirteenth century). By contrast, from the fifteenth century onwards, we can register a great tide of realist portraiture, not merely of rulers and dignitaries but of the urban and cultural elites in general: medics, lawyers, merchants, academics, writers, artists, actors, buffoons.

Numerous factors, economic, social and cultural, may be adduced as contributing to this new attention to the individual. The emergence of urban, commercial societies in Italy and the Low Countries in the late Middle Ages, and the secularization of values that accompanied this development, encouraged more robust and affirmative attitudes to human attainment and human potential. At the same time, increasing wealth and the rise of consumer culture produced new material vehicles for self-expression, through dress, jewellery, ornament, art. Developments within religious culture may also be adduced, such as the spread of the practice of individual, private ('auricular') confession in the thirteenth century, which, it has been speculated, encouraged the development of more self-conscious forms of subjectivity.[9] Even technological advances, for example in mirror-making, had a part to play in fostering the new culture of individual selfhood. Convex glass mirrors were available in Europe from the fourteenth century, along with more traditional metal mirrors, but, from the fifteenth, Venetian mirror-makers evolved a new and clearer species of glass known as *cristallo*. In the sixteenth century, fresh technological advances allowed for the production of large-scale, flat *cristallo* mirrors, silvered with mercury. Renaissance man could see himself more clearly than his medieval forebears in a very literal sense.[10]

Also important in the development of Renaissance individualism, initially at an elite level, was the recuperation of classical culture. This refamiliarized Renaissance thinkers with the sophisticated resources Graeco-Roman culture had evolved for representing the individual. In addition to the tradition of realist portraiture, evinced most accessibly through portraits of emperors on Roman coins, classical literature offered a rich and articulated body of writings that served to represent historically identifiable individuals, whether objectively or subjectively, ranging from biographies like Plutarch's *Lives* and dialogues featuring historically identifiable speakers, like Plato's or Cicero's, to the gossipy, informative letters of Cicero and Pliny and Horace's autobiographical verse epistles. All these writings contain an element of portraiture, or self-portraiture, and the first-person writings, in particular, engendered an enticing illusion of knowing a complex and distinctive self from within.

The significance of humanism as a cultural frame for the re-emergence of individualism is well illustrated by the fact that some of the earliest realist representations we have of identifiable individuals in this period stem from the contexts in which humanism first flourished. The Paduan banker Enrico Scrovegni, a contemporary and compatriot of the early fourteenth-century humanist Albertino Mussato, discussed in Chapter 2, commissioned no fewer than three portraits of himself for his funerary chapel, the famous Arena Chapel, frescoed by Giotto. In addition to a painted donor portrait by Giotto, Scrovegni is represented in two anonymous sculptures, one a reclining tomb portrait, the other a free-standing statue, both remarkable for their precocious naturalism.[11] At the end of the century, still in Padua, the first realist portrait medals of the Renaissance were struck, representing Francesco I Carrara and his son.[12]

The humanist context was also important for the re-emergence of modes of realist literary portraiture and self-portraiture. Petrarch is the outstanding figure here, important especially for his vast collection of letters, written over a period of some 40 years, from the 1340s, following his discovery of Cicero's letters to Atticus in Verona. In the early fifteenth century, Leonardo Bruni wrote the first neo-Ciceronian dialogue featuring speech-portraits of contemporary intellectuals, and the first self-standing humanist biographies (of Cicero, in 1413, and of Dante and Petrarch, in the 1430s). In 1438, Leon Battista Alberti composed the first humanist autobiography, written in the third-person form of Caesar's *Commentaries*. Other classical autobiographical genres revived by the humanists included the Horatian verse epistle, the pastoral eclogue, and the love elegy in the manner of Catullus, Ovid, or Propertius, the latter cross-fertilizing with a existing tradition of love lyric rooted in the medieval Christian culture of courtly love. These revived classical (and classical-medieval fusion) genres became some of the most widely practised literary forms of the Italian Renaissance in the sixteenth century, serving as the prime humanistic vehicles for the crafting of idealized social selves.

Visual and literary portraiture developed across the fifteenth century with equal impetus and sometimes in parallel. Petrarch was not only the founding figure in the humanistic literature of self-representation, but he was also the first poet to celebrate the art of portraiture in verse, in two famous sonnets describing a supposed portrait of his beloved Laura by the Sienese artist Simone Martini. Alberti, the author of the first humanist autobiography, also sculpted the first artistic self-portrait of the age, on a bronze plaque of the 1430s. As the tradition of visual portraiture developed, painters sought means to vivify their portraits, partly in order to counter poets' jibes that painting was limited to surfaces, while poetry could convey a person's inner moral qualities and mental life. Thus the profile format of early portraiture, based on ancient coins, gave way to the three-quarters and the full-view portrait; painters incorporated suggestions of movement and fugitive expressions such as smiles to enhance the sense of human presence and suggest temporality; and stage-setting became common in portraits, with 'props' like books, antiquities, and letters introduced to evoke sitters' intellectual and emotional lives.

In addition to portraiture, by the sixteenth century, new vehicles had developed for individual self-expression, reflecting the spread of consumer culture. Fashion was one. Castiglione's *Book of the Courtier* advises that a man should follow 'usage' in dress, but acknowledges that such usage varies widely in modern Italy, to the extent that 'anyone is free to dress as he wishes'.[13] It is quite clear from Castiglione's discussion, however, that dress is viewed both as a key form of self-expression and a potential minefield, if mismanaged. A man must 'decide how he wishes to seem, and to be considered by others, and dress accordingly', knowing that poor choices may lead him to be regarded as foolish or lacking in taste.[14] Castiglione's letters to his mother, who acted as his main wardrobe mistress, document very well the attention to detail needed to follow this prescription, in a culture in which a fashion dynamic was beginning to establish itself, with the result that clothes needed to be not merely of fine quality, but also to correspond to the latest stylistic shifts. A plaintive letter of 1509 records that 'since I had that marten-fur lining made, the fashion [*usanza*] has arrived here of cutting garments more amply, so that I'm finding it much too short for the type of things we wear now'.[15] Castiglione requests a cloak from his mother in Mantua as a matter of urgency, claiming that a garment of sufficient quality is not to be found in Urbino, where he is stationed. His only alternative would be to seek one out in Rome at an exorbitant price.

Perhaps the most striking manifestation of the Renaissance culture of individualism was the popularity of 'emblems' or 'devices', which constituted a kind of individual heraldry to complement the traditional collective heraldic imagery worn by noble families or chivalric orders. Emblems consisted of an allegorical image accompanied by a motto, in Latin, Greek, or Italian. They were intended to express the moral qualities or personal philosophy of a given individual, and, more implicitly, his erudition and wit. One of the earliest and most famous emblems is that of Leon Battista Alberti: a winged eye, shedding thunderbolts, accompanied by the cryptic motto, *quid tum?* ('What then?' or 'So what?'). The image, Alberti explained, represents the divine capacity to survey all things, his inspiration as philosopher and artist, while the motto, a Virgilian allusion, has sometimes been taken as an ironic reference to Alberti's illegitimacy.[16] Originating in humanist circles in the fifteenth century, the practice of devising emblems was popularized in the sixteenth, to the point of becoming a positive craze. The wealthy had emblems woven into their garments; sculpted on the reverse of portrait medals; painted on their tableware. By the second half of the sixteenth century, printed compendia of emblems were available glossing the emblems devised by prominent figures, making this aristocratic practice of public self-definition available to a wide public.

Quite how rich the repertoire of vehicles for the expression of individualism was by the sixteenth century is best illustrated by a famous example. Isabella d'Este Gonzaga, marchioness of Mantua, won herself a Europe-wide celebrity far in advance of that which her status, however exalted, would automatically have conferred on her. She was one of the first dynastic consorts in Italy to reach out beyond the 'safe' formula for cultural self-expression that had established itself as a norm for aristocratic women, centred on the patronage of convents and other ecclesiastical institutions. Instead, Isabella's prime energies in the field of art patronage were concentrated on antiquity collecting and the crafting of domestic space to project a learned and sophisticated humanistic self-image—forms of self-expression largely limited before her time to men.[17] Her various *studioli* and other palace spaces, decorated by artists of the calibre of Andrea Mantegna and Antonio da Correggio, are justly some of the most-studied interiors of the period.[18] Besides paintings proclaiming Isabella's moral virtues, such as Mantegna's image of an armed Minerva, goddess of wisdom, expelling a horde of grotesquely rendered vices, Isabella's *studioli* were studded with ingenious emblems and with a famous motto, *Nec spe nec metu* (with neither hope nor fear), which positioned Isabella as a Stoic sage.

In addition to these more oblique cultural self-portraits, Isabella was a serial commissioner of literal, physical portraits (which often recycled previous images of her, as she did not have the patience to sit long). Among the most famous was a portrait medal of 1498 by Giancristoforo Romano, showing Isabella in her mid-twenties, with a learned reverse showing an allegory of Peace, together with an inscription that Isabella commissioned from the poet Niccolò da Correggio (having rejected an earlier proposal by Correggio on the revealing grounds that it was not unique to her). The medal was widely distributed, and other portraits were almost certainly based on it, including a famous drawing by Leonardo now in the Louvre. Giancristoforo Romano was also responsible for a marble bust of Isabella, now lost, and probably for a highly idealized terracotta statue of her now at the Kimbell Art Gallery in Fort Worth, while a lost painted portrait of her by Francesco Francia as a youthful beauty survives in a copy she ordered from Titian at the end of her life. Other artists' efforts pleased her less, almost certainly because their representations were less idealizing. An early portrait of her by Mantegna was destroyed on her orders with the irate comment that 'he has portrayed us so ill that it does not resemble us in the least'.[19]

In addition to these more established means of self-expression, Isabella d'Este pioneered others, especially fashion. Her iconic status in this regard may be measured by a 1515 letter from her son Federico Gonzaga, temporarily stationed at the French court as a political hostage, asking for a fashion doll or dolls, illustrating 'the fashions that become you, in shirts, sleeves, undergarments, outer garments, dresses, headdresses, and hairstyles'.[20] Federico notes that this was at the request of the king of France, François I, who wanted this information so that he could use it to have clothes made for the ladies of his court. Federico also seems to have been besieged by the French court ladies themselves, intrigued by accounts of Isabella's prolific palace perfume laboratory; in a letter of 1516, he requests from her 'perfumes in large quantities to give to these ladies ... and sufficient gloves [to perfume, as was the custom], and a jar of hand soap that is large enough to give to many women, and, again, oils, powders, and waters'.[21]

As this episode illustrates, a powerful individual 'brand image' such as Isabella d'Este forged could have considerable currency within an increasingly fashion-conscious Europe. Co-ruler of a small Italian state, Isabella exploited her taste and ingenuity to lever herself soft power within one of the most powerful courts in Europe. She managed her brand cannily, noting in one letter of 1516 that she would be happy to release a sought-after recipe for an ointment to the queen, but not just to any lady of the court.[22] Further evidence of Isabella's reach is offered by a fascinating letter from the Mantuan ambassador in Naples in 1507, reporting on the reactions of the queen of Spain, Germaine de Foix, and the daughters of the Spanish Viceroy of Naples, Gonzalo de Córdoba, on seeing Isabella's medal by Giancristoforo Romano, with its classicising portrait and humanistic reverse. The queen, in the ambassador's report, comments not only on the beauty of the image, but the indications it gives of Isabella's 'great intellect', of which she had heard very often.[23] Although there is clearly a large element of flattery here, we can also read this as a response to the novelty of the image that Isabella presented, and the possibilities she revealed to her aristocratic observers of how they might fashion themselves in turn.

IDENTITY AND PERFORMANCE

A useful concept in understanding the way in which Renaissance Italians of the social elite constituted and articulated their social identities is the rhetorical notion of ethos. Together with logos (reasoning or argument) and pathos (the management of emotion), this was one of the key components of rhetorical persuasion, within the Aristotelian-Ciceronian tradition of eloquence. A speaker's ethos is composed both of the cultural capital he brings to his speech from his external reputation, and the impression of character he creates for himself through his speech and gesturality. These should be carefully calculated to project qualities such as dignity, intellect, sincerity, and poise. The notion of ethos implies an element of conscious and artful performance, of acting: a parallel Cicero underlines in his dialogue *De oratore* when he has a speaker declare himself 'not the actor of another's persona, but the author of my own'.[24] Importantly, ethos had a relational and interactive aspect, very different from our own, more stable notion of a person's 'character'. The orator was instructed to modulate his speech according to the audience he was addressing and the circumstances of his speech, and his ethos must vary accordingly. Flexibility was hence a core element in the orator's skill-set. Rather than a sole, God-given character, he needed to be able to dispose of a repertoire of 'characters' almost in the literary sense, finely calibrated to different occasions and agendas.

This notion of identity as flexible, malleable, performative is one of the most distinctive and intriguing features of Renaissance elite culture. One important philosophical work of the period, a speech by Giovanni Pico della Mirandola popularly known as *Oration on the Dignity of Man* (1486), places the potential for self-metamorphosis at the very core of what it is to be human, comparing man to the shape-shifting ancient sea-god Proteus. For Pico, God had created all creation on a ladder of ascending dignity (the 'scale of being'), with angels at the top, followed by animals, plants, and inert matter. All were fixed in their positions in this quasi-feudal, static structure, with no possibility of deviating from their God-given nature. Man alone, created last, when this structure was already in place, was endowed with the freedom to craft himself as he wished. According to his moral choices, he may descend to the level of a beast, or he may rise through philosophical contemplation to attain union with the divine. In the words Pico gives to God, in a stirring address to the first man, Adam: 'We have made you neither of heaven nor of earth, neither mortal nor immortal, so that you may, as the free and extraordinary shaper of yourself, fashion yourself in the form you will prefer.'[25]

While Pico develops his notion of man's chameleon nature in an essentially optimistic manner, emphasizing the philosopher's ability to transcend his mortal state, others regarded this same capacity for change with greater wariness. A popular moral theme of the day was man's capacity for simulation and dissimulation. 'Our souls harbour so many dark nooks and recesses', a speaker notes in Castiglione's *Book of the Courtier*, 'that it is quite impossible for human prudence to discover the simulations that lurk within.'[26] A recent study argues that a key cultural feature of the period was an enhanced awareness of the distance between potentially conflicting 'inner' and 'outer', 'private' and 'public' selves, reinforced in the climate of increasing religious intolerance in the second half of the sixteenth century, when many Italians of heterodox belief retreated into a prudent 'Nicodemism' (outward conformity to the dominant religion).[27] Within political life, Machiavelli, in *The Prince*, notoriously identified an ability to simulate and dissimulate flawlessly as a key professional skill for the ruler. Where Pico had spoken of man ascending to the nature of the angels or descending to that of the beasts, Machiavelli argues that the prince must learn to be a 'centaur', a simultaneous amalgam of man and beast.[28]

Conceiving of Renaissance elite identities as a form of rhetorical performance can be helpful in understanding the portraiture of the period, though here, of course, the performance is a dual one, a collaboration of artist and sitter. The crafting of ethos in Renaissance portraiture often has an emphatic, even a hyperbolic quality, so that the portrait serves simultaneously as an evocation of an individual and an encapsulation of the qualities of an ideal type, whether prince, cardinal, humanist, lover, poet. Good examples are offered by Titian's 1530s portraits of the duke and duchess of Urbino, Francesco

Maria della Rovere and Eleonora Gonzaga (Figs 25 and 26). The duke, a well-known *condottiere*, or mercenary captain, is figured as the epitome of the Renaissance warrior, clad in dark gleaming armor, with a splendid, dragon-crowned helmet behind him. His assertive virility—one of the most striking features of the image is the superabundance of phallic weaponry with which the duke is surrounded—is sharply contrasted with the demure, contained figure of the duchess, the eldest daughter of Isabella d'Este. A pair of sonnets by Pietro Aretino in praise of the portraits, underlines the sharply differentiated ethos of the two sitters, he with terror gleaming from his brow and boldness in his eyes; she chaste, modest, and prudent, a figure whose inner moral harmony matches the harmony of Titian's palette. Both portraits depict the sitters performing to perfection their sharply differentiated gender roles.[29]

The difference between Renaissance and modern notions of self and identity is well illustrated by the different expectations sixteenth-century readers and modern readers bring to first-person genres such as lyric poetry. The post-Romantic reader tends to approach lyric poems as sincere expressions of the writer's thoughts and emotions, and as windows on a writerly self conceived of as unique and individual; hence our preoccupation with originality of 'voice'. When we approach them with these expectations, most Italian Renaissance lyrics appear stereotyped in their treatment of emotion, while their adherence to a common lexicon and style, imitated from Petrarch's love poetry, makes individuality of voice at first difficult to discern. For much of the twentieth century, critics tended to dismiss this entire lyric school as artificial and inauthentic, only recognizing merit in poets who could be construed as rebels against Petrarchist norms. It is only relatively recently that scholars have begun to approach this body of poetry with a more sympathetic and historicizing perspective, recognizing that the poetic 'I' of Renaissance Petrarchism was a very different construct from the poetic 'I' we look for today. Renaissance readers turned to poetry in order to enjoy the spectacle of a flawless performance of what was essentially a collective, consensually defined identity.[30] Poets individualized themselves within this code through their mastery of language and the subtlety with which they manipulated their inherited repertoire. Renaissance verse is no more a record of what poets 'really felt' than Renaissance portraiture is a straight record

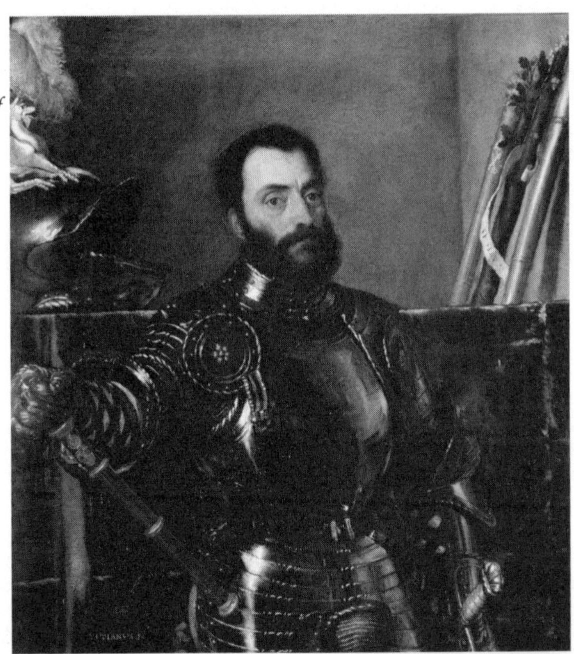

Fig. 25: Titian [Tiziano Vecellio], *Francesco Maria della Rovere, duke of Urbino*, 1536–8.

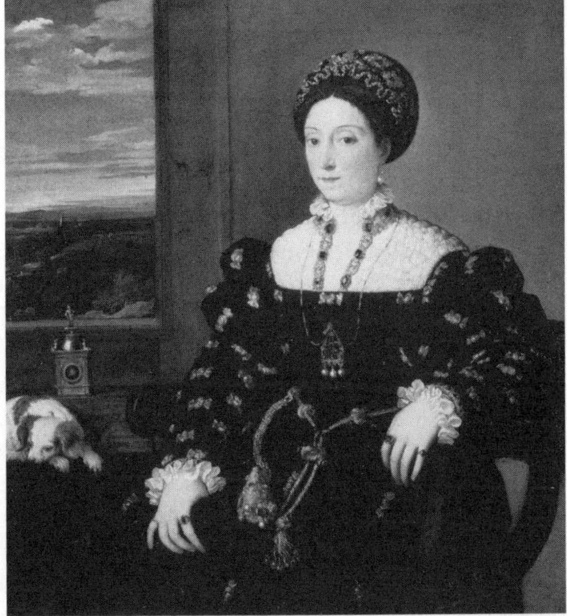

Fig. 26: Titian [Tiziano Vecellio], *Eleonora Gonzaga, duchess of Urbino*, 1537–8.

of what sitters really looked like. Both register less an expression, than a self-conscious enactment, of self.

THE SOCIAL DYNAMICS OF INDIVIDUALISM

A useful term in discussing Renaissance identity, much in use in scholarly discourse, is 'self-fashioning': a concept that originated in an influential 1980 book by the literary scholar Stephen Greenblatt.[31] Influenced by the French cultural theorist Michel Foucault, Greenblatt was concerned with the ways in which state agency inflected the construction of identities—so that the subject of the verb 'to fashion' in the original conception of the term is society and power, rather than the person being fashioned. Today, the term 'self-fashioning' is generally used in a rather different sense, to indicate the way in which Renaissance men and women consciously or unconsciously crafted their social personae: a process profoundly influenced by cultural norms and power structures, but also allowing for some degree of individual agency. Here, I propose to use the term with a more specific significance, to pick out those forms of identity construction that give salience to the individual self rather than the collective self: the 'I', rather than the 'we'.

One immediate thing that we may note if we survey the Renaissance Italian culture of self-fashioning, understood in this limited sense, is that the practice is not evenly distributed. Some social groups were distinctly more concerned with the expression of individuality than others. At one extreme, we may point to members of a powerful social group such as the Venetian patriciate, possessed of an unusually stable and prestigious collective identity, which was rigorously reinforced. The patriciate was a closed class, confined to a fixed number of families, the oldest of which could trace their ancestry back for many hundreds of years. They were the only Venetian citizens who could participate in government, although a lesser elite class, the 'original citizens' (*cittadini originari*) were entrusted with running the civil service. The patriciate practised something close to formal endogamy, allowing patrician status only to the legitimate offspring of patrician fathers married to women of appropriate status. Patricians and original citizens were even distinguished from their fellow Venetians by a corporate dress code. After the age of

25, men of these classes were required to wear a long black robe (with colour variations for governmental office holders) whenever they appeared in public—a rule so sedulously observed that men claiming citizen status often produced witnesses to testify that they and their fathers and grandfathers had not been seen wearing class-inappropriate clothes.

As the detail of dress suggests, the expression of individual identity was regarded with a certain suspicion in Venetian patrician culture, not least for political reasons. As one of the last surviving republics in a land in which most cities had fallen into the hands of the most ambitious of their citizens, Venice regarded with suspicion any attempt by a powerful individual to distinguish himself too sharply from his class. Venetian patricians were rarely active or creative self-fashioners, and the class produced relatively few strikingly individualized figures capable of serving as cultural role models to those outside their own immediate context. Compared to their aristocratic peers to the west and south, Venetian patricians tended to style themselves, and have themselves portrayed, in a relatively uniform manner. Only gradually, as wealthy Venetians began to invest more heavily in land and villas on the mainland, and to become more culturally assimilated with the mainland aristocracy, did the discipline of their corporate ethos begin to fade.

An exception who proves the rule of Venetian patrician 'collectivism' is the poet and humanist Pietro Bembo, the most famous Venetian patrician of the sixteenth century and one of the most influential cultural figures of the age. Bembo came from one of the most distinguished patrician dynasties of the city and was the son of a prominent diplomat. Like any talented man of his background, he might have been expected to advance to a career in the service of the Venetian state. Instead, Bembo struggled to find acceptance among his peers, spending his late twenties and early thirties being proposed for diplomatic and governmental posts and being rejected for each by substantial majorities, despite his father's political influence. A proposal put forward in December 1500 that he be sent as Venetian ambassador to Hungary was defeated by 142 votes to 17.[32]

It seems likely that this diffidence reflected a perception of the young Bembo as somehow not quite 'one of us'. Rather than spending his early years assiduously building up his contacts in Venice, as young patricians were supposed to, Bembo had spent much of his youth outside the city, spending two years, for example, studying Greek in Sicily, and a further two or three enjoying the glamorous court culture of Ferrara. Where Venetian patricians characteristically prepared for their political careers by gaining business experience or studying law, Bembo's interests were literary and philosophical, more than practical, and took a vein more characteristic of contemporary court culture. One of his earliest works, written during his Ferrarese sojourn, was a vernacular philosophical dialogue on love set at the tiny court of Asolo, seemingly inspired by an unhappy love affair. Bembo published it in 1505 with a dedication to Lucrezia Borgia, duchess of Ferrara, with whom his name was romantically linked. The following year, now in his mid-thirties, Bembo came to what was an extraordinary, even scandalous decision for a Venetian patrician, entering into the service of a foreign ruler, the duke of Urbino. At the same time, he began his path to an ecclesiastical career by taking minor orders: a choice that led to important posts such as that of papal secretary in his mid-forties, and cardinal, at the end of his life. Although Venice eventually recognized Bembo's immense cultural prestige, and conferred on him the office of civic historian and director of the Library of San Marco, he did not settle back in the city, preferring the university city of Padua instead.

Important as a poet, as a critic, and as a linguistic theorist, Bembo was also a master of self-fashioning, leaving highly curated collections of published verse and letters and a rich legacy of visual representations. Five portraits survive of him, three from the period of his cardinalate (a splendid painting by Titian showing Bembo gesturing eloquently in his cardinal's robes (Fig. 27), and a bust and a medal by the Tuscan, Veneto-based sculptor Danese Cattaneo); and two from an earlier time (a painting by Lucas Cranach the Younger and a medal by Valerio Belli, showing on the reverse Bembo poetically reclining in a pastoral landscape, dressed in a toga). Two other portraits, by Raphael and by Titian, are recorded, while there is evidence that Bembo also sought a medal-portrait from Benvenuto Cellini.[33] Where literary self-portraiture is concerned, Bembo's verse collection, first published in 1530, played a key role in shaping the characteristic sixteenth-century format for such volumes, mingling love poetry in the Petrarchan manner with occasional verse addressed to aristocratic friends and patrons, so as to show off the poet both

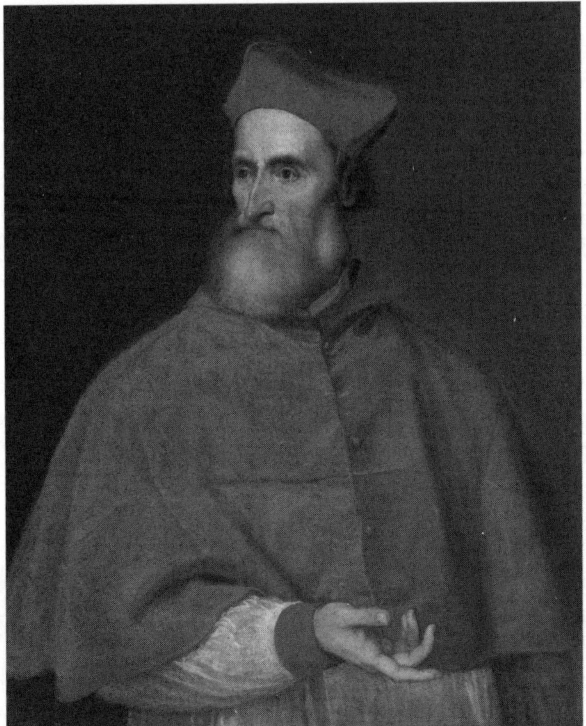

Fig. 27: Titian [Tiziano Vecellio], *Cardinal Pietro Bembo*, *c.* 1540.

as melancholy love-obsessive and well-acquainted man about town. Bembo also well exemplifies the role of collecting in humanist self-fashioning. His house in Padua was famed for its remarkable collections of Roman coins, inscriptions, and statuary, and for its rich library, which included treasures such as a fourth-century illustrated fragment of Virgil, one of only a handful of illustrated codices to survive from the ancient world.[34]

As the example of Bembo illustrates, some social environments in Italy—notably the courts—were better suited than others to individual self-expression. This was true for men, but it is even more markedly so for women of the social elites. Venice, again, marks a kind of extreme. It was noted in Italy for the seclusion in which it kept its noblewomen, and the strictness of the mores it imposed on them. Chastity, modesty, and submissiveness were the qualities most prized in Venetian wives, while cultural attainment and social sophistication seem to have been relatively undervalued. If we except the errant Bianca Cappello, who eloped at the age of 15 with a Florentine banker and became the lover and finally wife of Grand Duke Francesco I de' Medici, it is difficult to think of any Venetian noblewoman of the fifteenth or sixteenth centuries who became a cultural celebrity during her lifetime, or who was sufficiently distinctive as a personality to act as a role model for others. It is primarily the courts which produced women of this type, as we saw with the figure of Isabella d'Este.

In addition to these geocultural considerations, a further general point that may usefully be made about the practice of individual self-fashioning in Renaissance Italy is that some of the most virtuoso self-fashioners in this period were men and women whose social status was relatively fluid or ambiguous. Leon Battista Alberti, whom we noted above as a pioneer of autobiography and self-portraiture, offers an intriguing example of this dynamic at work. Alberti was born into one of the wealthiest and most powerful Florentine merchant-banking dynasties, but his family had been exiled from Florence for political reasons, and he was born in Genoa, to a Genoese mother. Alberti was, moreover, illegitimate and, although he was raised and educated in a manner befitting a man of his patrician status, he was never legitimized. He made his career in the papal court, and in various other court settings, relying on his intellect and talent to make his way, more than family connections. He never lived for an extended period in Florence, although he visited the city after the Alberti family's exile was revoked. His life was hence very different from that of a man of his class born legitimately and residing for his entire life in his city, embedded from birth in the social and familial networks he would remain in until old age. Although Alberti was highly successful in career terms, enjoying the patronage of popes and princes, he remained deliberately disengaged from certain powerful, identity-shaping social choices. He never married, nor did he embrace full clerical status, taking only minor religious orders. The same is true of Petrarch, another key figure in the history of Renaissance self-fashioning, and another deracinated Florentine bachelor, born to a family in exile.

A further very striking example of a figure of ambiguous background who crafted himself a memorable, distinctive, and

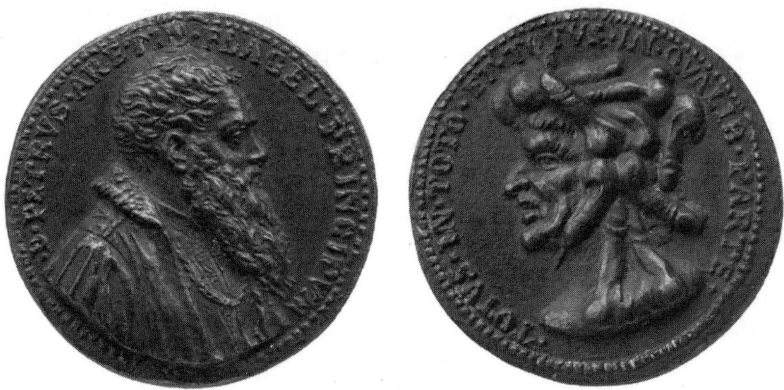

Fig. 28: Anon., portrait medal of Pietro Aretino with a reverse of a satyr's head made up of phalluses.

highly individualized persona is Pietro Aretino, name-checked above as the author of a letter on Titian's portraits of the duke and duchess of Urbino. Aretino came from a humble background; he was the son of a shoemaker of Arezzo who abandoned his wife when the young Pietro was a child. Pietro was raised by his mother, who had become the mistress of a wealthy nobleman, and he clearly received some form of education, although nothing like the refined humanist education of a man like Alberti. It is not clear that he even studied Latin. Initially trained as a painter, Aretino made his career mainly as a prodigiously prolific writer for the press, known for his letter-collections, his comedies, and his satirical and erotic writings. After a youth spent mainly at the papal court in Rome, and a brief spell in Mantua, Aretino lived for most of his mature life in the printing capital of Venice, where it was possible to make an independent career as a professional writer. He never married, and made no secret of his libertine lifestyle; one of his many portraits, a medal, depicts on the reverse a satyr's head concocted, Archimboldo-style, out of an agglomeration of phalluses (Fig. 28).[35] One of the most distinctive figures of the age, Aretino excelled as a self-publicist, mesmerizing his contemporaries by the spectacle of his hyperbolic enactment of self. In an age that revered politeness and decorum, he created himself a deliberately outspoken persona, as a fearless speaker of unwelcome truths (the poet Ariosto coined for him the epithet 'the scourge of princes'). In an age that saw study and imitation as the chief means to developing style, he proclaimed himself the 'secretary of Nature', writing spontaneously what came to his pen.[36] In many ways, Aretino was the antithesis of the kind of polite, polished, courtly self to which so many of his contemporaries aspired, and a figure like Bembo was more influential as a role-model. Only with the Venetian libertines of the seventeenth century did Aretino's irreverent and provocative style come to acquire a new appeal.

CONCLUSION

'Uniqueness'—the basis of Burckhardtian individualism—was certainly a concept available to Renaissance thinkers. The encomiastic literature of the time was replete with bold claims for the singularity and unrepeatability of the person being praised. Sonnets, funeral orations, florid book dedications never tired of repeating that the subject of praise was rare, singular, matchless, unique of his kind. The poet Bernardo Accolti was celebrated with the nickname *l'Unico Aretino*, 'the Unique Aretine'—a title that must have lost something of its lustre when Pietro Aretino rose to the height of his fame. The poet, singer, and philosopher Tarquinia Molza, one of the most accomplished women of the later Renaissance, proudly chose *l'Unica* as her academic name when she was elected to the Parmese 'Academy of the Unnamed' (*Accademia degli Innominati*).

Given this, it seems difficult to deny a degree of truth to Burckhardt's thesis about the Italian Renaissance as an age of individualism. The aim of the present chapter has been to attempt to ascertain precisely how far that individualism went. It certainly did not constitute a kind of proto-modern atomism, in which relational and collective identities were attenuated. Most Renaissance Italians were deeply embedded in social contexts that called such common identities to the fore. Only, perhaps, in an avant-garde social context such as the cosmopolitan circles surrounding the print shops of Venice, where Pietro Aretino played out his extraordinary career, do we begin to see something approaching the kind of environment where a more modern 'individual' might thrive.

The present chapter has concentrated on self-fashioning within the elites, but it is a question worth asking how far down the social hierarchy this practice extended. Interesting recent work in social history suggests that modes of material self-expression associated with the Renaissance elites, such as fashion, domestic luxury, and fine dining, had found some purchase within the households of upper artisans by the mid-sixteenth century. Inventories of artisans' homes in Siena in 1549–50 record a tailor, Pietro, as possessing a gilded marble bowl, a gilded *all'antica* cup, two gilt knives, and a gilt fork—the utensils presumably to be used in tableside carving—while a shoemaker, Girolamo, had a display credenza decorated with an ornamental basin, a tablecloth, and a textile hanging emblazoned with his family coat of arms.[37] In Venice, there is evidence of servant-class women running into debt by renting clothes and jewellery, presumably of a higher quality than the work clothes with which their employees supplied them, while literary texts comment on artisans' wives dressing sumptuously in gold chains and pearls.[38]

There are intriguing suggestions, as well, that the practice of portraiture was beginning to spread beyond the elites by the mid-sixteenth century. Pietro Aretino snobbishly complained in 1545 that 'tailors and butchers' were appearing in portraits, while the art theorist Giovanni Paolo Lomazzo commented reprovingly in 1584 that such works were being commissioned by 'plebeians and the base' (*plebei e vili*).[39] It is not easy to find empirical evidence to bear out these claims that artisans commissioned portraits, although a noteworthy exception is discussed in Chapter 5, in the form of Giovanni Battista Moroni's *The Tailor*. While Moroni's sitter is portrayed with the tools of his trade, however, making identification simple, it does not seem obvious that all artisans commissioning portraits would wish to be portrayed in this manner. It is quite possible that some of the many sixteenth-century portraits of unidentified sitters that we find labelled in galleries as 'Portrait of a Man', or even as 'Portrait of a Gentleman', silently attest to this tradition of artisan portraiture, just as some works labelled 'Portrait of a Lady' may represent ambitiously dressed artisans' wives.

5

RENAISSANCE MAN

RENAISSANCE MAN/RENAISSANCE MEN

As we saw in the last chapter, there are limits to the utility of discussing 'Renaissance man' in the abstract. As with Italian Renaissance culture in general, identity-formation in Italy was geographically, or geoculturally, inflected. Class also fundamentally influenced identity formation, as did gender, age, profession, religion, military status. A basic division existed between clerical and lay identities, but there were also salient distinctions between the secular and monastic clergy, and, within the latter category, among the different orders of monks, canons, and friars. Similarly, in the lay world, a Ferrarese courtier might have quite different cultural values from a Venetian patrician, a Bolognese university professor, a Neapolitan artisan.

To give some sense of the diversity of Renaissance identities, the present chapter will be devoted to considering three important and characteristic Italian Renaissance social types, based on the criterion of profession: the merchant, the courtier, and the artist, with the last term understood in the broadest possible sense, including all skilled professionals within the creative and performance arts. These three categories of 'Renaissance man' are, of course, far from exhaustive, but a discussion of them will help give a sense of how class and professional context inflected identities more generally. It will also provide useful insight into the ways in which initially low-status social groups succeeded in engineering themselves an enhanced social standing across the course of the fifteenth and sixteenth centuries. Looking back from the vantage point of modern, Western societies, Italian society at this time looks markedly hierarchical, with a high degree of what social anthropologists call ascriptive inequality (i.e. inequality determined by individuals' 'ascribed status', the social status into which they are born). This is true to a large extent, but it is also true that the precocious rise of urban, commercial economies in Italy made for some degree of social mobility. A literate, urban, skilled worker was in a far better position to improve his status through his own agency ('achieved status') than an uneducated peasant.

A useful instrument in investigating professional identities such as those that interest us here is what the literary scholar Thomas Greene termed 'institutes': prescriptive writings defining the human qualities and virtues necessary for a successful practitioner of a given trade.[1] The institute was a much-practised genre of writing in this period, taking its cue from classical writings such as Cicero's *On the Orator* and Quintilian's *Oratorical Education*, which set out to define the attributes and intellectual formation of the perfect orator. We have texts from this period crafting the perfect citizen (Matteo Palmieri), the perfect cardinal (Paolo Cortesi), the perfect ambassador (Ermolao Barbaro), the perfect courtier (Baldassare Castiglione and several others), even the perfect courtesan (Pietro Aretino, parodying Castiglione and the whole genre). Treatises forming the perfect prince, often called 'mirrors for princes', are so common as to rank as a genre in themselves. Although obviously idealized—by definition—such writings have much to offer to the study of Renaissance identity-formation. Generally written by insiders (with the exception of works on princes and cardinals), they can give us a good sense of how at least the most reflective practitioners of a given profession wished to be regarded, and how they socially positioned themselves and their trades.

THE MERCHANT

One of the most characteristic professional types of Renaissance Italy was the merchant: a ubiquitous figure in the late-medieval and early modern urban landscape, especially dominant in republican contexts. Much of the vast wealth Italy generated between the thirteenth and the sixteenth centuries derived from commerce and from banking—the latter virtually an Italian invention—and merchants played a notably more significant role within Italian social and political life than they did elsewhere in Europe, with the exception of the Low Countries and perhaps Germany. Much social snobbery surrounded the practice of trade, in Italy as elsewhere, and Italian aristocrats felt free to sneer at merchants' ink-smeared fingers and preoccupation with lucre. Nonetheless, the wealth-creating power of the Italian commercial and financial sectors, over a long period, lent the figure of the merchant much cultural capital, especially if he was engaged in banking and in large-scale international trade. The Medici, until the 1430s one wealthy Florentine merchant-banking family among others, were *de facto* rulers of Florence by the later fifteenth century and formal rulers of the city by the early sixteenth. By 1600, the family held the title of grand dukes of Tuscany, and had produced two popes and two queens of France.

Internationalism was characteristic of Italian commerce and banking in these early centuries of 'merchant capitalism'. Italian merchants, often generically referred to as 'Lombards', were a familiar sight in cities throughout Europe by the late thirteenth and early fourteenth centuries, and Italian merchant-bankers played a vital role in supplying the rulers of Europe with loans (which they did not always repay). Especially dramatic is the history of the so-called 'super-companies' of early fourteenth-century Florence, run by the Bardi and Peruzzi families, which flourished in the late thirteenth and early fourteenth centuries before collapsing dramatically in the 1340s, just prior to the Black Death. The Peruzzi family, which traded in textiles and grain, as well as financial services, had 14 international branches in addition to its central office in Florence, ranging from Paris, London, and Bruges in the north, to Majorca in the west, and Cyprus, Rhodes, and Tunis to the east and south. The Bardi operation was even more geographically expansive, with branches in Seville, Constantinople, and Jerusalem.

Merchants were generally educated to a high level, predominantly at 'abacus schools' geared specifically to practical commercial skills. They formed a highly literate social group, although, unlike notaries, lawyers, and clerics, their culture often leaned towards the vernacular, rather than Latin. Writing was a key element in the merchant's skill-set. The merchant Giannozzo Alberti in Leon Battista Alberti's dialogue *On the Family* advises the aspiring merchant that he should always have his fingers stained with ink.[2] Florentine merchants, in particular, left an impressive legacy of practical writings of all kinds, often referred to by the generic terms *ricordi* or *ricordanze*. These encompass account books and annotations of business techniques, but also autobiographical jottings, genealogical information, notes on public affairs and civic history, moral and political axioms—essentially, the encapsulated patrimony of professional and personal experience a merchant wished to hand on to his heirs. The educational impulse in these writings justifies us in seeing them as a kind of dispersive 'institute', collectively delineating the knowledge base and the moral qualities of the ideal merchant. A more formal merchant institute is Benedetto Cotrugli's *On Trade and on the Perfect Merchant*, written in 1458 and printed for the first time in 1573.[3]

The merchant identity that emerges in these writings is a distinctive one, forged in part to counter negative cultural stereotypes of the merchant as grasping and avaricious, or as sordid—and potentially even sinful—in his focus on monetary gain. The late-medieval Italian church had made its peace with mercantile activity, condoning the search for profit when it could be seen to be of benefit to the common good, and to result from industriousness and prudence on the part of the merchant. Classical moral philosophy reinforced this culture of virtuous merchant capitalism through the notion of 'magnificence'. This encompassed religious charity, civic philanthropy, and architectural patronage, which was seen as contributing to the public good of a city through embellishment, even if the buildings concerned were intended for private use. More broadly, as Cotrugli notes in his discussion of merchant ethics in the third book of *On Trade*, mercantile activity benefits cities by importing goods necessary for their physical survival and comfort, by stimulating the arts through the export trade, and by augmenting the public coffers through tax.[4] Merchants grow cities and expand their wealth through their 'glorious industry', whereas aristocrats and rentiers practise mere sterile consumption and see their fortunes decline over time.

Especially within republican cultures such as Venice, merchants were praised for combining this kind of civic-directed magnificence with a certain degree of personal austerity. Cotrugli represents the merchant's life as an arduous and physically exacting one, requiring him to undertake long journeys, work long hours, and sometimes go without food or other physical comforts. Sobriety and temperance figure high on Cotrugli's list of the virtues proper to the merchant: he should be chaste, modest in his speech, sparing in his consumption of food and particularly wine, and he should shun all extravagance in dress. Revealingly, in one passage, Cotrugli refers to the merchant's body as an instrument or tool, essential to his profession in the same manner as a hammer to a blacksmith.[5] A similarly instrumental view underlines the global thesis of good management (*masserizia*) that Alberti gives to his speaker Giannozzo in *On the Family*. In its original and literal meaning, the term *masserizia* applies to the frugal management of material resources within a household, but Giannozzo extends it to apply to the management of the merchant's three great personal resources of mind, body, and time.[6]

The medieval merchant mentality has sometimes been caricatured in the past as secularizing and rationalistic, in a manner that prefigures modernity. This captures some aspects of mercantile identity, most obviously in respect of the value accorded to worldly goods, which stand unashamedly at the centre of the merchant's activities. However, to suggest that this worldliness signifies a diminution of religious sentiment is anachronistic. The Florentine silk merchant Marco Parenti opened what is effectively an account book in 1447 with an invocation to God, the Virgin, and Saints Nicholas, John the Baptist, John the Evangelist, Peter, Paul, Mark, Mary Magdalene, Catherine, 'and all the Evangelists, and Apostles, and saints, male and female', devoutly auguring that all he inscribes in the book will be to their honour.[7] Benedetto Cotrugli devotes a full quarter of his treatise to instructing the merchant in his religious duties (including an interesting section on issues of conscience arising from business). Cotrugli concludes the work by sternly warning that no merchant should continue in his profession after the age of 50; rather, he should at that age retire to the country and devote himself to preparing his soul for death.[8]

An interestingly pragmatic attitude to the role of religion in the merchant's life is evinced in a passage of the *Ricordi* of the Florentine wool merchant Giovanni Morelli, written between 1393 and 1411. Describing his revered and long-dead father, Morelli notes that he devoted his energies in the early years of his business career to winning 'the love of God' through his charity and good works, as well as 'the friendship of good and respected and powerful men'.[9]

This investment in the spiritual capital of human and divine good will then enabled him to survive harder times. God figures here as an actor in the social world, participating in laws of *amicitia* similar to those that bound human patrons and clients. The calculation is certainly a rational one, but it may hardly be characterized as secularizing on that account.

Although the practice of trade—and often, in the republics, governmental service—naturally occupied the main energies of merchants, there is much evidence that they participated with interest in the broad culture of humanistic learning. While few practising merchants were 'literary humanists', to use a term recently introduced by the historian Brian Maxson to signify those who engaged with classical study in a concerted, quasi-professional manner, numerous merchants qualify for Maxson's category of 'social humanists'. In Maxson's definition, these were men who showed an interest in classical culture; who had contacts with the learned world of the literary humanists; who owned or read classical and humanistic texts, in the original or in translation; and who sometimes acted as patrons of humanistic learning, or received dedications of humanistic works.[10]

A recent study of two fifteenth-century vernacular works transmitting Aristotle's teachings on ethics, addressed to two Venetian merchants of the patrician Giustinian family, allow a glimpse into this lively divulgatory culture of humanism, which has been relatively little studied to date.[11] The two works, one from the 1430s, the other from the 1460s, differ in the level of intellectual engagement they require of their readers: one is a translation, via the Latin, of Aristotle's *Nicomachean Ethics*; the other, a translation of the much briefer and simpler pseudo-Aristotelian *Book of Virtues and Vices*. The latter text, in particular, through the translator's notes, makes a marked effort to relate its teachings to the dedicatee's professional culture, alluding, for example, in the discussion of prudence, to the widespread custom among merchants of sending their sons for a stint at a foreign branch of their firm, in the interest of broadening their knowledge of the world. The note continues with a literary analogy that seductively glamourizes and classicizes the Venetian merchant lifestyle; the apprentice merchant is compared to Homer's wandering hero Ulysses, who sees 'many cities and many customs of men'.[12] This vision of the merchant as 'universal' and broad in experience and competence finds a match in a passage in Cotrugli, where he notes that 'the grave and worthy merchant should not be like the needle, which is a base tool, since it knows how to do nothing but sew'.[13]

THE COURTIER

Although it is coherent to speak of a 'Renaissance merchant', particularly with regard to patronage, personal style, and learned interests, the social type of the Renaissance merchant has deep medieval roots. The twelfth and especially the thirteenth centuries saw merchants and guildsmen rising to prominence within the central and northern Italian republics, where they established themselves ultimately as the dominant political class. The thirteenth and fourteenth centuries also saw the development of some of Italian business culture's key technical instruments, such as double-entry book-keeping, mercantile insurance contracts, letters of credit, bills of exchange. Boccaccio, whose father worked for the Bardi bank, and who himself started out as an apprentice in the bank's Naples branch, gives a vivid portrait of fourteenth-century mercantile life in his *Decameron*, to the extent that the Boccaccio scholar Vittore Branca termed the work 'the epic of the merchants'.[14]

By contrast, the figure of the courtier, another key protagonist of the Renaissance, emerged as a defined social type much later. The Italian city-republics had already begun to give way to *signorie* by the later thirteenth and fourteenth centuries, but the courts of these early *signori* were relatively modest entities, consisting of little more than the immediate *famiglia* or household of the lord. The only exception, to the south, was the royal court of Naples, ruled by the French Angevin dynasty, and an important conduit for French cultural models. It was in the later fourteenth and fifteenth centuries, as the precarious *signorie* of the centre and north of Italy began to consolidate their power, that the courts began to grow in size, splendour, and ambition. An expansionist development of this period was the tendency for courts within courts to proliferate; in Ferrara, by the time of Ercole I d'Este, who ruled from 1471–1505, besides the duke's own court, which amounted to over 500 employees, his wife Eleonora d'Aragona, and his three brothers and four sons all had their own substantial entourages, ranging from 25 to 140 employees.[15]

As the courts rose in size and ambition, they assumed an ever-higher cultural status in Italy as centres of learning and artistic, musical, and dramatic production, coming to rival more established republican cultural powerhouses such as Florence. This was all the more so when the papal court returned to Rome from a long period of 'exile' in Avignon in the early fifteenth century, and successive popes set themselves to rebuilding Rome as a great cultural capital. Accompanying these material changes, we see the court assuming an increasing discursive salience across the course of the mid-fifteenth century, as shorthand for a particular way of living, of speaking, of styling oneself: 'a main reference point in the organization of upper-class consciousness'.[16] Often, the court was presented negatively, as a place of corruption and insincerity, continuing a medieval tradition of writing on the 'miseries of courtiers'. A classic of this miserabilist genre is Enea Silvio Piccolomini's treatise *De curialium miseria* of 1444. More innovatively, the Florentine humanist Lapo da Castiglionchio, in his *De curiae commodis* (*On the Benefits of the Court*), 1438, uses the dialogue form to dramatize the contradictory reality of the papal court: from one perspective, a sink of sensuality and corruption; from another, a cosmopolitan and innovative environment, magnetically attractive both for its sophistication and the possibilities it holds out for material advancement.[17]

The salaried members of Italian courts, in their mature, fifteenth-century incarnation, included practitioners of a wide range of professions, ranging from musicians and dance masters to cooks, stablemasters, secretaries, and accountants. A fundamental division was between non-noble professionals and service staff and aristocratic courtiers closer in status to the ruling lords. The latter were traditionally conceptualized as 'companions' (*comites*) to their lords, although by the sixteenth century the status gap between princes and even their most elite courtiers was beginning to become too extreme for this traditional designation to have much real force. Princes' most distinguished followers were often minor lords themselves, with feudal estates and titles, and their aristocratic prestige lent them value as representatives of the prince, whether as governors, military commanders, or diplomats—the latter role increasingly important as the practice grew of maintaining resident ambassadors at other Italian and foreign courts. Many of these humanistically educated noble courtiers took a leading role in the literary life of the courts, although this did not exempt them from more mundane duties. The greatest Italian poet of the early sixteenth century, Lodovico Ariosto, complains bitterly in his *Satires* that his Este masters in Ferrara cared nothing for his poetry, rewarding him only for more utilitarian services such as scurrying across the country on diplomatic errands, or serving as governor in the remote and mountainous province of Garfagnana, assailed on all sides by 'thefts, murders, hatred, vendettas, rage'.[18]

It is the ethos and persona of the aristocratic courtier that is the chief concern of Baldassare Castiglione's *Book of the Courtier*, justly the most famous Italian Renaissance 'institute', and a work of vast, European diffusion, after its publication in 1528. The work takes the form of a dialogue on the perfect courtier, and the perfect court lady, held among a group of predominantly noble courtiers in the court of Urbino, in the Marches, in 1506. As befits its subject-matter, *The Courtier* is an immensely urbane work, with none of the earnest didacticism of a treatise like Cotrugli's *On Trade*. The task of discussing the perfect courtier is presented as an after-dinner 'game', pursued across four evenings in the apartment of the duchess of Urbino, and punctuated by dancing. Consistently with the game format, much laughter accompanies the dialogue, and the discussion is vivified by wit and sex-war banter among the male and female courtiers. The work's considerable classical erudition is worn lightly. When one of the speakers begins to employ technical Aristotelian philosophical terminology in the course of a discussion of gender difference, he is reprimanded by the sharp-tongued mistress of ceremonies, Emilia Pio, who tells him to speak in a language all can understand.[19]

Castiglione's analysis of the virtues and qualities of the courtier gives us a term to describe the work's deliberately (and deceptively) casual and 'light' air: *sprezzatura*. This, we learn half-way through the first evening's discussion, is the secret of attaining the prime quality of the perfect courtier, 'grace'.[20] The literal sense of the word is something like 'a disdaining' (from the verb *sprezzare*, to disdain). What is disdained is effort, difficulty, labour; the ideal is to perform every courtly activity, from dancing to public speaking, swordplay to lute-playing, with perfect ease, as if it were something entirely natural, acquired without practice or thought. The ideal derives from rhetoric; Cicero advises in his *Orator* that the orator cultivate a certain 'diligent negligence' (*negligentia diligens*), to lessen his listeners' consciousness of his craft and hence their suspicion of being manipulated.[21] Castiglione carries the ideal of *sprezzatura* into effect in his writing. Manuscript evidence shows that he worked intensely on *The Courtier* from 1508 to around 1524, revising the work minutely at every level from structural edits to word-by-word fine-tuning, yet in the dedicatory letter he speaks of having written the dialogue in a few days (*pochi giorni*), following the death of the duke of Urbino in 1508.

The notion of *sprezzatura*, and the disdain for any semblance of hard work it implies, serve accurately to measure the distance that separates the human ideal of the courtier from that of the merchant. In the formulae of theorists like Cotrugli and Alberti, and in the writings of merchants themselves, the merchant's outstanding qualities are defined as *diligenza*, *sollecitudine*, *industria* (diligence, vigilance, industry). These are to be proudly placed on display, not disguised. Similarly, money, which stands at the heart of the merchant's activities, whether in terms of accumulation or proper and virtuous expenditure, is banished from the discourse of the courtier. Although Castiglione's anxious letters home to his mother in his years of court service show him to have been far from immune from monetary concerns, talk of money is entirely absent from *The Courtier*, except for a revealingly worded warning, on the first evening, that any man who engages in warfare for gain rather than glory is 'not a gentleman, but the basest of merchants' (*vilissimo mercante*).[22]

Another detail that can help reveal the cultural gulf between the identities of merchant and courtier is their very different attitudes to the body. Cotrugli requires good looks in the perfect merchant, as Castiglione does in the courtier, and both authors recommend sobriety of dress and dark colours, as conferring an air of gravity and dignity. Castiglione, however, allows his courtier to dress in more exuberant clothes at jousts and festivities, while Cotrugli's merchant has a single, sober, and businesslike register. Indeed, Cotrugli expressly forbids jousting and dancing to the merchant, as lightweight and inappropriate distractions. Fundamentally, Cotrugli conceives of the merchant's body in functional terms, as a tool of his trade (an 'instrument', as we saw), while the body of Castiglione's courtier is aestheticized. Grace, agility, elegance are required of him because it is a crucial part of his job to give pleasure to the eyes. This is apparent in the initial discussion of the need for the courtier to excel in sports and physical exercises, especially the key gentlemanly and martial arts of swordsmanship, wrestling, and horsemanship, but also swimming, running, tennis, and vaulting on horseback. At first, the speaker relates the need for excellence in these pursuits to the courtier's military career (consistently with medieval chivalric ideals, his 'principal profession' is assumed to be soldiery). Soon it is remarked, however, that military exercises and sports are often practised in peace time, and before audiences of civilians and of ladies and great princes. It is in these peace-time contexts that the aesthetic dimension of athleticism comes to the fore.[23]

Underlying all these differences in the merchant's and the courtier's ethos is their very different social positions. Important though relations with the powerful were to the Renaissance merchant, he was essentially an independent entrepreneur, dependent predominantly on his own efforts for success or failure. The courtier, by contrast, was a dependent, if a gilded one, reliant at a fundamental level on favour—the favour of his prince, most importantly, but, also of those figures analysts of the courts have called 'threshold patrons', men and women known to have the ear of the prince.[24] The courtier also needed to win the respect of his peers, of the ladies of the court—presented in the dialogue as an especially exacting audience—and even of the 'vulgar hordes', the *moltitudine*, who attended some larger events, such as jousts. To perform successfully before such multiple and overlapping audiences, the courtier must possess an expert grasp of social dynamics. He must be hyperconscious of how others see him, and acutely aware of the means by which collective judgments are reached. These are not always rational, as Castiglione observes. 'Just as in many other things, Fortune has immense power over men's judgments.'[25] A prince may arbitrarily take against the most talented of men and the entire court will swing behind his bias. Similarly, if the prince takes the most inept of men into his favour, he will instantly become the darling of the court.

In this treacherous environment, it is not sufficient for a courtier to possess substantive qualities, in terms of skills, education, and achievements. He must also be a master of appearances, capable of ensuring that his qualities are always seen in the best possible light. The advice *The Courtier* offers on this is sometimes controversial, as when the speaker on the second day advises that the courtier should attempt to orchestrate his acts of valour on the battlefield so that he performs them when he has the best audience, preferably directly before the eyes of the prince. Similarly, at jousts, he must attempt to ensure that he is among the first to appear in the lists, since the spectators' attention will be keenest at the outset of the event.[26] Most deviously of all, it is suggested that the courtier might make light of the skill in which he most knows himself to excel—say, dancing—and to pretend to set more store by another activity, perhaps music or jousting. This will allow him to startle those watching, when they see how well he performs in his second-string activity, and it may induce this audience to imagine him an even greater master in his 'true' art.[27]

The element of calculation and seduction in the courtier's personality did not escape notice. Within Castiglione's dialogue itself, certain of the speakers express qualms that the courtier's rhetorical suppleness may sometimes amount to deception; and the stereotype of the wheedling, flattering, treacherous, backbiting courtier was a popular stereotype of the period. Despite these suspicions, however, the influence of the suave and polished model of behaviour Castiglione teaches in his treatise was considerable. Courts were key political and social environments in the entire early modern period, both in Italy and across Europe, and the glamour and prestige that attached to them guaranteed that cultural and social practices originating in them attained considerable diffusion elsewhere. The sociologist Norbert Elias, in an influential work, posited that the courts of Renaissance Europe were the principal *loci* for what he called 'the civilizing process', meaning the spread throughout society of a distinctive model of social behaviour characterized by high levels of self-consciousness, bodily self-control, and *politesse*.[28] Although Elias's claims have been questioned by medievalists, who push the origins of the civilizing process back in time and emphasize the role of monasteries in transmitting ideals of 'civilized' behaviour, few would doubt the role of the courts in diffusing polite manners, especially in the age of print. The reception of *The Courtier* confirms its purchase on contemporary readers' imagination. The work was published more than a hundred times in the century that followed its first appearance, and it was translated into six languages (French, Spanish, German, English, Polish, and Latin).[29]

THE ARTIST

Both the courtier, as envisaged by Castiglione, and the merchant, as envisaged by Cotrugli, are unquestionably men of the social elite: the former, an aristocrat, the second, a wealthy patrician. In his exaltation of the merchant's contribution to society, Cotrugli is careful to note that his paean relates not to 'plebeian and vulgar' merchants, but rather to what he calls 'the glorious merchant', the large-scale merchant or merchant banker engaged, like Cotrugli himself, in international trade. This distinction was one consistently maintained in Renaissance Italy, and it may be found also in Cicero's *On Civic Duties* ('trade, if small, must be considered sordid; if grand and copious ... it must not be scorned').[30]

What of the professional identities of lesser men, the 'sordid' and 'mechanical' smaller merchants, shopkeepers, and artisans? One group among these figures, visual artists—painters and sculptors—has been very thoroughly studied, and presents a striking case of a professional cadre whose status changed significantly across the period we are looking at here. Until the late thirteenth and early fourteenth centuries distinctly of the artisan class, artists began a long process of upward social mobility that saw at least the most successful artists enjoying remarkable material advancement and acclaim by the sixteenth century. At the very apex of the profession, it is possible to point to figures such as Raphael, who enjoyed such social prestige that a cardinal, Bernardo Bibbiena, was eager to offer him a niece in marriage, while Castiglione himself was proud to boast of him as a friend. Several painters purchased or were granted honorific noble titles; a few more substantial offices or benefices. Andrea Mantegna was made a papal count by Pope Innocent VIII in 1469; Titian, a Palatine count by the Emperor Charles V in the 1530s.[31] Pope Clement VII appointed Sebastiano del Piombo to the lucrative office of keeper of the seal for papal correspondence (the nickname 'del Piombo' means 'of the lead' or 'of the seal'). The sculptor Leone Leoni, another protégé of Charles V, built himself a magnificent palace in a noble quarter of Milan, with a life-size cast of the Capitoline equestrian statue of Marcus Aurelius in its courtyard.[32] Michelangelo was buried in Florence in 1564 in a ceremony ordered and funded by the city's ruler, Duke Cosimo de' Medici, and on a scale reminiscent of the exequies of statesmen or great military leaders.

Although, at a basic level, the elevation of the status of artists simply reflected market forces—artistic talent was in high demand—the process was accompanied by an ideological repositioning of art itself within the hierarchy of human activities. Because of the element of manual application involved, painting and sculpture had traditionally been classed as a 'mechanical' (or manual) craft, and been socially devalued accordingly. Across the course of the Renaissance centuries, these activities were gradually redefined as 'liberal' arts, arts worthy of the attention of gentlemen, or, in the original Roman formulation, of free men. Alberti's treatise *On Painting* already argues the case for this in the 1430s, but the process of redefinition was a long one. Castiglione innovatively endorses painting and drawing as a suitable accomplishment for his courtier, but he prefaces this endorsement by having his speaker acknowledge that drawing 'may today seem a mechanical art and ill suited to gentlemen', before going on to note the far higher status accorded to the visual arts within the classical world.[33]

The fame attained by a few artists from non-artisan backgrounds (most notably Michelangelo, who descended from a Florentine family of government officials, and claimed more distant and improbable descent from the counts of Canossa, who welcomed the connection) helped bolster the 'liberal arts' credentials of painting and sculpture in the course of the sixteenth century. So also did the development of Neoplatonic models of art theory that located artistic creativity in the intellectual moment of conception of a work of art, rather than in its manual realization: a development, again, closely associated with Michelangelo and with intellectuals in his circle. The status of painting and sculpture as liberal arts was given a degree of formal recognition with the foundation of the first artistic academies, in imitation of the literary academies so popular in this period: the Accademia del Disegno in Florence in 1563, an academy of the same name in Perugia in 1573, and the Accademia di San Luca (St Luke was the patron saint of artists) in Rome in 1577.

Writings by artists, in which the Italian Renaissance is rich, give a vivid sense of a growing confidence in the status of their profession. As we saw in Chapter 3, Cennino Cennini already claimed in the late fourteenth or early fifteenth century that some painters were drawn to the profession not for the financial gain it could hold out, but through 'nobility of spirit' (*gentilezza d'animo*). The phrase echoes the notion developed by thirteenth-century intellectuals in the Italian city-republics that true nobility is defined not by birth but by qualities of mind. Lorenzo Ghiberti incorporates an autobiography, as well as a history of classical and modern art, in his *Commentaries*, probably written in the 1430s and 40s—a notably assertive gesture, at a time when the subjects of biographies were more usually intellectuals, statesmen, and generals.

Drawing on Vitruvius, Ghiberti prescribes an ambitious educational programme for the artist, incorporating literature, geometry, mathematics, history, medicine, philosophy, astronomy, and anatomy (the last an addition to his Roman source). It is unlikely that many artists attained such 'universality', but the figure of the artist-intellectual began to become familiar in the later fifteenth century. Prior to Leonardo da Vinci, the most salient example was Piero della Francesca, who was born into a reasonably moneyed merchant family in Borgo San Sepolcro, in the north-east of Tuscany, and probably received an early education in commercial arithmetic, like most merchants' sons. In adulthood, Piero developed advanced mathematical interests and wrote three treatises on mathematics, geometry, and perspective, one of which, on polyhedra, was incorporated in the mathematician Luca Pacioli's famous treatise *On Divine Proportion* (1490s; printed 1509). In the sixteenth century, while the connections between art and mathematics persisted, a tradition also began to emerge of artist-poets, notably in Florence and Rome, with Michelangelo and Agnolo Bronzino the most salient examples. Michelangelo's standing as a poet was honoured in Florence in 1547 when the poet and intellectual Benedetto Varchi gave a lecture on a sonnet of his at Florence's state-sponsored literary academy, whose sittings were mainly devoted to readings of classic verse by Dante and Petrarch.

Giorgio Vasari's *Lives of the Artists*, already discussed in Chapter 3, helped set the seal on the cultural redefinition of the visual arts. The project is in itself a strong statement of the cultural importance of painting, sculpture, and architecture, and the dignity of their practitioners. The *Lives* collects an extraordinary amount of detailed information (of varying degrees of accuracy) about the activities and legacy of artists from the thirteenth century onwards. The work was splendidly printed by the ducal printer Lorenzo Torrentino, and with an editorial team drawn from the Florentine intellectual elite. The philologist Vincenzo Borghini compiled a vast and detailed topographical index, extraordinarily state of the art for the time. The proem to the second book of the treatise compares the enterprise to that of political and military historians, and classes the *Lives*, like the works of such historians, as a 'mirror of human life':[34] not merely a bare chronicle of events but effectively a work of philosophy, probing the hidden causes of the progress or decline of the arts, just as political historians probe civilizations' rise and fall.

One of the great thematic threads of the *Lives* is concerned with the professional ethos of what Vasari fondly calls 'his' artists (*i miei artefici*), to the extent that the work may be read, among other things, as a kind of artistic 'institute', outlining the virtues and qualities a perfect artist requires. Vasari does this according to the classic rhetorical procedures of epideictic oratory, defined as the rhetoric of praise and blame; his biographies of individual artists emphasize admirable traits and strongly castigate undesirable ones. In general, Vasari approves a disciplined and professional attitude in his artists, not dissimilar in some ways from that of the merchant as described by Cotrugli. Industriousness and commitment are highly valued qualities, as is prudence and good financial management; one of the most negative biographies in moral terms is that of Botticelli, who made good money through his art but frittered it away, dying crippled and in poverty. By contrast, Vasari's life of Pietro Perugino is prefaced by a homily on the value of poverty as a motivating force. Born into poverty and employed initially by a painter as an errand boy—formal apprenticeship required a payment to be made to the master for training—Perugino attained greatness as a painter partly on account of his ferocious work ethic, which led him to tolerate 'cold, hunger, discomfort, hard work, and shame' to attain his ambition.[35] His life illustrates the fact that 'one who is prepared to work continually, and not at nonsenses' can attain 'achievements, reputation, wealth, important contacts'.[36]

While the painter-businessman is a recognizable and lauded type in Vasari, other artists are constructed along more courtierly lines. Vasari's portrait of Raphael is particularly close to the cultural model inscribed by Castiglione, as is appropriate given the two men's celebrated friendship (Vasari's biography ends by citing the Latin elegy Castiglione wrote to mourn Raphael's death).[37] Raphael is portrayed as courteous and generous by nature, modest, handsome, and mannerly, and universally loved. Vasari especially attributes to Raphael the key courtly quality of 'grace': he is first introduced as 'the no less excellent than graceful Raphael Sanzio of Urbino',[38] praised for his 'graceful social charm' (*graziata affabilità*), and described as 'the most graceful Raphael' (*il graziosissimo Raffaello*). Raphael's courtly graces, in combination with his artistic genius, ensures a remarkable and meteoric career for a man who died at 37; he finished his brief life the darling of Leo X's Rome, living a lifestyle that Vasari describes as less akin to that of a painter than a prince.

Raphael's 'grace' has something of a redemptive role in Vasari's artistic theology. As he notes at the outset of the Raphael biography, prior to Raphael's generation, artists very often had about them some element of 'madness' (*pazzia*) and 'uncouthness' (*salvatichezza*), which led them to be abstracted and eccentric (*astratti e fantastichi*), hence damaging their reputation, however skilled they were in art. Vasari's accounts of fifteenth-century artists are rich in portraits of this eccentricity, in a manner that anticipates the later, romantic notion of the artist as a man outside social norms. For Vasari, unlike the romantics, eccentricity in artists is generally censured, although genius or good nature can occasionally excuse it, as in the case of Masaccio, who is said to have earned the pejorative suffix to his name ('Sloppy Tom') for his lack of attention to propriety in dress. A figure treated with particular severity is Piero di Cosimo, who, although he is credited with great intelligence and artistic originality, squanders the benefits of these gifts of nature through his personal oddities; from youth, he is seen to have a suspicious attachment to solitude and a dreamy and speculative mind, and, by his later life, he has become a positive recluse, lurking in his studio, unable to tolerate even the company of apprentices, surviving on an eccentric diet of boiled eggs, cooked up 50 at a time. Vasari twice speaks of Piero as 'bestial' or a 'beast', a term also applied to the spendthrift Botticelli. By contrast, Leonardo da Vinci and, still more, Michelangelo are said to embody man's capacity to rise to the level of the divine.

In tracking the progress of artists' manners, Vasari is of course to an extent recapitulating the macro-narrative of the rise in the status of the visual arts in general. More locally to Florence, however, he is also recording the implications for artists of the political change that had taken place in his city with the establishment of the Medici duchy. The fifteenth-century Florentine artist had naturally needed to cultivate relationships with patrons, within the city and beyond, but he was essentially an independent skilled artisan and small businessman, master of a *bottega* (workshop or shop), many of his key relationships being with his equals or inferiors. In sixteenth-century ducal Florence, by contrast, the ability to manouevre within the court system and to keep the favour of the ducal family and high-ranking court officials could be crucial to an artist's career. Vasari himself perfectly exemplifies the type of the courtier-artist. The son of a potter in Arezzo, he was rapidly taken under the wing of the Medici acolyte and cardinal Silvio Passerini, and was educated in Florence alongside two young members of the Medici family, Ippolito and Alessandro, in the 1520s. After a period working in papal Rome and elsewhere, Vasari returned to Florence in 1540 and won his way into the favour of Duke Cosimo de' Medici, who eventually entrusted to him the direction of most court-sponsored artistic and architectural commissions.

Looking back from these courtly heights, it is not surprising that Vasari found the fifteenth-century social type of the Florentine *maestro di bottega* distinctly archaic. Education, aspiration, manners, and social sense were increasingly key to a successful artistic career. Vasari's frustration with those artists who failed to adapt to the new world is vividly apparent in his exasperated biography of his own master, Andrea del Sarto, who, in Vasari's narrative, squandered an immense talent through timidity and lack of ambition. Vasari portrays del Sarto as pusillanimous and uxorious, sacrificing his social reputation through an ill-advised marriage to a manipulative woman, and preferring a quiet life in Florence with his wife to the possibility of celebrity and riches at the court of France, where he was invited by King François I. Art historians have questioned this long-influential version of del Sarto's biography, arguing that the artist's life choices were coherent and motivated, rather than resulting from 'baseness of spirit'.[39] In the *Lives*, however, the cautionary tale of Andrea serves to underline an important principle of Vasari's artistic ethics. For an artist to fail to capitalize on his talent in material and status terms was an unforgivable sin.

Reading Vasari, one has a clear sense of the status of the Renaissance artist as precarious and in need of constant, energetic renegotiation. The projection of a dignified social ethos was a crucial life skill for such men, both for themselves as individuals and for the status of their professions in general. Vasari's wrath at Andrea del Sarto's failure to profit from his talent needs to be read in this light. At its most extreme, this preoccupation with status and 'face' could take a considerable psychic toll, as we see in the case of the Florentine sculptor Benvenuto Cellini, whose autobiography, written in 1558–66 (though not published until 1728), is one of the most remarkable works of the age. Cellini's touchiness with regard to honour and status is one of the most marked traits of his generally extraordinary character, as the autobiography represents it, along with impulsiveness, violence, and an explosive and protean creativity that allows him quite literally to get away with murder. Although Cellini shows himself winning the esteem of popes, cardinals, dukes, and kings through his artistic genius, he also portrays his progress as continually thwarted by intrigues on the part of his rivals and ill-wishers. Especially memorable is his account of his time at the Medici court in Florence in the 1540s, represented as a treacherous labyrinth populated with malicious court officials and backbiting rivals: an environment where artistic excellence is sometimes trumped by flattery and manipulation, so that socially adept mediocrities thrive where a man of Cellini's talent and volatility might fail.

THE OTHER ARTISTS: THE *VIRTUOSI* OF THE COURTS

The tale of the rising social status of practitioners of the visual arts in the Italian fifteenth and sixteenth centuries is a familiar and a fascinating one, made more so by the fact that figures like Leonardo, Michelangelo, Raphael, Cellini are so alive to us still today through their artistic legacy. In reconstructing the cultural landscape of Renaissance Italy, however, it is useful to recall that painters and sculptors were not alone in this intriguing social trajectory; rather, it was common to an entire cohort of creative and performance artists, associated particularly with the courts. A recent study by the economic historian Guido Guerzoni speaks persuasively of a diffuse 'artistic presence' within Italian culture whose economic and social impact has been obscured by modern scholarship's focus on the anachronistic category of the 'fine arts'. This broader arts culture was impressive in its scale; Guerzoni's study of the Este court in Ferrara concludes that around 35 to 40 per cent of the total expenditure of the Este dukes, duchesses, and cardinals went on artistic and architectural patronage (including military architecture), and on the commission or purchase of other luxury items. Of this total, in years when there was not some exceptional event requiring lavish staging, such as a dynastic wedding, only 0.3 to 0.4 per cent went on painting and sculpture.[40]

Substantial numbers of people in the sixteenth century were involved in feeding the Italian courtly elite's insatiable appetite for beautiful objects and sophisticated diversion. Artists on the supply side included engravers, lapidists, goldsmiths, tapestry-weavers, ceramicists, intarsia workers, glass-makers, jewellers. Performers included actors, musicians, buffoons, dwarfs, professional dancers and dance masters (who also served as choreographers), and the multiple service staff associated with fine dining: chefs (*cuochi*), stewards (*scalchi*), virtuoso carvers (*trincianti*), cup-bearers (*coppieri*), and buffet-masters (*credenzieri*), who were charged both with serving and with managing the display of plate, glass, and napkins. Other skilled court professionals such as fencing masters, dog trainers, horse trainers, and falconers may also be placed in this broad category of skilled court professionals, as may the tennis coaches (*giocatori de balla*) we see employed in the fifteenth century by the tennis-mad Galeazzo Maria Sforza, duke of Milan.[41]

A backhanded tribute to the success enjoyed by professional court *virtuosi* of the type just described is the status anxiety we can see them awakening in their aristocratic 'betters'. 'What should I do?' Ariosto laments in one of his *Satires*, noting the lack of reward his poetry has won him at court. 'I can't dismember partridges in the air on a fork, nor place a leash on a hawk or a dog.'[42] The allusion to the carver's privileged position echoes a passage in Juvenal's fifth satire; yet the detail of 'aerial dismemberment' also references contemporary court reality: the showiest skill of the virtuoso Renaissance *trinciante* was to carve a piece of meat, such a roast fowl, aloft on a fork, slicing it thinly so that the meat rained down effortlessly on to the plates below. Castiglione takes care at various points in *The Courtier* to distinguish the figure of his 'perfect courtier' from men of lesser ascribed status. The notion of *sprezzatura* is first defined by distinguishing the aristocratic courtier's easy dancing style from the highly technical virtuoso dance style of the Urbino court's plebeian dance master 'Messer Pierpaolo', which would amount to 'affectation' if an amateur were to attempt it.[43] Similarly, the discussion of the type of wit appropriate to the courtier lays great emphasis on the importance of maintaining a certain dignity while jesting, without descending to the level of professional actors or buffoons.[44]

Professional court *virtuosi* seem to have come from quite diverse social backgrounds, often closer to those of artists than of writers or architects or composers. Those of highest birth status tended to be practitioners of 'gentlemanly' activities such as falconry and horse training, along with some of the highest of the table officials, such as the *scalco*, the steward or seneschal. Whatever their birth status, however, like painters and sculptors, court *virtuosi* of talent could attain considerable fame and prestige through the exercise of their artistry. Bartolomeo Scappi, chef to popes Pius IV and Pius V, seems to have held the highly visible office of papal mace-bearer (*mazziere*) and the papal title of Count Palatine at the end of his life.[45] The fifteenth-century dance master Domenico da Piacenza was given the papal title of Knight of the Golden Spur, while Fusoritto da Narni, *trinciante* to Cardinal Alessandro Farnese, could boast the title of 'Royal Knight' (Cavaliere Reale). Fusoritto's predecessor, Vincenzo Cervio, who acknowledges himself to have been low-born (*nato di umil famiglia*), speaks of having been awarded an office in the papal chancery by Cardinal Farnese worth 800 *scudi* a year, a vast sum—although he also complains that such justly liberal lords are scarce, and that some Roman prelates attempt to skimp by offering skilled carvers a stipend fitted for no more than a stable-boy.[46]

Like the men we today call artists, the Italian court *virtuosi* of the sixteenth century left a fairly substantial body of literature explaining and promoting their arts. Already in the fifteenth century, we can see a few dancing masters and cooks beginning to write treatises on their arts, which circulated in manuscript. The most important of the early dance manuals were written by Domenico da Piacenza and by the Jewish convert Giovanni Ambrosio, or Guglielmo Ebreo (the father of Castiglione's Messer Pierpaolo).[47] The most famous cook's manual of this time was by Martino da Como, who made his career in the household of Cardinal Lodovico Trevisan.[48] It was in the age of the press, however, in the sixteenth century that technical manuals composed by *virtuosi* rose to become something of a recognized genre. Some of the most important in the various fields are those of Cristoforo da Messisbugo (1549) and Bartolomeo Scappi (1570) on the art of the cook; Federico Grisone (1550) and Claudio Corte (1562) on horsemanship; Domenico Romoli (1560), Giovanni Battista Rossetti (1584), and Cesare Evitascandalo (1598) on the office of steward (*scalco*); Giovanni Francesco Colle (1532), Vincenzo Cervio (1581), and Evitascandalo again, on carving; and Fabio Caroso, on dancing (1581).[49] Some of these treatises, like Grisone's, Corte's, Scappi's, Cervio's, and Caroso's, went through multiple editions, and several, like Corte's, Scappi's, and Grisone's, were translated into various other European languages. Scappi's, in particular, is a physically impressive work, almost 500 double-sided pages long, and containing over 1,000 recipes. It is prefaced by an engraved author-portrait and followed by numerous illustrations, including an elaborate double-page spread depicting the ritual surrounding the serving of food to cardinals in a papal conclave, recalling Scappi's own prestigious service at the papal court (Fig. 29).

Although scholarship on this genre of writings has to date been confined to specialists in the various fields to which these treatises relate (food history, dance history, etc.), this body of literature has considerable sociohistorical interest when seen as a whole. Several of the manuals produced by *virtuosi* of the table arts have something of the character of 'institutes', in that they do not limit themselves to giving technical instruction in a given art, but also devote some space to discussing the status of the profession and the ethos of its practitioners. The earliest of the writers, the *trinciante* Giovanni Francesco Colle, candidly entitles his modest, 50-page volume *Refuge of the Impoverished Gentleman* (*Rifugio del povero gentilhuomo*), but he nonetheless emphasizes the dignity of the art, defining it in his dedicatory letter as 'artful and COURTLY cutting' (*artificioso e CORTEGIANO tagliar*). In the preface to the third book of his treatise, Colle makes a distinction between the crude and artless meat-cutting practised by butchers (*beccai*) and the choreographed and erudite cutting of *trincianti*, whose professional remit he pushes as far as to encompass a basic philosophical and medical knowledge of nutrition and diet.

Colle's successors were still more assertive in social terms. Cervio begins his treatise by noting that the offices of *trinciante*, *coppiere*, and *scalco* are the noblest of the court arts having to do with the

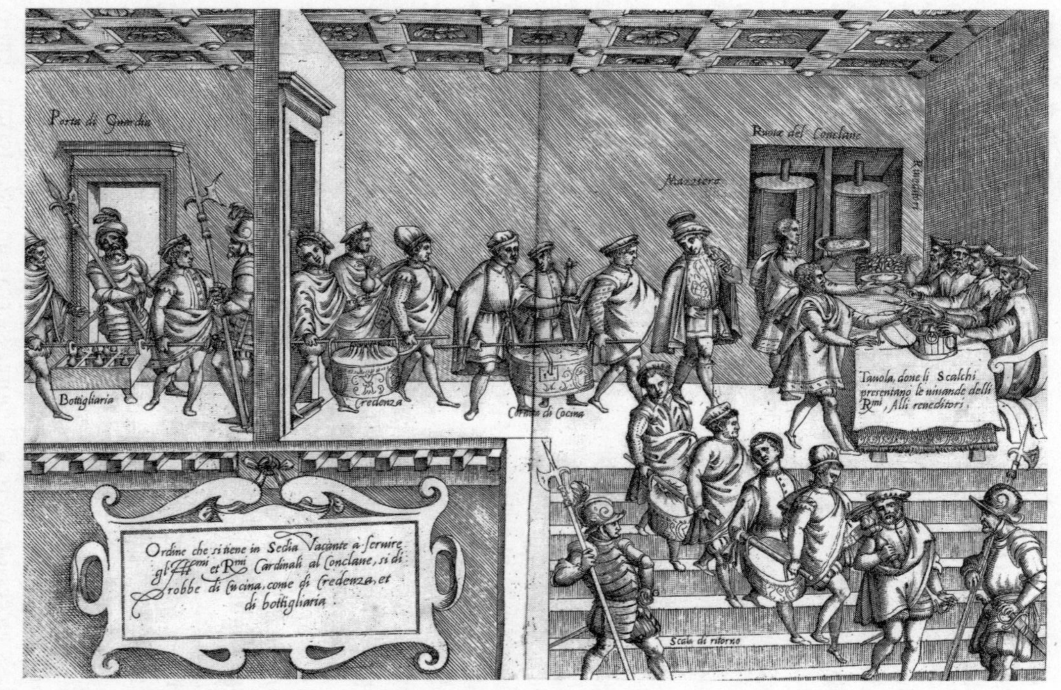

Fig. 29: Table service during a papal conclave. Illustration to Bartolomeo Scappi, *L'Opera* (Venice: Michele Tramezzino, 1570). Hampers and crates of food and drink are carried to an inspection table, before being placed on rotating containers (back right) and served to the room behind.

table, and that the post of *trinciante* is sufficiently honourable to attract the attention of noblemen, at least in theory, if not always in practice. Evitascandalo describes the office of *scalco* as the most important office of any noble household, above those of secretary and butler (*maestro di casa*), while Scappi opens his treatise with an extended analogy between the arts of the cook and the architect. Cervio goes as far as to suggest that gentlemen might wish to study carving at an amateur level, for recreational use, as Castiglione had recommended that the courtier study drawing. He illustrates this with an engaging anecdote about a Roman nobleman impressing his beloved at a summer dinner party by taking over a fork and knife from his carver and elegantly carving her a pheasant himself.[50]

Where professional qualities are concerned, Claudio Corte, the most ambitious of the *virtuosi*, insists that the horsemaster (*cavallarizzo*) must have a compendious literary education, such as he himself displays in the treatise, copiously citing literary sources in both the vernacular and Latin. Most of the others are less ambitious, insisting on more easily acquired qualities such as trustworthiness, cleanliness, and, in the case of the *trinciante* and *coppiere*, the confidence to perform publicly without self-consciousness and with a rock-steady hand. Some recommendations recall fragments of Castiglione's advice. Evitascandalo and Romoli would have their *scalchi* dress soberly in black. Cervio advises that his *trinciante*, like Castiglione's courtier, be neither too tall or too short. Scappi urges that the chef study the 'nature and qualities' of his prince, so that he may shape himself to harmonize with them as closely as possible. Several of the *virtuosi* recommend that the perfect practitioner of their art should be noble of birth, or at least noble in their manners—a sleight of hand that allows them to suggest a Castiglionesque social elitism while allowing for meritocracy in practice. Even Corte, who expresses a strong preference for his *cavallarizzo* to be noble, acknowledges that 'there are those who, though born commoners, nonetheless have manners fit for the noblest of men' (121v).[51]

It is not only in points of detail that these court art 'institutes' invoke the spirit of Castiglione and other authors of Renaissance conduct literature. The titles of Corte's and Cervio's treatises, *Il cavallarizzo* and *Il trinciante* (*The Horsemaster* and *The Carver*) seem deliberately intended to echo the title of Castiglione's dialogue, which, although originally published as *The Book of the Courtier*, was more usually entitled simply *The Courtier* (*Il Cortegiano*) from around the 1540s onwards. Corte explicitly cites both Castiglione's *Courtier* and Cicero's *On the Orator* to justify his methodology in describing the perfect form of the *cavallarizzo*, despite the impossibility of attaining this ideal in practice.[52] Domenico Romoli excuses the brevity of his chapter-long description of the office of the *coppiere* by noting that a full treatment would require no less time than was needed by 'Count Baldassare' to describe his perfect courtier.[53]

The use the *virtuosi* make of Castiglione in their writings points to a more general reception dynamic. Although one of Castiglione's agendas in *The Courtier* seems to have been to erect a wall between 'true' gentleman courtiers and the mass of non-noble court professionals, this effort was doomed to failure in practice. The democratizing dynamic of print culture transformed what had originally been intended as an elite text, to be circulated in manuscript to a select, coterie readership, into a work that exposed the secrets of courtly self-fashioning to an expanding vernacular public extending to urban professionals, merchants, literate upper artisans—and, of course, the lesser *virtuosi* of the courts. Successive editors of the work facilitated its utility as a textbook for hasty readers who might have been frustrated by the elegant obliquities of Castiglione's argument. Before long, the work was available in editions furnished with marginal notes and indices translating Castiglione's carefully nuanced suggestions into something more closely resembling rules, while later conduct books such as Giovanni della Casa's *Galateo* and Stefano Guazzo's *Civil Conversation* provided behavioural advice in a more folksy and less intimidating manner. By the later sixteenth century, a literate court professional like Corte's *cavallarizzo* might aspire to the same kind of cultural poise Castiglione required in his aristocratic courtier. Corte acknowledges this half-jokingly, having his interlocutor in the dialogue that occupies the third book of his treatise accuse him of making his horsetrainer 'brother to the Courtier' (*fratello del Cortegiano*).[54]

RENAISSANCE MAN AT WORK

As the evidence examined in the previous section suggests, traditional social distinctions were beginning to blur in some respects by the later sixteenth century. The Italian elite's vast investment in art, in the broad sense defined by Guerzoni, resulted in an enhanced appreciation of virtuosistic skill and ingenuity, in whatever form it manifested itself. This had consequences for a broader segment of society than the traditional focus on painters and sculptors would suggest. In addition to the examples considered so far, of practitioners of the fine and decorative arts and the table arts, we should also take into account skilled artisans in trades such as weapon-making, armour-making, and the manufacture of mathematical and scientific instruments—all apparently utilitarian crafts, but in fact often practised in Renaissance Italy with a high degree of aesthetic and design skill, in addition to marked technical ingenuity.[55] The ever-increasing material sophistication of Renaissance society gave rise to many new specialist professions in this period, such as that of damasceners within the internationally famous Milanese arms industry ('damascened' swords and armour, decorated with precious metals inlaid into a dark background of oxidized steel, were some of the most prized 'art weapons' of the day).[56]

Elite interest in the mechanical arts was, of course, for the most part limited to patronage and connoisseurship, but we even in this period find some evidence of a practical interest in 'mechanical' activities on the part of aristocrats. The most striking example is Alfonso I d'Este, duke of Ferrara, who is known to have practised metalwork, gun casting, and majolica work, as well as turning wood on a lathe. Alfonso was unusual in the extent of his practical craft interests, but a few manual arts gained reasonably broad aristocratic constituencies, particularly wood-turning, known as the *ars tornandi*. The Milanese turner Giovanni Ambrogio Maggiore, who had discovered a technique for turning one ivory ball inside another, was summoned to the court of Bavaria in 1573 by the heir to the dukedom, who had practical interests in the art.[57] Besides these instances of aristocratic amateur interest, we also find men of relatively elite status engaging with the mechanical arts more professionally. A prominent example is Vannoccio Biringuccio, son of a civil engineer in the employment of the Sienese government. An expert on mining and a renowned cannon founder, Biringuccio wrote a wide-ranging treatise on the 'arts of fire' (*La pirotechnia*, 1540), encompassing iron founding, ceramics, metal-working of all kinds, brick-making, even explosives and fireworks. Another 'gentleman mechanical' was Cipriano Piccolpasso, descended from a prominent patrician family from Bologna, though born in the majolica-making centre of Castel Durante in the Marches. Piccolpasso worked as a military engineer for some time, but he also ran a majolica workshop and composed the first monographic treatise on the ceramicist's art, *The Three Books of the Potter* (1548).

The very fact of the inscription in writing of craft techniques that had previously been passed on orally from father to son, or from master to apprentice, was a sign of the rising cultural status of such professions. Writing, analysis, theory all served to draw the mechanical arts into the sphere of the rational and discursive, and to underline the fact that these arts were not purely manual, but encompassed an intellectual dimension. The writers of technical treatises also emphasized this explicitly. Biringuccio consistently identifies 'good judgment' (*buon giudicio*) and 'talent' or 'intelligence' (*ingegno*) as core to successful craftsmanship. Another key element is *disegno*, 'the key that opens the door to all crafts' as Biringuccio defines it at one point.[58] The art of the ceramicist, for example, is said to be made up of a combination of *disegno* and alchemy (alchemy in respect of the importance that chemical formulae such as lustres and glazes played in the art).[59] *Disegno* was a charged term in Renaissance art theory, used by Vasari to designate the conceptual element in artistic ideation, as well as the material drawing in which the artistic 'idea' began to be sketched out in practice. Biringuccio uses the term in a more inclusive sense, signifying a capacity to inform and craft a material object, as well as conceiving of it—an 'organic', 'embodied' conception of creation, in which hand, mind, and eye worked in an integrated, non-hierarchical manner.[60]

The democratizing thrust of Biringuccio's treatise is most apparent in his treatment of the art of the blacksmith. This he initially speaks of with an air of disparagement, emphasizing the hard labour the craft involves and the filthy environment of the smithy. It is principally practised by 'people without *disegno*', 'crude and rustic folk'.[61] Across the course of his chapter, however, Biringuccio's tone changes, and a note of admiration creeps in. 'If this were not such a toilsome and indelicate exercise, I would think it most praiseworthy; when you consider that these masters turn out their pieces without any mould or plan, just relying on their eye and good judgment, shaping them and making them graceful just by force of beating, it seems a remarkable thing.'[62] Later in his discussion (288v), Biringuccio speaks of blacksmiths' skill levels as a factor in determining the nobility of their craft, along with the extreme utility of their products. The word he uses is *sapere*, a word usually employed to designate purely intellectual forms of knowledge or wisdom. In this context, it picks out a kind of practical, operative intelligence that can ennoble even the most physical of trades.

Similar instances of semantic drift are apparent in some of the discussions of the practical arts in Leonardo Fioravanti's 1564 *Mirror of Universal Knowledge* (*Specchio della scienza universale*), already cited in Chapter 3 for its celebration of the democratizing effects of print. Fioravanti's title is already significant; where the term *scienza* was generally reserved for theoretical bodies of knowledge, Fioravanti implicitly extends it to the practical arts, opening the work with a discussion of the liberal and mechanical arts, the latter including carpentry, weaving, mirror-making, shoe-making—any human activity that incorporates a body of technical knowledge, or 'secrets', in the language of the day. Similarly, in his individual chapters, Fioravanti appropriates language generally associated with learned contexts to describe artisanal, skill-based knowledge. The Venetian tailor Maestro Giovanni is praised, for example, for his stupendous *esperienza* and *dottrina*; his Treviso counterpart Maestro Cesare Vaghetto for his *scienza* and *esperienza*.[63] *Esperienza* in both cases indicates practice, but *dottrina* ('doctrine') and *scienza* generally have cognitive-intellectual associations. Fioravanti identifies good judgment and *disegno* as two of the main constituents of the tailor's art, along with the more manual element of sewing and its associated skills. His treatment presages the still more intellectually ennobling discussion of the profession that we find in the Venice-based tailor Giovanni Pennacchini's 1650 *The Nobility and Antiquity of Tailors*, where geometry and colour semiotics are added to the tailor's necessary skills.[64]

Although no tailor-authored treatise such as Pennacchini's survives from the sixteenth century, Fioravanti represents tailors themselves as having a robust sense of the dignity of their profession, to the extent that he feels himself called on to deliver a moral lecture warning them not to 'glory so much in their art' since, 'even though it is fine and elegant, ... it is not of that ingenuity (*ingegno*) and status that they] think'.[65] It is interesting to juxtapose this passage with the Lombard artist Giovanni Battista Moroni's famous portrait of a tailor dating from the late 1560s or early 1570s, a few years after Fioravanti's *Specchio* was published (Frontispiece). Moroni's painting shows the artisan at work, preparing to cut a cloth and—in a brilliant conceit—eyeing up the viewer with an air of concentration as if to gauge his size for the garment he is making. The device seems calculated to dramatize the moment of *disegno*, before the moment of the garment's material rendition, underlining the common element that the arts of painting and tailoring shared. The cloth Moroni's tailor is cutting is black, indicative of the status of his clientele; black was much favoured by the Renaissance elites, and many of Moroni's noble sitters sport sumptuous black garments. The tailor himself is also elegantly dressed, in a buff-coloured doublet, 'bombasted' (lined and stuffed) scarlet hose, and a white shirt frilled at the neck and cuffs. He even wears a sword belt with a sliding buckle, a notable mark of status, originally associated with the aristocracy, though increasingly appropriated by those of lesser rank. These were unlikely work clothes, even for a well-heeled master artisan, and Moroni has done nothing to detract from the posed nature of the portrait; there is no allusion to a workshop setting other than the props of scissors, cloth, and uncluttered table (perhaps that of his client, rather than his own). The tailor's dress seems intended as an advertisement of his wares—or rather, perhaps, a proud exhibition of his artistry; yet they are a gentleman's clothes, and Moroni portrays him modelling them with dignity and poise.

The process of democratizing rehabilitation of the mechanical arts that we see in Biringuccio and Fioravanti reaches a kind of apotheosis in a remarkable work of the late sixteenth century, Tommaso Garzoni's *La piazza universale delle professioni umane* (*The Universal Piazza of Human Professions*), published in Venice in 1585. Unlike most of his predecessors, Garzoni was not a practitioner of the mechanical arts himself; rather, he was a cleric, a Lateran canon—improbable though that may seem, given the worldly, and even racy, character of many of his writings. *The Universal Piazza* is typical of Garzoni's writings in its exuberant, proto-Baroque title and its encyclopedic pretensions; it forms a kind of trilogy with Garzoni's *Theatre of the Various and Diverse Brains of the World* (1583) and his *Hospital of Incurable Madmen* (1586). While the *Theatre* attempts to codify the different types of human character, and the *Hospital* the various species of madness, the *Piazza* offers an overview of professional and trade identities: a semi-serious, semi-satirical, moralizing anthropology of late-Renaissance man viewed through the particular lens of work.

As recent scholarship has stressed, Garzoni's *Piazza* makes an interesting comparison with traditional 'vertical' descriptions of society, with kings and emperors at the apex, the nobility below, and merchants, artisans, and peasants beneath.[66] As the metaphor of the *piazza* suggests, Garzoni's vision of society is essentially horizontal, with the social 'estates' jostling and elbowing one another in a single, crowded space. In this vision, birth into a particular estate is less defining of human value than the proper use of the talents with which one has been endowed. Nor does Garzoni fully maintain the traditional hierarchical distinction between the sciences and liberal arts on the one hand, and the mechanical arts on the other. On the contrary, some of the professions that emerge with most honour in his book are technical arts such as ship-building, printing, clock-making, and weaponry. Developing the logic of writers of technical treatises such as Biringuccio, Garzoni explicitly contests perceptions of the mechanical arts as purely manual in character, defining them instead as 'arts that involve both the intellect (*ingegno*) and the hand'. Indeed, emphasizing the conceptual element in mechanical activity, Garzoni makes technological innovation part of the definition of the term. 'Not all trite and commonplace artisans (*artefici*) can be properly called mechanicals, but only those who use their intellect to address immense emerging difficulties, in the interest of the common good.'[67]

This last criterion, of contribution to the common good, is fundamental in Garzoni's treatise. While his chapter on mirror-makers includes a fascinated long description of the manufacture of glass mirrors at Murano, and while he acknowledges that the trade requires both 'intellect and industry', Garzoni is forced to dismiss it on moral grounds as a trade catering essentially to 'worldly diversion'.[68] The cooks, carvers, cupbearers, and other ministers to Renaissance gourmandizing discussed earlier in this chapter are similarly given short shrift. Moving down the moral ladder, Garzoni's 'professions' include those of thief, prostitute, pimp, vagabond, charlatan, murderer, and professional idler (*ozioso di piazza*). These are the sections of the treatise where Garzoni's satirical wit, and his anti-hierarchical instincts, are most apparent. The chapter on thievery does not simply encompass discussion of the kind of lower-class, often socially marginal, figures who tended to populate the gallows of Renaissance cities. Garzoni also finds room for princes, the prototypical thieves, in that their main profession consists of occupying the territories of others, and for writers, who freely plagiarize the works of their predecessors (surely a wry self-reference, given Garzoni's own gargantuan indulgence in such 'thieving').[69] Renaissance man, for Garzoni, is driven by a kind of promiscuous creative energy, capable of devising societally useful technological innovations on the one hand and ever-new schemes for trickery and mischief on the other. As moralist, Garzoni approves of the proper use of human ingenuity and disapproves of the improper. As writer, he seems to divert himself equally in exploring the secrets of both commendable and disreputable trades.

MAN THE INVENTOR

In an intriguing passage in Vanoccio Biringuccio's treatise on the 'arts of fire', the author takes the pretext of a discussion of brick-making to embark on an extended meditation on the anthropology and psychology of material progress. Starting in the prehistoric world, Biringuccio narrates the way in which primitive man first slept like an animal under the open skies, before gradually acquiring the habit of manufacturing crude huts using natural materials such as rocks and earth and tree trunks. Having acquired a measure of comfort and security through this means, Biringuccio's early man expands his ambitions to embrace 'superfluity' and 'pomp'; still in his earthen hovel, he begins to dream 'not of huts, but of houses and palaces and the greatest of cities'.[70] This vaulting fantasy of ever-expanding luxury is presented as arising from an innate human impulse towards 'insatiability': 'always wanting more than we have; never contenting ourselves with what we have'.[71] In the case in question, the desire for 'more' leads primitive man to exert his intelligence and observational powers to work out what it would take to go beyond the building materials provided by Nature (earth, stone, and wood) and gradually to evolve the means to mix mortar and fire bricks.

Biringuccio's narrative has humanistic roots, following in the tracks of classical writers such as Cicero, Lucretius, and Vitruvius, who represented the early history of humankind as one of evolution from an initial, primitive, quasi-bestial lifestyle to a civilized one. Lucretius's *On the Nature of Things* is Biringuccio's most likely source, since it encompasses discussions of primitive metallurgy and other early uses of fire. Biringuccio's attitude to the urge to luxury is distinctive, however, differing sharply from Lucretius's more moralizing stance. The desire for 'pomp' and 'superfluity' is not posited here as a late development in society and a harbinger of decadence and corruption; rather, Biringuccio presents the luxury impulse as something natural and innate in man from his hut-dwelling days, and, moreover, as something commendable. Biringuccio describes the brick, the end result of primitive man's dreams of future cities, as 'an invention ... more divine than human in its effects'.[72]

This positive attitude to material progress and to the psychological drives that produce it is characteristic of Biringuccio's treatise as a whole, even if he shows a degree of understandable ambivalence when discussing recent advances in weapons technology towards the end of the book. At the beginning of the treatise, Biringuccio justifies the fact that the work will reveal 'secrets' previously jealously guarded by craftsmen, on the grounds that this provision of 'fresh knowledge' will help generate 'fresh inventions', which will supply further 'fresh knowledge' in turn.[73] As Pamela Long has underlined, this tradition of technological innovation within the mechanical arts importantly presages the development of experimental science in the seventeenth century. The hierarchical division between *techne* (technical or craft skill) and *episteme* (theoretical knowledge) here begins to break down, as 'mechanical' labours are credited with the ability to generate new forms of theoretical knowledge.[74]

A celebratory attitude to technological progress similar to that which we find in Biringuccio underlies the decorative scheme of the study (*studiolo*) that the alchemist-prince Francesco I de' Medici constructed in his Florentine palace to house his cabinet of curiosities in the 1570s, one of the most strikingly original pictorial schemes of the age.[75] The theme of the *studiolo* scheme is bifold: a celebration of the creativity of Nature and of man, articulated into four sections themed to the four elements, earth, water, air, and fire. Alongside mythological scenes relating to the marvels of nature (such as Vasari's beautiful *Perseus and Andromeda*, illustrating the origins of coral, from the blood of a slaughtered sea monster), the *studiolo* also includes paintings celebrating technological inventions, either ancient (purple dye, glass) or modern (gunpowder), and others figuring technological spaces, such as a wool factory, a bronze foundry, a diamond mine, and a goldsmith's workshop (Fig. 30). Francesco had himself portrayed several times in the sequence: once in an alchemist's workshop, sleeves rolled up and indistinguishable from his assistants, in terms of dress; the other on the margins of Giovanni Maria Butteri's *The Glassworks*, where he is seen scrutinizing a recently made goblet. This spectacularization of technology, while unusual, was not quite unique to Francesco's *studiolo*. Among the entertainments laid on for the French king Henri III during a state visit to Venice in the 1570s was a temporary glassworks mounted on piers in the lagoon, with Murano glass-makers performing their skills in public, leaving their noble audience 'astonished and filled with delight'. The spectacle was illuminated, allowing the glass-making to be watched after dark, a significant technological achievement in itself.[76]

These points are worth underlining, as a long-rooted scholarly cliché sees late sixteenth-century Italy as a backward-looking, static, elitist culture, increasingly rigid in its social hierarchies and in a state of economic decline. Italian historians have often described this period as one of 'refeudalization', reaching back beyond Italy's vibrant early-Renaissance commercial culture to a distant, aristocratic, landed past. In cultural terms, one sign of this shift was the vogue enjoyed in the Italian courts by a genre such as pastoral drama: a form of comedy, or tragi-comedy, set in the fantastic ancient setting of Arcadia, with a cast made up of 'aristocratic' shepherds and nymphs, whose elegant loves are contrasted with comic business involving 'plebeian' goatherds and satyrs.[77] Pastoral has its roots in the classical mythological narrative that saw man's origins in a simple, pastoral setting, during the so-called Golden Age, prior

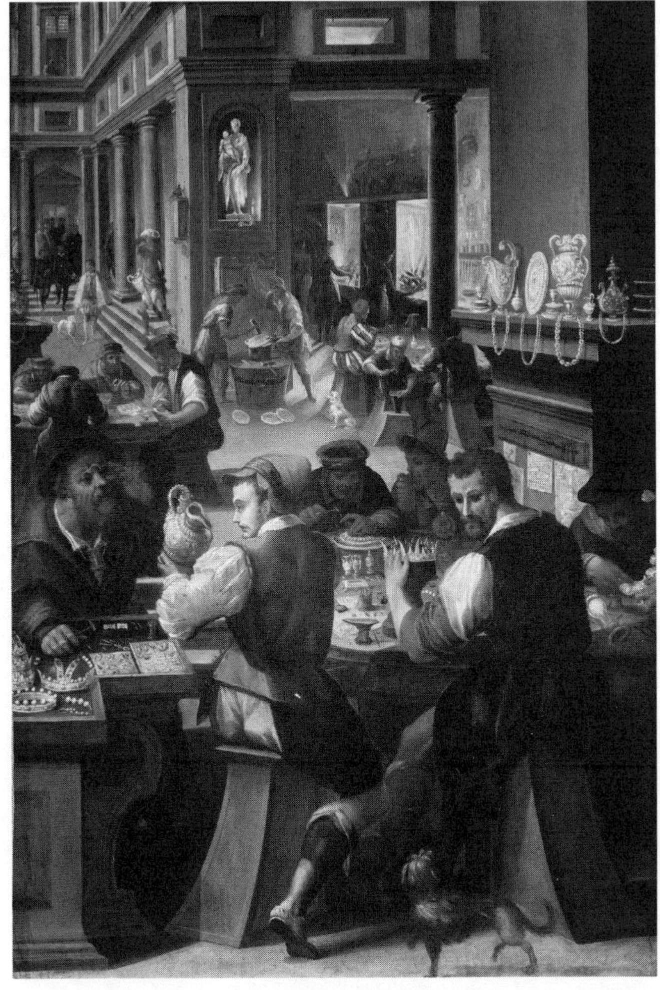

Fig. 30: Alessandro Fei, *The Goldsmith's Workshop*, *c.* 1570. Studiolo of Francesco I de' Medici, Palazzo Vecchio, Florence.

to such corrupting technological advances as the development of navigation, the rise of cities and commerce, the invention of money. Human material inventiveness of the kind celebrated by Biringuccio is demonized in this alternative narrative of human origins, which paints technological and material progress as inevitably accompanied by a concomitant moral decline.

Although critics have often seen pastoralism's nostalgia and its fastidious distaste for the modern, urban, money-driven world as representative of later sixteenth-century aristocratic attitudes in general, it is important to recall that this set of attitudes co-existed with other, very different, even antithetical value systems. Within the increasingly articulate culture of the mechanical arts and their gentleman admirers, man's material powers of invention were celebrated, not reviled. Nor did social status depend entirely on 'feudal', ascriptive factors, such as those that divided noble shepherds from base-born goatherds in pastoral; a respectable social standing might rather be achieved through exertion and talent. Even within the princely courts, which have often been stereotyped as the prime *loci* of 'refeudalization', these two cultures existed in parallel. Indeed, as Guido Guerzoni has argued, the culture of 'magnificence' and conspicuous consumption that dictated such a high percentage of expenditure in the courts, rather than sapping the Italian economy, as traditional models have sometimes suggested, served instead to stimulate that economy's thriving and innovative luxury goods sector, which Guerzoni sees as having laid the basis for Italy's modern-day, technological-aesthetic investment in design.[78]

6

RENAISSANCE WOMAN

Although Jacob Burckhardt's bold assertions about the emergence of a new model of individualistic selfhood in the Italian Renaissance have been endlessly debated by scholars, a simpler and less contentious point has largely escaped notice. Whether or not it saw the birth of a new 'Renaissance Man', the Italian Renaissance quite indisputably saw the birth of a new model of woman. In 1300 or 1350, it would have been difficult for the best-informed observer to cite examples of women outside religious life who contributed to literary and intellectual culture as producers, rather than as consumers, with the exception of a handful of female troubadours and distant memories of a few classical poets like Sappho. By 1600, the figure of the secular female writer was well established in elite public consciousness in Italy, and educated readers could cite a tradition of women's writing dating back several generations. The first all-female anthology of poetry, incorporating the work of more than 50 writers, dates to 1559; the first biographical dictionary of women writers to 1620.[1] The same arc of time, and more specifically the later sixteenth century, saw the emergence of secular women as artists, as musical performers, as composers, as actresses. The figure of the creative woman, the *virtuosa*, is one of the Italian Renaissance's most clearly documentable cultural novelties, and one of this period's most potent anticipations of modernity.

A further important development in women's history in this period, with strong causal connections to that just noted, is the emergence of new ways of thinking about gender and about women. Across the course of the fourteenth to the sixteenth century, a body of theory emerged framed to counter traditional visions of women as 'weak vessels': less rational than men, and more prone to sin. The new theory instead argued that women were men's equals by nature, no less rational than men and no less capable of virtue. Rather than seeing men's social dominance as justified by biological differences between the sexes, the new thinking attributed this dominance to social and cultural factors. Women were kept in an artificial position of inferiority by their inferior education, by cultural conditioning, and by a lack of professional opportunities. If girls were given the same opportunities as their brothers, they would prove themselves the equals of their male peers. Towards the end of the sixteenth century, the Venetian writer Moderata Fonte, or Modesta Pozzo, voiced this intuition through a powerful simile, comparing women's talent and capacity to a buried seam of gold in society, undiscovered and hence invisible. If brought to the surface, it would gleam in the world just as brightly as any other gold.[2]

By the time Fonte was writing in the 1580s and 1590s, sufficient empirical evidence was available to give credibility to her 'buried gold' analogy, as this period saw perhaps the high point in the rise of the *virtuosa*. Fonte's literary career coincided with the artistic career of Lavinia Fontana, one of the earliest professional women artists; with the emergence of virtuoso court singers such as Laura Peverara; and with the striking artistic trajectory of Isabella Andreini as actress, theatrical impresario, dramatist, and poet. One of the reasons why gender and women's history have rarely held a key place in narratives of Italian Renaissance culture is that traditional periodizations that locate the end of the Renaissance in 1527 or 1530 or 1550 miss the crucial late-sixteenth moment that saw the climax of the long-running narrative of women's emergence as cultural protagonists. The same is true to a lesser extent with the associated narrative of the emergence of proto-feminist thinking on gender in this period. Although the new thinking on women was largely the product of late fifteenth- and early sixteenth-century humanists, and we find it enshrined already in a work of the 1520s like Castiglione's *Book of the Courtier*, it was in the mid- to late sixteenth century that this new model of thinking about gender, once limited to the courtly avant-garde, became widely disseminated throughout society. It is principally in the later sixteenth century, moreover, that women began to contribute themselves to public debate on gender, most notably in the writings of Moderata Fonte and her younger Venetian contemporary Lucrezia Marinella.

GENDER AND SOCIETY IN RENAISSANCE ITALY

As we have seen with every aspect of Italian Renaissance culture, women's roles, and societal conceptions of gender, varied considerably from region to region and from city to city. Women's roles and social identities also differed very sharply according to their social status, in a manner that precludes generalization. Even a fundamental question such as what education women received cannot be answered without a detailed breakdown by social standing and context. A study by Sharon Strocchia of fifteenth-century Florentine convent schools shows girls of the commercial and banking elite, along with notaries' daughters and the daughters of a few aspirant artisans and shopkeepers, receiving a basic education, incorporating vernacular reading skills, but not necessarily extending to writing ('split literacy').[3] Strocchia's research suggests a society cautiously opening up to the idea that literacy could enhance a woman's marriage prospects and improve her performance in managing her household, but still deeply conflicted about the dangers that access to written materials might pose to a woman's moral virtue. At the same time, however, in the same city, Lucrezia Tornabuoni, wife of Piero de' Medici and mother of Lorenzo de' Medici, the effective rulers of the city from the 1460s to the early 1490s, was very publicly cultivating a literary persona, without any obvious damage to her reputation. Five religious narrative poems survive by her, together with a number of sacred songs (*laude*). Two other Florentine women within the Medici circle also attained literary recognition. Antonia Pulci, who married into a family of Medicean poets, composed a number of popular religious dramas that continued to be republished throughout the sixteenth century. Alessandra Scala, daughter of the chancellor, Bartolomeo Scala, won renown for her classical learning, and corresponded in Greek with the great humanist Angelo Poliziano.

Although they were outliers by Florentine standards, women like Tornabuoni, Pulci, and Scala would have been considerably less unusual in other contexts in Italy, where female literacy and erudition had a longer and more socially embedded tradition. In the princely courts of central and northern Italy, and in some of the great early humanist centres like Padua and Verona, a robust tradition of female learning evolved at least from the late fourteenth and early fifteenth centuries. A striking early figure within this tradition is Battista da Montefeltro, born into the ruling family of Urbino and married to the lord of Pesaro, Galeazzo Malatesta. Battista is the first woman in Italy known to have delivered a Latin oration in public, and she left a sizeable collection of Latin letters and of religious vernacular verse. She was the recipient of an important early humanistic treatise on education, Leonardo Bruni's *On Studies and Letters*, dating from the 1420s, which outlines a programme of Latin learning suitable for the well-educated noblewoman, incorporating both the study of patristic writings and of classical literature. Although her erudition was exceptional, Battista's correspondences with her sister Anna and her sister-in-law Paola Malatesta Gonzaga show her not to have been the only educated woman in her circle. Later women in these same families also distinguished themselves for their learning. Paola Malatesta's daughter Cecilia was educated at the prototypical humanist school run by Vittorino da Feltre, highly unusual as an educational institution in this period that educated girls alongside boys. Battista da Montefeltro headed what became a dazzling dynasty of erudite women, stretching down to Vittoria Colonna, the most famous female intellectual of the first half of the sixteenth century.

Another famous female intellectual dynasty of the fifteenth century was that of the aristocratic Nogarola family in Verona. This produced the most impressive female humanist of the century in Isotta Nogarola, exceptional as an instance of a woman who chose not to marry or enter a convent, but to lead a scholarly life in the secular world. Both Isotta's sister, Ginevra, and her aunt, Angela, were also noted for their erudition, and Angela left a body of writings that are some of the earliest by any Italian woman to survive. Isotta Nogarola has sometimes been presented by feminist scholars as a tragic example of fifteenth-century humanism's hostility to the notion of the educated woman. After a brilliant early scholarly career, following her decision not to marry and the appearance of a slanderous work questioning her virtue, she is said to have been forced into a reclusive life confined effectively to a 'book-lined cell'.[4] This seems unduly pessimistic as an interpretation of her life, and to reflect an exaggerated idea of how challenging and controversial the figure of the learned woman was in this period within the kind of aristocratic circles in which Nogarola moved. The evidence is, rather, that Nogarola continued to engage actively with the world, corresponding with male humanist intellectuals and contributing to public debate, as with the written oration she sent to Pope Pius II at the time of the Council of Mantua in 1459. Nogarola even seems to have delivered an oration herself in person on one occasion in Verona, at the invitation of the city's humanist bishop: a Latin sermon in praise of St Jerome.[5]

The difference in educational patterns that we can observe between Florence and the courtly and aristocratic circles of Battista da Montefeltro and Isotta Nogarola reflects a marked different in women's roles within the mercantile republics of Italy and the princely courts. The Italian republics, mainly oligarchic by the fifteenth century, entrusted political power to a fairly narrow elite of wealthy men, who alternated in power and were elected to office. Women were excluded both from office-holding and from voting, and, although women's social networking and charitable engagement doubtless helped consolidate male political alliances and client systems, this was all essentially 'behind the scenes' activity. Women were largely invisible in public life, and the ethos that was required of them was that of a modest and chaste wife, a loving mother, and a capable household manager. Showier, non-domestic virtues such as erudition, conversational brilliance, artistic and literary connoisseurship, musical or poetic talent, were either irrelevant to a wife's social value, or were positively frowned on, as signs of flightiness. Any girl of the Florentine or Venetian patriciate with intellectual aspirations would probably have been best advised to enter a convent, where traditions of study, drama, and music were well established and socially condoned.

Things were very different in the courts, where the centrality of the dynastic system in the transmission of power meant that the ruler's family was much in the public eye, and where the ruler's wife, in particular, was among the most salient figures of the court. Women did not rule Italian states except in special circumstances, such as in their husbands' absences, or as regents for sons too young to accede. Such special circumstances were not particularly unusual in Renaissance Italy, however, where many princes were *condottieri*, whose military careers often kept them absent from their states for long periods, and where marriages, especially second and subsequent marriages, often paired young women with much older men. For this reason, women bred to princely marriages needed to have an education sufficient to allow them to substitute for their husbands where necessary, and they needed to cultivate a 'princely' ethos, sufficiently authoritative to sustain the exigencies of rule. Battista da Montefeltro's career as *signora* of Pesaro offers a telling illustration of this point. The political ineptitude of her husband, Galeazzo Malatesta, constrained her to take a leading role within the government and diplomacy of the city, along with Galeazzo's brothers. Eventually, when her husband left Pesaro after selling his lordship to Alessandro Sforza, the husband of his granddaughter Costanza Varano, Battista remained behind to manage the transition, and ensure that the city passed safely into Costanza's and Alessandro's hands.

Even when her husband was alive, at home, and competent, the role of a princely consort required a degree of showiness far in advance of that of a patrician wife within a republic. On multiple occasions—feasts, ceremonies, weddings, funerals, diplomatic visits—she needed to be seen alongside her husband and to converse with important visitors, representing the dignity of the state in the same way as the prince. At the very least, taste in dress, courtly manners, and articulacy were required of a princely consort, in addition to a patrician wife's domestic virtues. As the courts became larger and more sophisticated, across the course of the fifteenth century, dance skills and musical ability became increasingly sought-after qualities in court ladies, while, especially after 1500, some princely consorts showed their taste, intellect, and learning through such activities as art collecting, architectural patronage, and the commissioning and composition of verse. Education was not an optional extra for such women; it was a necessary professional competence.

Although the role of the dynastic consort was an exceptional one, the aristocratic practice of educating women was not limited to the ruling families, as the example of the Nogarola family suggests. As the size and complexity of the courts grew, princely consorts increasingly surrounded themselves with an entourage of noblewomen as their ladies-in-waiting, who frequently came to play an important role as cultural 'brokers' by virtue of their closeness to their mistresses: a relationship we see immortalized in Castiglione's *Courtier* in the figure of Emilia Pio. Talented young girls might also be invited to court to share in the education of the daughters of princes. This was the case with two notable Italian female intellectuals, Caterina Vigri, or St Catherine of Bologna, in the fifteenth century, and Olimpia Morata in the sixteenth. Both were educated at the court of Ferrara as companions to daughters of the Este family. Late in the sixteenth century, we see a fascinating document of this custom in a published treatise of 1586 by a Piedmontese gentleman, Annibale Guasco, addressed to his 11-year-old daughter Lavinia, who had just obtained a post at the court of Savoy, in the entourage of the recently arrived bride of the duke. Before instructing Lavinia in the mores of the court, Guasco recalls in detail the rigorous education to which he subjected her, which left her possessed, among other things, of superb musical skills, beautiful handwriting, mastery of the abacus, and the capacity to beat her father at chess.[6]

The special place of the courts within the history of women's engagement with elite culture was, of course, not simply an Italian story. Cultured queens and other ruling women constitute a well-known feature of late medieval and early modern European history. What was different in Italy, however, and what contributed immensely to the diffusion of court manners and mores throughout society was that, instead of a single royal court, as we find in many other European nations by the fifteenth and sixteenth centuries, Italy had multiple courts. Moving east from the Alps, in the 1490s, just before the Wars of Italy reshaped the Italian political map, we find the courts of Savoy, Monferrato, Milan, Mantua, Ferrara; then, to the south, Forlì, Pesaro, Rimini, Urbino. Further south was the great court of Naples, seat of the only Italian-based dynasty to bear the title of king. This list includes only the larger courts, not the very numerous smaller feudal estates, in the north and the south, from whose rulers the great powers of Italy drew their ranks of military captains, diplomats, and courtiers, and with whom they frequently tied themselves in kinship through the marriage of younger or illegitimate daughters and sons. It also excludes quasi-courtly regimes in cities that remained formally republics, such as those of the Bentivoglio family in Bologna and the Medici in Florence.

The proliferation of courts meant, most obviously, a proliferation of dynasties, a proliferation of entourages, and a proliferation of women educated for court life. It also resulted in an intense cultural rivalry between courts, manifest especially at showpiece events such as weddings, which demanded flamboyant expressions of princely magnificence. Precisely on account of this competitive dynamic, the courts proved a productive habitat for women's cultural activity: here was a field, like art patronage, architectural patronage, spectacle, in which a court might seek to excel. By the late sixteenth century, this showcasing of female virtuosity was beginning in some cases to take on a quasi-institutional character. Ferrara in the 1580s had a famous and influential female vocal consort, the *concerto delle donne*, made up primarily of non-aristocratic singers imported into the court for their talents. The same court featured a female dance ensemble, the *balletto delle donne*, sponsored by the duchess, Margherita Gonzaga, and including aristocratic ladies-in-waiting among its participants, along with several members of the *concerto delle donne*.[7]

The extent of women's engagement with elite culture in the Italian Quattrocento and Cinquecento was obscured until recently by the fact that twentieth-century scholarship on the Italian Renaissance, especially in the field of social history, concentrated disproportionately on Florence and Venice, probably the most conservative major cities in Italy in terms of attitudes to gender and women's education. It is still not unusual to read generalizations about women in this period being confined to the domestic sphere; about literacy in women being regarded as an index of sexual availability; about female education consisting purely in needle skills and the ability to read simple religious texts. All these statements may have a degree of validity when applied to Florence and Venice, especially in the fifteenth century, but they are all highly misleading when applied to Italy as a whole.

RETHINKING WOMEN

With the rise of the courts and the increasing visibility of the court lady as a social type, traditional philosophical models of sex difference began to come under pressure, and new models of thinking about sex and gender began to evolve. We can see signs of this already from the late fourteenth century, but the key period is the late fifteenth and the early sixteenth centuries. Unsurprisingly, the initial locus for this revolution in gender thought was the princely courts. By the mid-sixteenth century, however, the new thinking had become widely disseminated throughout the Italian urban elites.

In order to understand this segment of intellectual history, it is necessary first to have a grasp of the Aristotelian model of thinking on sex and gender, which was hugely influential in shaping Western thought on these issues from the thirteenth century onwards. First evolved by Aristotle and his followers in fourth-century BCE Athens, and appropriated and Christianized by the medieval scholastics, this formed the basis of thinking about sexual difference within a number of key university disciplines, including natural philosophy, medicine, law, and theology.[8] It also informed writings on subjects such as household management, where the pseudo-Aristotelian *Economics* was one of the key classical sources. The dominant feature of this model of thinking is what is often termed 'gender essentialism': the notion that the sexes have different capacities, rooted in intrinsic, or essential, biological differences, and that these biologically differentiated capacities determine their societal roles. Within Aristotelian thinking, this essentialism has a strongly evaluative dimension. Women are not merely different from men in their intrinsic capacities, but inferior to them, so that their natural role in society is one of obedience and submission.

The cardinal point in Aristotle's theory of sex difference is found in his writing on reproduction in animals, where he argues that the female is a defective version of the male. At the moment of conception, Nature always aims to produce the perfect form of the species, the male, but, for many medical and circumstantial reasons, ranging from the age of the parents to the direction of the wind, this precarious process may fail and a female be produced instead. In the case of humans, this results in a being deficient in the specific human virtue of rationality, as well as the more general animal virtue of strength. Although women do not lack reason, their reason is feebler than men's, just as their bodies are weaker. Nature has fitted them to lesser tasks than men in the conduct of politics and the governance of cities; essentially, man is framed to command, women to obey. As a consequence of this thinking, women's virtue-system was conceived of as complementary and opposite to men's. Eloquence was praiseworthy in man, as it was needed for leadership, while the corresponding virtue in woman was silence. Fortitude and courage were key virtues in men, while women were held to be naturally timorous and so were not judged by the same measure. Within the household, man's stronger and more active nature fitted him to work outside the home, earning household revenue through warfare or commerce, while a woman's more sedentary nature equipped her to remain within the domestic world, conserving and managing the wealth her husband has gained.

The Aristotelian notion of women as inferior beings, and as timorous and weak by nature, did not gel easily in all respects with late-medieval Christian culture, with its deep reverence for the Virgin Mary and its panoply of valiant female martyr saints. The Christian tradition, however, had its own, strong vein of misogyny, centring on a demonization of female sexuality, and encapsulated in the Genesis story of Eve's fatal temptation of Adam, which brought about the Fall. Aristotelian thinking worked with the grain of this, providing a 'scientific' explanation for the association of women with sensuality and moral corruption. Within Aristotelian thought, the relative weakness of women's reason made it more difficult for them to master their bodily appetites, so that they remained prey to unruly sexual urges, as well as being generally volatile, unpredictable, and impulsive. All in all, Aristotle's system was sufficiently compatible with other influential ways of thinking about sex difference to supply a robust philosophical legitimization of current social beliefs and values—at least in republican political environments, where the roles of men and women differed relatively little from those in Aristotle's Athens.

Justly famous as a statement of Renaissance republican ideals concerning gender roles is Leon Battista Alberti's shrewd, semi-caricatural account of one Florentine patrician's 'training' of his wife in the third book of his 1430s dialogue, *On the Family*.[9] The passage is Aristotelian in its basic philosophical premises, drawing on Aristotle's *Politics*, and pseudo-Aristotle's *Economics*, as well as a dialogue by Xenophon on household management. Alberti brings these classical sources into dialogue with contemporary Florentine experience, however, giving the task of speaking on marriage to Giannozzo Alberti, one of the most sharply characterized speakers in his dialogue—an older, garrulous, opinionated, somewhat folksy figure, whose account of his marriage is rich with details of fifteenth-century Florentine domestic life.

After enjoying his listeners' compliments on the sagacity of his wife, who was apparently well known for her efficient management of their household, Giannozzo gives a detailed narrative of ways in which he socialized her to this role after her first arrival in his household as a young bride. The dialogue makes clear that Giannozzo's own age at marriage was 30, the norm for upper-class Florentine men. We are not told the age of his wife, Nicolosa Pazzi (who tellingly remains nameless in the text), but, going by norms, we should probably imagine her as much younger, most likely between 15 and 17. Giannozzo tells his listeners how he led his young wife through the house to show her his possessions, with the exception of his books and his personal and business writings, which he defined as strictly out of bounds to her. Following this, he lectured her on the need both to be chaste and to maintain the strictest appearance of chastity; this entails remaining as silent and modest as possible in public and avoiding any form of cosmetic beautification. As a dutiful girl, already well indoctrinated in the need for obedience by her parents, Giannozzo tells us that Nicolosa followed this doctrine religiously, except on one social occasion, when she forgot herself slightly; she greeted her guests laughing and talking, and her colour was high, leading her husband to suspect she had applied rouge. This deviance he quickly corrected, not through a direct reprimand, but by mock-innocently asking her whether she may have accidentally smeared her face in some way. He then followed up the lesson with the cautionary tale of a 30-year neighbour who already resembled an old woman, so much had she ruined her skin through the use of cosmetics. Giannozzo contrasts this ruined hag with the fresh-faced women of the Alberti family, whose unadulterated beauty stands as an index of their moral purity.

Giannozzo Alberti's complacent account of his wife-taming has become a locus classicus for feminist scholarly critiques of Renaissance patriarchal oppression—and not without reason. His insistence on chastity as women's core virtue (Nicolosa is made to reiterate three times over that she will never invite another man to her bed) is familiar from many other Renaissance texts, both literary and non-literary. Giannozzo's insistence on the *appearance* of chastity is equally familiar, as is the fact that the curation of appearances is not limited to the fields of dress and personal adornment, although these are of course crucial. Along with personal vanity and a concern with self-beautification, sociability and readiness of speech are also regarded as important 'warning signs' of a woman's potential unchastity. The party at which the otherwise docile Nicolosa makes her ill-advised venture into the world of cosmetics is also the only moment in the text at which she reveals a vivacious and outgoing social self. Another wifely tendency against which Florentine husbands are put on guard in the dialogue is a propensity to show interest in the world outside the household. Giannozzo approvingly quotes another Alberti patriarch who corrected his wife's tendency to pry into his movements outside the house by pointing out to her that women who show too much interest in the world of men may be suspected of having too much interest in men themselves. Giannozzo's own jealous protection of his books and papers from his wife is perhaps motivated by similar reasons, as well as his stated concern with women's inability to keep a secret—a familiar topos in the literature of the time.

Although Alberti's treatment of gender roles has often been taken as paradigmatic for the Renaissance in general, it will be clear from the preceding discussion of women's roles within the courts that it was nothing of the kind. The Aristotelian model that saw women as fitted by nature for submission to men was radically ill-suited for a political system in which a woman might, at times, exert supreme power in the state. The notion that women's reputation was best protected by curtailing their social interactions was similarly ill-matched to an environment like the court, in which mixed social interaction was the norm. A different theoretical model was required to describe and legitimize the different social practices of the courts. This evolved gradually, across the course of the fifteenth century, largely through the writings of humanists working in court contexts or enjoying court patronage. This tradition of thought reached maturity in the early sixteenth century, when it first began to be disseminated in print. The episode as a whole offers an excellent example of the way in which the Italian humanists' polemics with scholasticism led to fresh models of thinking. It also illustrates very well the close connection between humanist thought and its social and patronage contexts.[10]

Initially, the new humanist model of thinking on gender took a largely narrative, descriptive, empirical form. Early works in this tradition are mainly collections of paradigmatic examples of women of classical or biblical antiquity who were celebrated for achievement in fields typically thought of as male preserves, or who manifested

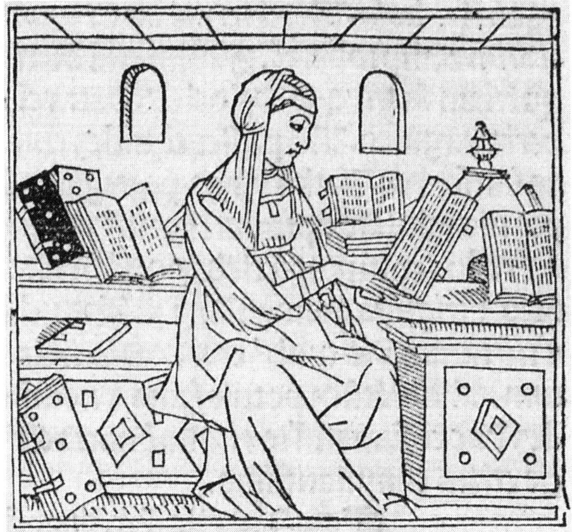

Fig. 31: Anon., woodcut illustration to Jacopo Filippo Foresti, *De plurimis claris sceletisque* [sic] *mulieribus* (Ferrara: Laurentius de Rubeis, 1497), fol. CLIr.

'masculine' moral capacities such as fortitude, constancy, prudence, and sexual temperance. This tradition of writings on 'famous women' was initiated by Boccaccio in the 1360s, and it gained new impetus in the fifteenth century when humanists became acquainted with a classical precedent for such collections, Plutarch's *The Virtues of Women*. Initially strictly 'ancient'—Boccaccio's *Famous Women* features a sole modern example, Queen Joanna I of Naples—such collections later expanded their reach to encompass modern examples of high-achieving ladies. The climactic work of the fifteenth-century tradition, a vast compendium of 1497 by the Augustinian canon Jacopo Filippo Foresti, pulls together classical heroines, medieval saints, and modern courtly women, reconstituting a genealogy of female excellence stretching from the present day to the earliest times.[11] Illustrations to texts in this tradition, both in manuscript and print, helped to give imaginative life to the new female archetypes. A striking instance is the woodcut of a female scholar used in Foresti's volume to illustrate the figures of Angela and Isotta Nogarola, and of the early Christian poet Proba (Fig. 31). This shows an elegantly dressed woman seated before her desk in a spacious study, with books piled and propped around her, several of them open, in a way suggestive of advanced scholarly labours such as commentary or manuscript collation.

Looked at collectively, as a tradition, the fourteenth- and fifteenth-century 'famous women' treatises serve implicitly to undermine the Aristotelian essentialist theory of sex difference by providing a mass of counter-examples to the thesis of women's intellectual and moral defectiveness. This implicit proto-feminist argument could be more or less stressed, depending on the individual author. Boccaccio, for example, is notoriously ambiguous, sometimes presenting his outstanding women as exceptions that prove the rule of women's general weakness, though at others suggesting that classical heroines' high achievements should inspire contemporary women to follow their lead. In general, however, it is possible to trace a marked trend towards more assertive positions with regard to women's capacities across the course of the fifteenth century, until, at the turn of the sixteenth, we find humanists beginning to counter Aristotelian theory explicitly. The first traces of this development are found in the writings of humanists associated with the courts of Ferrara and Mantua, and closely associated with the circles of those courts' powerful princely consorts, Eleonora d'Aragona and her daughter Isabella d'Este. The same patronage circles were responsible for Jacopo Filippo Foresti's famous women compendium, published in Ferrara in 1497 with a dedication to Eleonora's sister Beatrice d'Aragona.

A key feature of the new humanist theory of sex and gender was its anti-essentialist bias. Women's subordination to men was not explicable in this theory by biological differences that made them intrinsically unsuited to leadership roles. Male superiority was rather a matter of custom, entrenched by differential educational practices and social expectations. If society were differently configured, there would be no reason why women should not successfully inhabit male roles. Where Aristotle had taken men's dominion over women as a model for legitimate political rule in his *Politics*, Renaissance theorists sometimes figured it as a 'tyranny' or arbitrary rule. When a spokesman for the Aristotelian position in Castiglione's *Book of the Courtier* contests that women's natural defectiveness may be inferred from the fact that they instinctively wish they had been born men, a pro-feminist speaker replies: 'the poor things do not wish to be men in order to be perfect, but to have some freedom and to escape that dominion that men have claimed over them *by their own authority*' (my italics).[12]

Castiglione's dialogue is important in the history of the humanist profeminist tradition of thought, as the first work to bring to a wide, Italian and European public what had previously been a relatively arcane and avant-garde courtly model of thought. The third book of *The Courtier* contains a lively debate on the theoretical issue of sex and gender, incorporating both the earlier humanist tradition of argument by example and the more recent tradition of explicit anti-Aristotelian polemic. The profeminist position is mainly voiced by Giuliano de' Medici, son of Lorenzo de' Medici and grandson of the poet Lucrezia Tornabuoni. Giuliano argues against the Aristotelian theory of women's defectiveness both by pointing out the weaknesses in Aristotle's thinking and by emphasizing his differences from Plato, whose radical vision of the ideal polity in his *Republic* envisages men and women sharing equally in the governance and defence of the city. Aristotle had argued that the root cause of women's defectiveness was a lack of vital heat at the moment of conception, which left them cold and moist in their physical composition, rather than hot and dry, like men. In mental and moral terms, this translated into a certain sluggishness and passivity in woman, contrasting with alertness and agency in men. Giuliano counters this by pointing to other passages in Aristotle where he appears to see the perfect entity as temperate, rather than hot: a state Giuliano argues is closer to that of women than to men, whose excessive heat inclines them to impulsiveness and violence. Giuliano also questions the notion that physical strength and mental excellence inevitably go together, pointing both to empirical evidence and to internal contradictions within Aristotle's writings.[13]

In addition to his theoretical discussion of sex difference, Castiglione also includes in *The Courtier* an influential sketch of the ethos and manners of the court lady. To the jeers of a small hard core of misogynists in the court circle, who serve to underline the novel and still controversial character of the ideal proposed, Giuliano de' Medici sets forward an ideal of the court lady as educated, musical, sociable, and possessed of the same moral virtues as a man. Although she must be chaste, she need not manifest her chastity through the kind of rigorous demureness and self-effacement envisaged by Giannozzo Alberti. A lady who is too timorous to speak in public or who becomes flustered if the conversation turns mildly salacious will look uncouth in the worldly context of the court. The court lady's prime professional attribute is conversational 'affability', defined as a capacity to modulate her speech according to circumstances and to combine wit and vivacity with decorum, modesty, and poise.[14] Castiglione embodies Giuliano's ideal of the court lady within the dialogue in the two principal female speakers, the dignified and authoritative duchess of Urbino, Elisabetta Gonzaga, and her livelier second-in-command and sister-in-law, Emilia Pio, whose sarcastic asides and witty sparring with the male speakers of *The Courtier* contribute much to the dialogue's dramatic life.

Despite his insistence on the moral and intellectual equality of the sexes, Castiglione's Giuliano de' Medici distinguishes quite sharply between masculine and feminine social identities. Robustness and virility are attractive in the male courtier, but the female courtier should be aesthetically more delicate. Beauty is more important in the court lady than the male courtier—though he, too, must be handsome—and Castiglione's speakers are even prepared to countenance some cosmetic embellishment, as long as it is sufficiently discreet. Both male and female courtier must be expert dancers, but the court lady should leave the more vigorous styles of dancing to men, focusing on grace. Similarly, she risks seeming too masculine if she indulges in energetic physical activities and sports. There are similarities here to the Aristotelian model of a dichotomized, gendered system of virtues, but with the fundamental difference that femininity and masculinity are conceived by Castiglione less as intrinsic, biologically determined 'essences' than as social and aesthetic styles to be self-consciously assumed.

In practice, Castiglione's prescriptions for gendered behaviour at court seem to be somewhat conservative with regard to contemporary practice. A speaker in the dialogue, indeed, Castiglione's cousin, Cesare Gonzaga, contests Giuliano de' Medici's constraints on the court lady's physical activity as unnecessarily restrictive, noting that he has often seen women 'play tennis, wield arms, ride, hunt, and perform almost all those exercises we might expect of a knight'.[15] Where dancing is concerned, it is difficult to square Giuliano's insistence that women limit themselves to movements compatible with feminine 'delicacy and softness' with accounts of the choreographed battle scenes staged by the Ferrarese *balletto delle donne* in the

1580s, where the aristocratic dancers performed cross-dressed and in armour. Closer to Castiglione's own day, an admiring description by Paolo Giovio of a solo Hungarian dance performed to great applause by the young Vittoria Colonna, marchioness of Pescara, at a royal wedding in Naples in 1517, sounds considerably showier and more physically exuberant than anything Castiglione's Giuliano would condone.[16]

An interesting vision of the qualities of the court lady, complementary to Castiglione's yet differing in some regards, is offered by a collection of female courtly biographies by Giovanni Sabadino degli Arienti, written in Bologna in the 1480s. Arienti's *Gynevera, or On Famous Women*, is dedicated to Ginevra Sforza, wife of the city's effective ruler Giovanni Bentivoglio, and it presents itself not merely as an entertaining collection of narratives but as a didactic 'mirror' for Ginevra's own self-fashioning. Arienti's noble ladies are a composite of traditional feminine virtues, such as modesty, chastity, and devotion to family, with fresher ones, such as erudition, eloquence, and physical and moral courage.[17]

Turning to Arienti's biographies from Castiglione, one immediately striking feature of them is how physically active many of Arienti's subjects are. Cleofe de' Lapi of Cesena is praised for her falconry skills, which are said to have equalled those of a professional falconer, while Diana Saliceto is lauded for her expertise as a horsewoman and huntress (along with witty conversation, Arienti tells us, 'the forest was her joy').[18] Several women are praised for their military skills. The sharp-tongued, cross-dressing Bona de Vultulina, or Bona Lombarda, first catches her aristocratic lover's eyes as a shepherd girl when he sees her fighting with her young male peers. When he is moved by her loyalty to marry her, she fights alongside him, as well as taking control of the administration of his lands. The term 'virago', from the Latin *vir*, man—'a manly woman'—is a compliment in Arienti's book, in a way that differentiates him sharply from Castiglione. Ursina Visconti is characterized as impressive in her movements, and a fast speaker; 'a virago in many respects', as she demonstrates most notably when she defends her husband's fortress at Guastalla from an invading Venetian army.[19] Interestingly, this virility is not seen as detracting from Ursina's moral exemplarity as a woman. She is also characterized as civilized (*humana*), as liberal and charitable, as a strict and devout Christian, and as chaste.

Along with physical prowess, Arienti's biographies also place much emphasis on intellectual and artistic attainment in his women. We hear of the renowned Latin eloquence of Battista da Montefeltro, Costanza Varano, and Isotta Nogarola; of Angela Nogarola's poetic talents; and of Diana Saliceto's conversational brilliance and wit. Costanza Sforza Gonzaga is commended for her keen interest in literature, her compendious knowledge of sacred and classical history, and her taste for literary debate, besides being credited for inventing a new style of figurative embroidery in gold and silver thread and silk, representing 'meadows with diverse flowers and leaves; woods with many different trees, and animals picked out in relief, looking quite real'.[20] In other cases, Arienti highlights more utilitarian fields of knowledge. Giovanna Bentivoglio Malvezzi and Ippolita Sforza are both praised for their shrewd understanding of statecraft. Arienti's detailed biography of his Bolognese compatriot Giovanna is especially striking as a portrait of a political woman, fiercely committed to the furtherance of her family's interests. On several occasions, we see her raising troops for Bentivoglio campaigns (Arienti tells us his father was among her conscripts); and we see her counselling her exiled brother 'with great art and cunning' on how to regain his state.[21] On one occasion, after a victory against the rival Canetoli faction, Giovanna is seen to out-Machiavel the men of her family, counselling that the Canetoli leadership should be eliminated in its entirety so that they can never trouble the Bentivoglio again.

In an interesting gesture, Arienti concludes his collection with a tribute to his late wife Francesca Bruni, a Bolognese woman of relatively high status—higher than his own—but not of the exalted aristocratic level of most of his subjects. Arienti's biography of Francesca is interesting as a counterpoint to Alberti's portrait of the ideal Florentine bourgeois wife. While she is not given the heroic and virile qualities of many of his aristocratic women, nor any particular intellectual distinction, Francesca is portrayed as an intelligent and sociable woman, as well as a chaste, loving, and pious one. Arienti mentions her taste for hearing the verses of Virgil (presumably in translation) and he notes that her reading embraced Pliny's *Natural History* in the vernacular, as well as sacred works. Of her social skills he notes that she was pleasant in her dealings with visitors to the house, welcoming them in such a way 'as to make the smallest bird into a falcon'.[22] She was also committed to her husband's literary labours, urging him on in his composition of *Gynevera*, in particular, so that the work may almost be seen as a posthumous tribute to her. We are at a considerable distance here from Alberti's portrait of a wary Florentine husband assiduously hiding his books and writings from his wife.

DEPICTING THE NEW WOMAN

It was not solely through theoretical writings and biographical compendia that the new humanistic discourse on women circulated. The theme of women's prowess and moral exemplarity was also taken up in literature and art. Where art is concerned, we see the 'famous women' theme taken up in a series of panels painted by Ercole de' Roberti for the Ferrarese court in the 1480s showing three classical heroines (Lucretia, Portia, and the wife of the Carthaginian general Hasdrubal), all probably chosen to compliment the virtues of the duchess Eleonora d'Aragona. In Mantua, in the 1490s, Andrea Mantegna painted a further series, in a *trompe l'oeil* classicizing style, probably as a tribute to Isabella d'Este. The women featured there are the biblical Judith; Dido, queen of Carthage; Artemisia, queen of Caria; and the Roman Vestal Virgin Tuccia, who proved her chastity through the miracle of carrying water in a sieve. Notable in the Mantegna sequence is the presence of two female rulers, both of whom were also celebrated for their devotion to their husbands. Dido is almost certainly portrayed not in her Virgilian guise, but in an alternative tradition stemming back to antiquity and championed by Petrarch and Boccaccio, which has her suicide motivated by her desire to keep faith with her dead husband Sichaeus, when she has come under pressure to marry again.[23]

Where literature is concerned, perhaps the most interesting development of this period is the prominence given to warrior women in the great chivalric romances of Matteo Maria Boiardo and Lodovico Ariosto, *Orlando innamorato* and *Orlando furioso*, both written for the Ferrarese court. These popular and hugely entertaining works tell the tale of the Carolingian-era battles of Christians against Saracens, though with much influence also of Arthurian tales of wizardry and love. The chief female character in both poems is Bradamante di Montalbano, a Christian knight who falls in love with a Saracen warrior, Ruggiero, whom she eventually marries, after many vicissitudes and after Ruggiero's conversion. Following a device used by Virgil, Bradamante and Ruggiero are represented as distant ancestors of the ruling Este family of Ferrara, so that Bradamante may be read as an indirect portrait of the contemporary ladies of that line.[24]

With Boiardo and Ariosto, as with Castiglione and Arienti, we are looking at innovative representations of women crafted by men, but by the early sixteenth century, secular literary writings by women themselves were becoming more frequent. Women had been writing in Latin and publicly circulating their works since the late fourteenth century, but in minuscule numbers. In the later fifteenth century, they participated in the growing vogue for vernacular poetry, especially in the courts. By the first decades of the sixteenth century, we start seeing the earliest literary productions of Veronica Gambara and Vittoria Colonna: the two most famous women writers of the sixteenth century, and the female figures who were most instrumental in disseminating the model of the culturally distinguished court lady beyond the world of the courts.[25] Both Gambara and Colonna descended from distinguished lineages of intellectual women. Veronica Gambara was the great-niece of Isotta Nogarola on her father's side and niece of Castiglione's Emilia Pio on her mother's, while Vittoria Colonna was descended through her mother from the great female intellectual lineage of Battista da Montefeltro. Both were prominent for political, as well as intellectual reasons. Gambara ruled the small state of Correggio as dowager countess after her husband's death, while Colonna was the wife of a prominent Spanish-Neapolitan general, Ferrante d'Avalos, and a leading member of one of the greatest Roman baronial families.

Colonna's earliest surviving poem, a verse letter to her husband, offers an interesting instance of the self-fashioning of the Renaissance 'New Woman'.[26] The poem was written in the wake of the terrible battle of Ravenna of 1512, in which both Colonna's husband and her father, fighting on the side of the Spanish army, were taken prisoner by the French. The form of the verse epistle, written by a woman to her absent husband or lover, was a familiar one in humanistic literature, modelled on the Roman poet Ovid's *Heroines*, a collection of such letters written in the voices of famous women of classical mythology. Late fifteenth-century humanists revived the genre, penning epistles in the voices of the wives of contemporary princes and generals. Colonna seems to have been the first woman to write one herself, taking specifically as her model Ovid's letter from Penelope to Ulysses, one of the few of Ovid's letters where the heroine writing was a lawful wife, rather than a lover.

In her *pistola* ('epistle'), as it is sometimes called, Colonna portrays herself on the island of Ischia, near Naples, living with the island's ruler, her husband's aunt, Costanza d'Avalos. The young Vittoria, around 20 at the time the poem is set, is seen anxiously awaiting news of her husband and father, lighting candles before every shrine on the island; then, after a series of fearful portents—sudden storms, a boiling sea, sinister howling of night-birds—the grim news of their captivity arrives. For much of the poem, the gender polarities familiar from Ovid's *Heroines* are observed. Men are rash, daring, courageous, active, addicted to war and the pursuit of glory, while women are timorous, emotive, waiting anxiously on the sidelines, their lives consumed almost entirely by thoughts of love.

The end of the poem, however, registers a sharp change in perspective, when Colonna's poet-figure reproaches her husband for leaving her behind when he went to war. She invokes famous loyal Roman political wives like Pompey's Cornelia and Cato's Marcia, who bravely accompanied their husbands in their war against Caesar, and the legendary Hypsicratea, wife of King Mithridates of Pontus, who followed her husband into battle disguised as a squire. Colonna's invocation of Hypsicratea ushers in a different ideal of wifely potential than her earlier, more lachrymose one: 'A wife should follow her husband wherever he goes ... Let the one risk what the other risks; let them be equal in life and in death.'[27] The ideal here is very close to Boiardo's and Ariosto's representation of the affianced Bradamante and Ruggiero, or to Arienti's descriptions of *condottiere* couples in which both husband and wife showed themselves capable of military action. It is possible that a portrait medal representing Vittoria Colonna and Ferrante d'Avalos, he with a fanciful classicizing helmet, she with a classicizing hairstyle and with one breast bared, is intended to allude to a famous warrior couple of Greek mythology, the hero Theseus and the Amazon Hippolyta, whose story had been popularized in Italy through Boccaccio's romance *Teseida*, the source for Chaucer's *Knight's Tale*.[28]

Although it would be attractive to imagine that Colonna was proposing to her husband a literal reliving of the Mithridates-Hypsicratea relationship, it seems much more likely that the spousal equality in arms she was advocating was to be understood on a more symbolic level. By penning the *pistola*, and hence personally inhabiting the author-position readers of Ovid's *Heroines* were accustomed to seeing occupied by a male author ventriloquizing women's voices, Colonna was already making a notable claim to 'virility'. Renaissance thinking identified two principal routes to worldly glory, 'arms' and 'letters'—military prowess on one hand; literary, scholarly, or philosophical eminence on the other. Although intellectuals debated which of these two routes was superior, both were essentially seen as equal in dignity, and both were still seen at this time as predominantly limited to males. The *pistola* praises d'Avalos as a hero on a par with the ancient prototypes of Achilles and Hector, but at the same time it establishes his wife as a poet capable of sustaining comparison with Ovid. This model of d'Avalos and Colonna as a heroic couple, excelling respectively at arms and letters, became enshrined after d'Avalos's early death in 1525, when Colonna's mourning verse for him began to win her national fame as a poet. Already in 1532, in the final edition of his *Orlando furioso*, Ariosto presents Colonna as the archetypal woman writer, as well as the epitome of the devoted wife.[29]

RENAISSANCE WOMAN BEYOND THE COURTS

Down to around the 1520s or 1530s, literary composition remained the preserve of aristocratic women from the same courtly circles as Veronica Gambara or Vittoria Colonna. After this, however, we can note signs of a broader participation by women in literary culture, becoming more marked as the vernacular rose to challenge Latin's primacy as the dominant literary language in Italy.

A fascinating instance of the dissemination of the courtly ideal of the culturally active woman is offered by the small city of Siena in the 1530s to 1550s, home to a famous literary academy with a strong commitment to the promotion of high-quality vernacular literature, the Academy of the Thunderstruck (*Intronati*).[30] Siena was ruled as a republic, yet we do not find the rigid gender roles there we saw theorized in Alberti's *On the Family*. On the contrary, perhaps to differentiate itself from Florence, its traditional rival, and perhaps also due to its close ties with courtly Naples in these years, Sienese patricians seem to have made it a point of pride to cultivate a courtly model of culture. Mixed social interaction on the courtly model played an important role in elite Sienese culture, with its taste for *veglie* or 'vigils', evening parties enlivened by games. The courtly ideal of the witty, sociable, culturally engaged woman was rapidly domesticated, and it began to be celebrated in literary works. One intriguing dialogue of the 1530s, surviving only in manuscript, shows a Sienese woman with a reputation as a poet, Atalanta Donati, entertaining a *veglia* with an improvised commentary on a popular song: a parody of the wordy, erudite commentaries on Petrarch that proliferated in these years. The work is one of the few Renaissance dialogues featuring real-life speakers that shows a woman taking the dominant role in the conversation. In Castiglione's *Courtier*, although the duchess of Urbino and Emilia Pio direct the discussion, they are not among the principal speakers themselves.[31]

Atalanta Donati was not the only woman in Siena to gain fame as a poet in these years. On the contrary, Sienese women's literary creativity became a source of pride in the city and something of a trademark. One of the first things the English traveller Thomas Hoby recorded in his account of a visit to Siena in 1549 is that 'most of the women are well learned and write excellentlie well bothe in prose and verse'.[32] In the second half of the century, after Siena had lost its independence and been absorbed into the Medici duchy of Tuscany, the Sienese poet Girolamo Bargagli nostalgically recorded this brilliant season of Sienese culture in his *Dialogue on the Games that are Played in Sienese Veglie* (1572). One of the speakers in the dialogue recalls in particular the 'heroic and free manner of proceeding' of Sienese ladies in the last years of the republic, as if this were symbolic of Siena's free and heroic past.[33]

The female protagonists of Sienese culture in the 1530s–1550s were still noblewomen, though of the relatively broad class of the provincial urban nobility rather than great princely and baronial families such as the Colonna, Este, Sforza, and Montefeltro. The aspiration to participate in literary culture was no longer limited in this period to women of noble birth, however. Increasingly, from the 1540s, we begin to see women writers emerging from the urban professional classes, the daughters of lawyers, doctors, teachers, and also from the rising segments of society discussed in the previous chapter: merchants, shopkeepers, upper artisans. The social dissemination of the practice of women's writing was greatly stimulated by publishers, who began to see the potential market interest of this great literary novelty from the late 1530s onwards. The first printed volumes of verse by a female author that began to appear were unauthorized editions of Vittoria Colonna's poetry, of which 11 came out between 1538 and 1547, the year of her death. From 1547, works by other women began to follow, with the facile works of the Neapolitan Laura Terracina, in particular, proving a popular hit.[34]

A good example of a woman writer of this period from a non-aristocratic background is Chiara Matraini, author of an important collection of Petrarchist love poetry published in 1555, as well as, more unusually, a vernacular translation (via the Latin) of Isocrates's oration *To Demonicus*, a key statement of classical educational ideals. Matraini was born into a moneyed and politically ambitious family of weavers in the small republic of Lucca, in northern Tuscany. The family fell into disgrace when Chiara's brothers were involved in an uprising against the city's oligarchic elite in 1531, and, at the time of her emergence as a poet, she was a young widow of straitened means. Matraini's poetic talent appears to have been spotted by a writer closely associated with Venetian print culture, Lodovico Domenichi, who had previously been instrumental in the 'discovery' of Laura Terracina.

Matraini prefaces her printed verse collection with a polemical letter addressed to an anonymous male critic ('M. L.') who has questioned the propriety of a woman like her engaging in literature, and especially writing of love, suggesting that such pursuits were only appropriate in women of aristocratic descent. Matraini replies by defending the 'decency' of her background, but also by citing the alternative view of nobility that Italian intellectuals of non-noble background had advanced since the days of Dante: 'it is not antiquity of blood, nor power won through subjugation of others, nor gold or purple, but a mind shining with virtue that makes a man truly noble'.[35] The pursuit of literary excellence, in this view, was not limited to the elite; rather, as a virtuous exercise, it was itself constitutive of elite status, as it evinced the innate nobility of the writer's mind.

This same logic—writing as an ennobling activity—informs the verse of another notable non-noble Italian female poet of these years, Gaspara Stampa, the daughter of a jeweller from Padua. Stampa's mother moved to Venice with her family after the death of her husband, and Gaspara and her sister Cassandra began to acquire a reputation as virtuoso singers, performing at their mother's house and also at select gatherings of the Venetian cultural elite. Through these contacts, Stampa met and became amorously involved with a nobleman from the Venetian mainland, Collaltino da Collalto, a literary patron and small-time poet, and a soldier in the service of the king of France.

Stampa's bittersweet account of her affair with Collalto, published by her sister after Gaspara's premature death in 1554, in her late twenties or early thirties, has been recognized since the eighteenth century as one of the classics of Italian Renaissance literature.[36] Stampa portrays herself in a manner consonant with many of the speakers in Ovid's *Heroines* as the yearning lover of a flighty and treacherous beloved, forgotten back in Venice while her heedless soldier-lover pursues military glory in France. As in Ovid, however, the 'abandoned woman' is rhetorically empowered by her eloquence, even as she describes herself as vulnerable and abject. Medieval Provençal and Italian love lyricists had long established the notion that love for a noble object was ennobling in itself, while the very language of Petrarchist lyric—a stylized version of fourteenth-century Tuscan—bespoke the speaker's distance from the modern dialect of the 'vulgar hordes'. Stampa's poetry thus serves to bridge the status gulf between the humble poet and her aristocratic lover, while casting her in dramatic terms as a heroine of doomed love worthy to stand beside Ovid's Dido or Sappho.

In the sexual irregularity of her lifestyle, of which she made no secret, Gaspara Stampa had much in common with the figure of the courtesan, or *cortigiana*, a very distinctive Italian Renaissance social type, with no obvious medieval precedent and no real parallel in other European cultures at this time. Courtesans first emerged as a distinctive subset of exclusive sex workers in the papal court in the first years of the sixteenth century: an origin reflected in the term *cortigiana*, the feminine form of *cortigiano* ('courtier'). A famous prototype was Imperia Cognati (1486–1512), whose glamorous lifestyle is evocatively described in a *novella* by Matteo Bandello (3.42), which shows her inhabiting a palace with cloth-of-gold wall hangings and tables artfully strewn with musical instruments and finely bound books. The humanists who made up Imperia's circle were well acquainted with the ancient Greek figure of the *hetaira*, on which the type of the Renaissance courtesan was undoubtedly modelled. Within the papal court, essentially a congregation of nobly born clerical bachelors, the courtesan performed a similar cultural function to that performed by ladies of the type portrayed by Castiglione in the secular princely courts, serving as witty, culturally attuned conversational partners and as providers of refined musical and poetic entertainment. Within the more bohemian ranks of society, at least, courtesans' cultural credentials served to redeem them from the social slur of unchastity; hence the term we occasionally find used of them, *cortigiana onesta* ('honest, or decent, courtesan'): a striking turn of phrase within a culture in which, for women of the elites, 'honest' was virtually a synonym of 'chaste'.[37]

Two courtesans were among the leading female poets of the Italian Renaissance. The first, Tullia d'Aragona, had the fortune to live and write in the first half of the sixteenth century, when aristocratic men were happy to flaunt their association with fashionable courtesans. The second, Veronica Franco, was active in the stricter moral climate of the post-Tridentine period, when the profession was becoming of necessity more discreet.[38] Franco was Venetian and moved in the same kind of bohemian circles in Venice as Gaspara Stampa had a generation earlier, while d'Aragona, probably raised between Rome and Siena, led a peripatetic life, spending time in Venice, Ferrara, and Florence, as well as the two cities of her childhood. D'Aragona, the daughter of a courtesan, grandly claimed that her father was a cardinal from the former ruling family of Naples, though there is some evidence that her father was a dependent of the noble d'Aragona family who had been given the right to use the surname of the house he served. Franco was the daughter of a courtesan who had married into a 'citizen' family—a relatively elite though non-noble class, peculiar to Venice—and she was briefly married to a doctor before embarking on her courtesan career.

As was noted in Chapter 4, the most innovative self-fashioners of the Renaissance were often figures who combined social or cultural ambition with a relatively weak or ambiguous ascriptive identity. Courtesans fit this formula precisely, and one of the great fascinations of the writings of Franco and d'Aragona is watching a highly creative process of self-fashioning at work. Both women underline their social dignity by representing themselves in relationships of mutual respect with men of high social and intellectual status. Tullia d'Aragona's *Rime* of 1547, the first printed volume of Petrarchist verse by a woman other than Vittoria Colonna, showcases the poet's brilliant social circle as much as it does her poetic talent. Although it contains a short sequence of love poems, its main focus is correspondence verse (the full title of the work is *Verses by the Lady Tullia d'Aragona and by Others to Her*). The volume has been described both as a 'virtual salon' and a 'self-promoting autograph book'.[39] The work elegantly enacts in print the social and cultural functions of the courtesan in facilitating elite male sociability and literary production, and it maintains a high level of decorum throughout. It is dedicated to the duchess of Tuscany, Eleonora of Toledo, who had recently been instrumental in gaining d'Aragona exemption from a law Eleonora's husband, Duke Cosimo I de' Medici, had introduced constraining prostitutes to identify themselves by wearing a yellow veil, precisely on the grounds of her literary talent ('let her off as a poet', the duke's secretary laconically scribbled on a plea she had submitted for exemption).[40]

Veronica Franco's verse, published almost 30 years later, in 1575, is very different in tone from Tullia d'Aragona's, in a manner that reflects the changing position of the courtesan in the stricter moral climate of the later sixteenth century. The introduction of pre-publication censorship would almost certainly have prevented a work by a known courtesan from being published officially, and Franco's *Terza Rima Poems* came out in a clandestine edition, as did her *Letters*, which were published in the same year. Like d'Aragona's *Rime*, Franco's works show her in conversation with a circle of high-status men, but their names are this time occluded, not displayed. Nor does Franco's collection attempt to maintain the same respectable tone as d'Aragona's; rather, making capital out of the necessity of clandestine distribution, it advertises the poet's sexual skills quite 'frankly' (Franco makes liberal use of this pun on her name). In addition to witty, self-dramatizing love poetry, Franco's *Terza Rima Poems* includes correspondence poems of various kinds, including a famous polemic against a poet who had written a vicious satire against her (unnamed in the volume, but in fact the louche and brilliant dialect poet Maffio Venier, the nephew of Franco's chief protector). A trademark of Franco's sprightly, provocative verse is her use of the metaphor of combat and specifically swordsmanship; in her riposte to Venier, she challenges him to a public duel in Tuscan, Venetian, or any other language he prefers. The metaphor is literalized in the 1998 film *The Honest Courtesan* (*Dangerous Beauty* in the USA): a zestful, though highly romanticized and inaccurate version of Franco's fascinating life.

A long-established cliché in Italian literary scholarship held that the tradition of women's writing came to an end after around 1560, and that Veronica Franco represented an isolated figure, the end of an impressive but short-lived flourishing of female creativity. This is strikingly inexact; in fact, the 1580s saw the beginning of an upswing in women's writing, lasting for around three decades, and characterized by a new breadth of range and boldness. While women's writing in the mid-century period was mainly limited to Petrarchist verse, together with letters and a few small-scale prose works, women in the later sixteenth century and the first years of the seventeenth extended their remit to include pastoral drama, chivalric romance, religious narrative, and epic. They were also more assertive in their authorial self-positioning, far more frequently writing their own letters of dedication and taking full ownership of their works. A survey of women's writing between 1580 and 1630 in Italy identifies around 200 known writers in this period, ranging from women with a single sonnet in an anthology to figures with multiple single-authored works to their name.[41]

A representative figure of this later moment in Italian women's writing is the Venetian Modesta Pozzo, who styled herself in her writings with the pointed pseudonym Moderata Fonte ('Moderate Fountain' in place of 'Modest Well'). Fonte was the first securely identified female writer to attempt a chivalric romance, in her youthful, unfinished poem *Thirteen Cantos of Floridoro*, published in 1581. Her other works are a short philosophical drama, acted before the Doge and Senate of Venice; two religious narratives on the passion and resurrection of Christ; and a long, two-book dialogue entitled *The Worth of Women*, published posthumously in 1600.

Fonte came from a cultivated and wealthy background, through not from Venice's ruling patriciate; she was the daughter and wife of lawyers, of the citizen class, which monopolized employment in the Venetian civil service. She was remarkable as the first Venetian woman from this kind of respectable background to gain fame as a writer in her home city, which was famed for the strict seclusion in which its upper-class women lived. Her relative and writing mentor, Giovanni Niccolò Doglioni, writes in the interesting biography that prefaces the printed version of *The Worth of Women* that Fonte felt constrained to pursue her writing only in hasty, snatched moments, out of deference to 'the false notion, so widespread in our city today, that women should excel in nothing but the running of the household' (*WW*, 9).[42] By Fonte's time, however, even in republican Venice, ways of thinking about women alternative to this 'false notion' were available, whether from books such as *The Courtier*, or personal contacts such as Doglioni (whose broad-mindedness may reflect the fact that his own family origins lay not in Venice but in the region of Friuli, to the north, whose elites were culturally close in many ways to the world of the courts).

The Worth of Women is a remarkable work: a strikingly original contribution to the long-running debate on women's status and role, and a lively and engaging dialogue that still reads very freshly today. The speakers are seven Venetian noblewomen of varying age and marital status: an elderly and a younger widow; three married women, including one newly married; and two young girls of marriageable age. The theme they decide to debate, in a light-hearted manner, is whether men are a good thing or a bad one, and the first book of the dialogue more or less keeps to this subject (although it also has much to say on the dignity of women). The second book embarks on an encyclopedic survey of general knowledge relating to the natural and cultural realms, mainly deriving from Pliny's *Natural History*, intended to illustrate the way in which women may be empowered by education and a virtuous curiosity about the world. The dialogue is given unity and vivacity by the recurrent theme of the relation of the sexes, which some of the speakers keep trying to bring back to the centre of the discussion, while others seek good-naturedly to thwart them. Prominent as a secondary theme throughout is a critique of the institution of marriage. The younger widow, Leonora, the host of the dialogue, and one of the unmarried girls, the learned and poetically gifted Corinna, both earnestly and repeatedly proclaim their intention not to marry (or remarry). Even the setting of the conversation conspires to foreground this theme. The women gather to speak in an idyllic garden created by Leonora's now deceased aunt, a wealthy woman who had chosen to remain single, and the garden's centrepiece is a fountain surrounded by allegorical figures spelling out the reasons for her choice.

Fonte is sufficiently skilful in her handling of the dialogue form for it to be difficult to be certain how seriously she means her anti-marriage polemic. Space is given in the dialogue to the pleasures of married life, as well as the trials, and Fonte incorporates a tribute to her own husband, Filippo Zorzi, who seems to have been supportive of her writing. Fonte's intent in *The Worth of Women* seems to have been less to polemicize than to use the humanist techniques of paradox and *serio ludere* ('serious play') to subject traditional ideas about women to critical scrutiny. Marriage was traditionally considered to be necessary for a woman, if she wished to remain 'in the world', outside the convent; yet intellectual men debated earnestly whether or not to take a wife, often concluding that the benefits of marriage were outweighed by the responsibilities it brought. The dowry system, whereby the family of a bride paid a substantial amount to her husband, tended to reinforce this notion of marriage as a benefit for women and a burden for men. The entire system rested on the unstated premise that women's mental and physical weakness made them unfitted to live without either the institutional support of a convent or the personal protection of a man. Once women were acknowledged to be men's equals, there seemed no reason not to speculate that a wealthy woman might choose to retain her independence and live a life on her own. Fonte's willingness to canvas this radical notion, however warily and humorously, edges the humanistic theoretical debate on women a few steps closer to the kind of interrogation of social realities that has such a key place in the modern tradition of feminist thought.[43]

RENAISSANCE WOMAN AND THE ARTS

By the time Fonte was writing her dialogue, it was becoming possible to point to achievements by women in a variety of fields of cultural production (indeed, *The Worth of Women* contains mentions of the singer Laura Peverara and the artist Marietta Tintoretto, daughter of the famous Jacopo Tintoretto). In certain of the performance arts, notably acting and virtuoso singing, women stood at the forefront of cultural innovation, and enjoyed a fame and status far greater than their male peers. The actress, singer, poet, and dramatist Isabella Andreini was one of the most famous cultural figures in Italy at the time of her death in 1604, and her fame extended well beyond the boundaries of her homeland; she died at Lyons, returning from a successful tour to the French court. Similarly feted and sought-after were singers such as Laura Peverara, Vittoria Archilei, Francesca Caccini—also a composer—and Adriana Basile. Women played a key role in this vital and innovatory moment in Italian musical and performance history: the period that saw the birth of opera, the maturing of the *commedia dell'arte* dramatic tradition, and the emergence of the new monodic style of vocal music that would lay the basis for the Baroque.[44] At the same time, with Lavinia Fontana, Italy had its first fully professional female painter, building on the precedent of Sofonisba Anguissola, whose artistic talent had won her a place at the Spanish court.[45]

The *virtuose* who excelled in music, art, and performance came from a broader range of social backgrounds than female writers. A few were aristocrats, such as Anguissola, who came from a noble, though financially straightened, family in Cremona, and the Mantuan singer Livia d'Arco. Tarquinia Molza, who sang with d'Arco in the Ferrarese *concerto delle donne*, was the highly educated granddaughter of a famous poet, while a third member of the consort, Laura Peverara, was the daughter of a wealthy merchant and intellectual who had worked as a tutor at the Mantuan court. More commonly, singers and painters came from families who specialized in these same arts. Lavinia Fontana was the daughter of a successful Bolognese painter; the engraver Diana Mantuana, the daughter of a Mantuan painter, sculptor, and engraver. The singer and composer Francesca Caccini was the daughter of Giulio Caccini, a famous musician in the service of the Medici, while the singers and instrumentalists Lucia and Isabella Pellizzari, who attained court posts at Mantua in the 1580s, were the sisters of a musician employed at one of the great theatrical academies of the day, the Accademia Olimpica of Vicenza. Actresses tended to come from more obscure backgrounds, and it has been conjectured that some of the earliest, such as Flaminia Romana, who rose to fame in the 1560s, may have been drawn from the ranks of courtesans. Although Isabella Andreini, married to a fellow actor, Francesco Andreini, established the type of the 'respectable' actress, later also embodied by her daughter-in-law Virginia Ramponi, it is inconceivable that an girl of elite background would have been encouraged to aspire to a career on the public stage.[46]

A fascinating early document of the emergence of the figure of the *virtuosa* is the anonymous *Life of Irene di Spilimbergo*, appended to a collection of verse published in 1561 to commemorate this young woman's premature death at the age of 19.[47] Irene di Spilimbergo was the daughter of a Venetian patrician mother and a nobleman from Friuli, north of Venice. According to her biography, Irene's mother, not especially well educated by her natal family, studied hard after her marriage and ensured that her daughter received an excellent education. Irene showed herself exceptionally talented from a very early age, turning her ambitions from poetry to music, then from music to drawing—which she studied with Titian—and finally from drawing to painting, inspired by seeing a portrait by Sofonisba Anguissola, which fired her with a desire for emulation.

An interesting feature of the *Life* is its unabashed celebration of Irene's powerful urge to excellence and artistic glory. She is said to be consumed by a 'virtuous envy' when other women are praised in her presence, and to be possessed by an ambition to become the outstanding female artistic *virtuosa* of the day. Irene is portrayed as effectively a martyr to her art when she contracts the fever that kills her as a result of rising early and working long hours in an unheated studio in an attic of her house. It is not difficult to imagine this being used as a cautionary tale, warning young girls off following in Irene's rash footsteps, but this striking secular hagiography does nothing of the kind. Irene's urge to glory and her all-consuming commitment to art are presented as entirely admirable and her death is lamented as the pure tragedy of a young life cut short. Nor is there any suggestion that Irene's devotion to her art 'masculinized' her or impacted negatively on her marriage prospects; on the contrary, her broad education and her artistic talent are said to have made her worthy to be the consort of a prince.

Another, equally interesting verbal portrait of an outstanding creative woman is the actor and poet Adriano Valerini's *Oration* on the death—reputedly by poisoning—of his colleague and lover Vincenza Armani (d. 1567), one of the first Italian actresses whose name has come down to us. Unlike Irene di Spilimbergo, it seems likely that Armani came from a relatively humble background, as Valerini gives no details of her parentage and speaks euphemistically of her innate nobility shining through the disadvantages of fortune. Like Irene, in Valerini's narration, Vincenza distinguishes herself by the variousness of her talents and by her will to succeed. She is first educated merely in the arts conventional to her sex, learning the art of embroidery so exquisitely as to rival the mythical Arachne herself.[48] Before long, however, the young Vincenza realizes that such skills are not sufficient to win her the fame she desires. She hence turns to reading, writing, and penmanship, learning all quite effortlessly and even acquiring an excellent knowledge of Latin, while at the same time working up her musical skills until she could not only play various instruments, but also sing and sight-read 'as well as the finest singer in Europe' (5v). More than this, she even made herself a composer, often setting to music sonnets and madrigals that she had written herself.

At the climax of his list of Armani's accomplishments, Valerini places 'the immortal light of brilliant eloquence' (6r). It was in persuasive speech and gesture that Armani truly excelled; and, in order that all should be able to enjoy and be inspired and morally elevated by her divine gifts, 'Heaven ordained ... that Vincenza ... devote herself to acting dramatic texts on stage'. This is strategic on Valerini's part: by equating acting with eloquence, he positions the acting profession, regarded by many at the time as disreputable, as a subspecies of the prestigious art of rhetoric. Valerini's account of Armani's acting draws on many commonplaces traditionally associated with oratory, such as the ability to stir the emotions of the listeners through her own feigned emotion (what Aristotle calls *pathos*), and the capacity to 'manipulate souls as she wished' (8r).

An aspect of Vincenza Armani's acting that Valerini especially emphasizes is her immense versatility: 'she transformed herself like a new Proteus according to each new turn of the plot'. This Protean quality extended to acting male parts as well as female, so convincingly that no one would have thought her a woman when they saw her appear in male garb. Armani appears in Valerini's description as an unexpected, low-born, female incarnation of the Renaissance ideal of universality: as miraculously omnicompetent as Castiglione's courtier, and a virtuoso self-fashioner, even across boundaries of gender. In the improvisatory culture of the *commedia dell'arte*, Armani can even claim distinction as a dramatist as well as an actor. Indeed, Valerini concludes by comparing her not only to the famous Roman actor Roscius, but to the greatest dramatists and pastoral poets of antiquity—Terence, Plautus, Sophocles, Euripides, Theocritus, Virgil. 'She was not only a great actress, but a great poet, as well, and a living lesson to her fellows actors in the true modes of art.'[49]

Although it would be easy to dismiss Valerini's panegyric of Vincenza Armani as pure hyperbole, consideration of the better-documented careers of Isabella Andreini and her daughter-in-law Virginia Ramponi offers evidence of the extraordinary versatility and talent of some of these early *virtuose* of the stage. Ramponi was not only the most famous actress of her day, but an extremely gifted singer, celebrated especially for an iconic performance of Monteverdi's *Arianna* at the court of Mantua in 1608, in which Ramponi stood in at short notice after the death of the singer slated to sing the lead role. Andreini was still more Protean, combining acclaimed skills in music and acting with considerable talent as a poet; she was the author of one of the most popular pastoral plays of the era, *Mirtilla*, and a writer of polished, witty, sensual madrigals that were widely anthologized after her death and set to music by numerous composers.

A detailed account of one of Andreini's most celebrated spectacles, *The Madness of Isabella*, which she performed at the wedding of Ferdinando I de' Medici and Christine of Lorraine in 1589—one of the most extravagant court weddings of the century—allows us to glimpse something of the star power that won the actress such fame.[50] This one-woman *tour de force* first showed Andreini's character, Isabella, in a state of love-induced madness, running around a city-centre stage-set accosting passers-by in French, Spanish, Greek, and 'many other languages'. During this first episode, Andreini sang a number of French songs, surprising and delighting the French bride. The second part of the performance featured Isabella in a series of imitations of her fellow (mainly male) *commedia dell'arte* actors, each of whom had a set comic character, with its own idiosyncratic speech patterns, gestures, and movements. After these antics, Isabella was restored to sanity through the ingestion of a magic potion, and the performance concluded with an 'eloquent and learned' disquisition on her part, on the perils of love and its deleterious effects on the lover. This ability to modulate kaleidoscopically through different registers was one of the trademarks of the *commedia dell'arte* first lady.

In addition to the performance arts, we can see a few women pursuing careers in the visual arts, despite the fact that women were generally excluded from participation in professional guilds. Examples of professional female artists in the late sixteenth century are the painter Lavinia Fontana, the engraver Diana Mantuana (sometimes erroneously called Diana Scultori), and the woodcut artist and lace pattern designer Elisabetta Catanea Parasole. Fontana made a very successful career in her native Bologna as a painter of portraits and religious narratives to commission, before moving to Rome towards the end of her life. Mantuana, also Rome-based, operated on a more market-led basis, as was usual for engravers, issuing engravings on mythological and religious subjects, and obtaining a papal privilege to produce and market her work. Elisabetta Catanea Parasole published a series of highly decorative *de luxe* lace-pattern books illustrated with her own woodcut images, as well as working on botanical illustrations for herbals. A cousin of Elisabetta's, Girolama Cagnaccia Parasole, also worked as a woodcut artist, although only one surviving work by her is known.[51]

An interesting feature of the lives and working practices of the artists just named is their relationship of collaboration with their respective husbands. Fontana's husband was a minor painter, Giovanni Paolo Zappi, who served effectively as agent and assistant to his much more famous wife. Elisabetta Parasole was married to another woodcut artist, Leonardo Norsini, with whom she collaborated on the illustration of one herbal. Diana Mantuana also collaborated with her architect husband Francesco Capriani, or Francesco da Volterra, on several projects, and seems to have worked closely with him on their arrival in Rome to publicize his activities and to help him establish his career. These three cases offer good examples of a phenomenon to which the literary scholar Victoria Kirkham has called attention: instances of husbands and wives both active in the same or different artistic fields, and collaborating or mutually assisting one another. Kirkham's prototypical example is the well-connected mid-century poet Laura Battiferri and her architect husband Bartolomeo Ammanati.[52] Other examples, from the performing arts, are Isabella and Francesco Andreini, and their son Giovanni Battista Andreini and his wife, Virginia Ramponi. The contrast is very sharp with the 'Aristotelian' model of domestic economy,

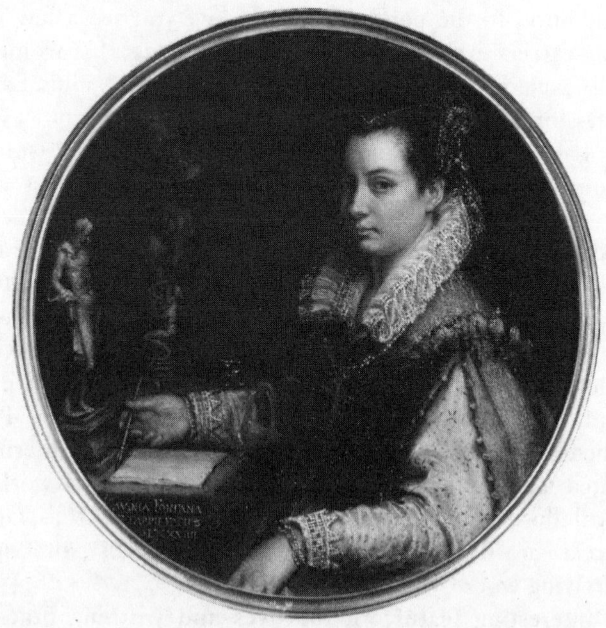

Fig. 32: Lavinia Fontana, *Self Portrait in a Tondo*, 1579. Oil on copper.

in which a husband's and a wife's activities and ethos are strictly dichotomized, and they operate in quite separate spheres.

Interesting visual evidence of the self-fashioning of a late sixteenth-century *virtuosa* is offered by a self-portrait by Lavinia Fontana in the Uffizi, dating to 1579 (Fig. 32). Fontana painted the portrait in response to a request by a Rome-based Spanish humanist, Alfonso Ciacón, who wanted it for a collection he was compiling of illustrious men and women.[53] Fontana portrays herself in a manner consonant with this flattering commission, as a wealthy, well-dressed woman and as an intellectual; she sits at her desk, in a study-like setting, surrounded by antique or *all'antica* statues and fragments, to be used as anatomical models for her art. A piece of blank paper lies before her on the table, and she wields a pen in her hand, whether to write a letter or to begin a sketch. No special effort is apparent in the painting to underline the sitter-painter's chastity or other specifically feminine attributes such as her modesty and demureness (although her piety is signalled by an oversize cross). Fontana looks out with a calm air of confidence: a professional, sure of her trade.

In the combination of references to the tools of her art with indicators of wealth and status, Fontana's self-portrait has something in common with Moroni's portrait of a tailor, discussed in the last chapter. Both represent socially aspirant artisans, confident of possessing a talent that society prizes. In the case of the Fontana self-portrait, moreover, we may see a conscious appropriation by a woman of a model of self-staging—in a study, at a desk, surrounded by the paraphernalia of learning—that had in the past been far more typically used for male sitters, and in which she herself had often portrayed male members of Bologna's intellectual elite. One of the chief arguments of this book has been that the Renaissance, as a cultural movement, penetrated more deeply through society than has often been assumed. Fontana's self-portrait makes the point very well. Detached from any attribution, it could serve as an illustration of Castiglione's ideal of the decorous, poised, cultivated court lady; yet what we are seeing here is not an aristocrat, nor even the wife of a wealthy merchant, but a hard-working painter's daughter from Bologna, capable of earning her lace ruff through her own toil.

THE RENAISSANCE IN THE CLOISTERS

This chapter has concentrated on secular women, as the secular *virtuosa* was the great cultural novelty of the era. Convents had a long tradition of fostering female learning, and there is nothing as specifically 'Renaissance' about the erudite nun as there is about the secular female painter or actress. Nonetheless, it would be misleading to imply that it was secular women only who participated in the cultural novelties of the Renaissance. 'Choir nuns', or *professe*, came from wealthy and prestigious backgrounds (unlike *converse*, who carried out the manual work of the convent), and their education was consonant with that of girls destined for marriage. Some nuns had even received a full humanistic education, like Cecilia Gonzaga, from the ruling family of Mantua: a star pupil at Vittorino da Feltre's school, who refused to marry, defying her father's wishes, and entered a convent after his death. A less famous example is Lorenza Strozzi, from a wealthy and erudite Florentine family, author of a collection of classicizing Latin hymns, drawing on Horace, which was published in 1588.[54]

The cultural production of Italian convents during the Renaissance was rich, especially in the fields of vernacular poetry, historiography, drama, and music. Theatre was a particular specialism, produced both for an internal, convent audience, and for invited spectators.[55] Nun artists are also known, perhaps most notably the Florentine Dominican Plautilla Nelli, who seems to have cultivated something like a school of painting in her convent, Santa Caterina di Siena.[56] Nuns were also active in some fields of skilled artisanal production, notably textile work, lacemaking, and printing. The earliest printing press in Florence, founded in the 1470s, was run by the Dominican nuns of San Jacopo di Ripoli, in conjunction with the friars of their brother-convent. The press published not only religious works but classical texts and a few modern secular writings, unexpectedly including Boccaccio's *Decameron*, with its numerous lewd stories featuring monks, friars, and nuns.

Like every other aspect of ecclesiastical life, convents were subject to close scrutiny following the Council of Trent, and stricter regulations were introduced to ensure that nuns were rigorously cloistered from the world. Behaviour within the convent was also carefully regulated, and closer constraints were placed on nuns' reading and their cultural activities in general. It does not appear, however, that this new and oppressive regime put an end to convent traditions of learning and culture, as has sometimes been suggested. A significant tradition of convent music continued in the post-Tridentine period, especially in Milan, with some nun composers winning considerable fame for their music, notably Claudia Sessa in the late sixteenth century and Chiara Margherita Cozzolani in the seventeenth.[57] Sacred poetry and drama also continued to flourish within the convents at this time. In some respects, the 'religious turn' in Italian culture inspired by the Counter-Reformation may have enhanced the appeal of nuns' cultural production for readers outside the convent. It is only after around 1550 that we begin to see nuns' writings beginning to be published; and the majority of convent writings that reached print publication appeared after the Council of Trent.[58]

A fascinating illustration of the extent of some nuns' cultural engagement is offered by the copious writings of Fiammetta Frescobaldi (1523–86), a nun at the Florentine convent of San Jacopo di Ripoli, mentioned above in connection with its printing activities. Born into an important Florentine merchant-banking family, Frescobaldi entered the convent at the age of 11 and took her vows at the age of 14. Her writings include various ecclesiastical histories, a history of the first millennium of the Christian era, translations of a number of Latin humanistic works, and a compendium of Francesco Guicciardini's *History of Italy*, now lost. Her most wide-ranging work, entitled *The Sphere of the World*, was a vast compendium of geographical and cosmological erudition, in nine volumes, of which three survive. A trademark of Frescobaldi's writings is her scrupulous recording of sources, which allows us to trace with a certain exactitude the works to which she had access in the convent. Besides Guicciardini—one of the most markedly anti-clerical historians of the age—these include Vasari's *Lives*, the architectural writings of Andrea Palladio, and the writings of explorers like Columbus and Vespucci. Frescobaldi also had scientific interests; a chronicle she wrote between 1575 and 1586 records eclipses, comets, meteorites, and sunspots.[59] Although Frescobaldi was clearly exceptional, the range of her interests was not untypical of elite Italian convent culture. History was one of the genres of writing most practised by nuns, and an interest in natural philosophy was not unusual in convents. Indeed, sixteenth-century nuns seem to have made something of a specialism of herbal medicine, even at times running apothecaries' businesses from their convents.[60]

It would be misleading to give too rosy an image of the cultural opportunities that Renaissance convent life offered women—just as it would also be misleading to underestimate the constraints and oppression under which many secular women laboured at this time. Despite the empowering rhetoric of sexual equality we often find in literary texts of the period, women were in practice very far from men's equals; they had fewer educational and professional opportunities and significantly less freedom of movement. It is inaccurate, however, to state that women did not participate in the cultural movement of the Renaissance, or that the only women who participated were a handful of aristocrats of the status of a Vittoria Colonna or an Isabella d'Este. The findings of the past few decades of scholarship have been transformative in this regard.

Conclusion

When did the Italian Renaissance end? Questions of this kind are always difficult, not to say impossible, to answer. Cultural history generally proceeds on a gradual, evolutionary basis, without dramatic points of transition. Elements of past traditions live on, even as new traditions emerge.

With this caveat, however, there are reasons to take the decade or so after 1600 as marking a cultural turning point from late Renaissance to Baroque. Certainly, the languages of literature and art changed at this time, in ways that contemporaries registered quite sharply. Although it is possible in retrospect to trace a gradualist history of the evolution of the Baroque style, reaching back into later sixteenth-century mannerism, nowhere in the sixteenth century do we see as strong a consciousness of a stylistic sea-change as we do after 1600. This is especially the case with literature, where the *Rime* of the Neapolitan poet Giovanni Battista Marino, published in 1602, were widely seen as ushering in a new and flamboyant style, which sharply polarized literary circles. It is not difficult to see anticipations of Marino's Baroque in certain poets of the later sixteenth century, yet this did not diminish his impact or readers' sense that they were seeing the dawn of a new age. Marino's aesthetic was one of rebelliousness, originality, daring, outrageousness, 'knowing how to break the rules' (*saper rompere le regole*). This marked a violent rejection of Renaissance Petrarchism, which had been rooted, precisely, in respect for rules and decorum and tradition. Marino underlined the point through his colourful lifestyle, which involved various stints in prison, and a narrow escape from death in a rival poet's assassination attempt.[1]

One way of seeing the culture of the Baroque in Italy, underlined by Marino's rule-breaking maxim, is that it marked a tilting of the cultural balance away from reverence for antiquity towards an exhilarated embrace of the new. As was emphasized in Chapters 2 and 3, these two impulses coexisted in Renaissance culture in a dynamic, dialectical, and highly fruitful relationship, with celebration of modernity on the rise across the course of the sixteenth century. The seventeenth century saw this latter trend coming to a head, with the 'quarrel of the ancients and the moderns' emerging as a formal topic of debate, often bullishly resolved in favour of the moderns. The academic and literary critic Paolo Beni pronounced the superiority of Tasso as epic poet to Homer and Virgil in a work of 1607, while, in 1620, the poet Alessandro Tassoni published an essay comparing 'ancient and modern intellects', the *Paragone degli ingegni antichi e moderni*, arguing for the superiority of the moderns in every respect, from science and art to music, agriculture, warfare, politics, and dress.

Although it would be easy, in this regard, to see the Baroque era as marking a continuity of trends already apparent in the Renaissance, in other regards, the relation between the two periods is one of inversion. Gender thinking and attitudes to women offer a dramatic example of this. After more than a century in which the dominant attitude to women in polite society had tended to be gallant and supportive, the Baroque saw a sharp backlash, with a revival of misogyny that swept away many of the cultural gains women had experienced in the long sixteenth century. The tradition of women's writing that had so flourished in the sixteenth century dwindled after around 1610, virtually drying up after 1650. Although some species of *virtuose* still flourished, in particular celebrity singers and a few painters, we see nothing like the critical mass of female creatives in all fields that marks the last decades of the sixteenth century. In particular, cultural activity by 'respectable' women was problematized, as the old slur associating literacy and intellectual curiosity in women with sexual profligacy was revived. Only after around 1690, as the vogue for the Baroque faded, to be succeeded by a new classicizing cultural movement called Arcadia, did creative women once more begin to receive the encouragement and social approbation they had come to enjoy 100 years before.[2]

In some quite clear senses, then, we can see the Renaissance as a cultural movement coming to an end in the early seventeenth century. In another sense, of course, it never ended. Many of the cultural novelties described in this book are still with us, though in much-changed guises. Histories of printing, technology, diplomacy, journalism, portraiture, philology, professional theatre, academies, collecting, and museum culture, all sink their roots into Renaissance terrain. So does the history of the creative woman in Italy, which frequently had recourse to Renaissance prototypes in reinventing itself in subsequent centuries. The ladies of the Arcadian Academy in the eighteenth century looked back quite explicitly to Vittoria Colonna and Gaspara Stampa in shaping their identity as modern female writers. Similar levels of scholarly and popular interest may be seen in Renaissance women poets during the late nineteenth century, when Italy lived its brief 'New Woman' moment.[3]

This book has made the case for a broader and deeper Renaissance than has generally been presented within scholarly literature, touching the lives of many men and women without the capacity to 'speak in *bus* and *bas*', to use Leonardo Fioravanti's impatient characterization of Latin. Burckhardt noted regretfully of the humanist revival of classical antiquity that it must be acknowledged as an 'anti-popular' movement, which had the effect of thrusting a wedge for the first time between the 'cultivated and uncultivated classes' (p. 121). The evidence examined in this book suggests that this is true only if we look at the initial moment of classical discovery and scholarship, not at the moment of dissemination and reception .

Of course, the democratizing processes discussed here had their limits. The broader Renaissance public considered here consists, at its lowest, of skilled artisans and shopkeepers; upwardly mobile courtesans, artists, and actors; and the more skilled and specialized 'mechanics' of the courts. These men and women might have been labelled 'base plebeians' by status-conscious nobles, but they stood very far from the lowest socio-economic ranks of Italian society; these were the literate, the urban, the clothed, and the fed, those sufficiently far from subsistence to afford books. Still, these vernacular stakeholders in Renaissance culture cannot be termed in any meaningful sense a social elite; nor can a movement whose ripples reached them be properly characterized as 'anti-popular'. Adding their voices to the conversation of the Renaissance can only enrich our understanding of the age.

Further Reading

Two excellent recent books of collected essays on Renaissance culture are John Najemy (ed.), *Italy in the Age of the Renaissance* (Oxford: Oxford University Press, 2004), and Michael Wyatt (ed.), *The Cambridge Companion to the Italian Renaissance* (Cambridge: Cambridge University Press, 2014). The first of these is more sociohistorically oriented, while the second is centred on cultural history. A geographically broader collection, with much interesting material on Italy, is Guido Ruggiero (ed.), *A Companion to the Worlds of the Renaissance* (Oxford: Blackwell, 2002). William Caffero, *Contesting the Renaissance* (Chichester: Wiley-Blackwell, 2010) is useful as a thematically organized bibliographical source-book.

As a straight historical survey of the period, Denys Hay and John Law's *Italy in the Age of the Renaissance, 1380–1530* (London: Longman, 1989) remains useful and readable, as does its continuation, Eric Cochrane, *Italy, 1530–1630* (London: Longman, 1988). Guido Ruggiero, *The Renaissance in Italy: A Social and Cultural History of the Rinascimento* (Cambridge: Cambridge University Press, 2104), ambitiously attempts a chronological overview of the thirteenth to the sixteenth centuries in Italy, combining social, political, and cultural history. As a history of the European Renaissance in general, John Hale's idiosyncratic and magnificently readable *The Civilization of Europe in the Renaissance* (London: Harper Collins, 1993) may be recommended.

Ronald Witt, *The Origins of Humanism from Lovato to Bruni* (Leiden: Brill, 2000), is becoming the standard history of humanism, though see also Christopher S. Celenza, *The Lost Italian Renaissance: Humanists, Historians, and Latin's Legacy* (Baltimore: Johns Hopkins University Press, 2005), on Neo-Latin literature, and

Brian Jeffrey Maxson, *The Humanist World of Renaissance Florence* (Cambridge: Cambridge University Press, 2007), on the social context of humanism.

As an overview of art history in this period, Stephen J. Campbell and Michael W. Cole, *A New History of Italian Renaissance Art* (London: Thames and Hudson, 2012), may be recommended. James Hankins (ed.), *The Cambridge Companion to Renaissance Philosophy* (Cambridge: Cambridge University Press, 2007), is an accessible guide to Renaissance philosophy (in general; not merely Italian). There is less of an obvious, one-stop work in the case of literary history, though the articles on 'Prose' and 'Verse' in Wyatt (ed.), *Cambridge Companion to the Italian Renaissance* (by, respectively, Jon R. Snyder and Deanna Shemek), make a good starting-point. For music, see Giuseppe Gerbino's essay in the same volume. For material culture, see Evelyn Welch, *Shopping in the Renaissance: Consumer Cultures in Italy 1400–1600* (New Haven: Yale University Press, 2005), and Michelle O'Malley and Evelyn Welch (eds), *The Material Renaissance* (Manchester: Manchester University Press, 2007); also Bella Mirabella (ed.), *Ornamentalism: The Art of Renaissance Accessories* (Ann Arbor: University of Michigan Press, 2011).

A bibliography relating to specialized areas of interest covered by this book can be found after the notes section.

Notes

Chapter 1: What? Where? When? Whose?

1 See Jacob Burckhardt, *The Civilization of the Renaissance in Italy* (1860), trans. S.G.C. Middlemore, with an introduction by Peter Burke (London: Penguin, 2004). All parenthetical references are to this edition.
2 John M. Najemy, *A History of Florence, 1200–1575* (Oxford: Blackwell, 2006), pp. 97–9.
3 Paolo Malanima, 'Urbanisation and the Italian economy during the last millennium', *European Review of Economic History* 9/1 (2005), pp. 101–2.
4 See Cesare Segre (ed.), *Volgarizzamenti del Duecento e Trecento* (Turin: UTET, 1953); Alison Cornish, *Vernacular Translation in Dante's Italy: Illiterate Literature* (Cambridge: Cambridge University Press, 2013).
5 For a survey of medieval renaissances, see Warren Treadgold (ed.), *Renaissances Before the Renaissance: Classical Revivals of Late Antiquity and the Middle Ages* (Stanford: Stanford University Press, 1984).
6 Najemy, *History of Florence*, pp. 45–6.
7 Robert Black, 'Education and the emergence of a literate society', in John Najemy (ed.), *Italy in the Age of the Renaissance: 1300–1550* (Oxford: Oxford University Press, 2004), p. 18. See also Ronald G. Witt, 'What did Giovannino read and write? Literacy in early Renaissance Florence', *I Tatti Studies* 6 (1995), pp. 83–114.
8 See Benjamin G. Kohl, 'The myth of the Renaissance despot', in Bernadette Patton and John Easton Law (eds), *Communes and Despots in Medieval and Renaissance Italy* (Aldershot: Ashgate, 2010); Philip Jones, *The Italian City-State: from Commune to Signoria* (Oxford: Oxford University Press, 1997).
9 See the relevant entries in the *Dizionario biografico degli italiani* (Rome: Istituto dell'Enciclopedia Italiana, 1960–). Dante (*Purgatorio*, XX, 79–81) compared Charles's bargaining off of his daughter to a corsair selling off female slaves.
10 Richard A. Goldthwaite, *Wealth and the Demand for Art in Italy, 1300–1600* (Baltimore: Johns Hopkins University Press, 1993).
11 This dynamic is underlined in Evelyn Welch, *Art and Authority in Renaissance Milan* (New Haven: Yale University Press, 1997).

12 See Peter Howard, *Creating Magnificence in Renaissance Florence* (Toronto: University of Toronto Press, 2012); Guido Guerzoni, *Apollo and Vulcan: The Art Markets in Italy, 1400–1700* (East Lansing: Michigan State University Press, 2011), pp. 29–43; Jonathan K. Nelson and Richard J. Zeckhauser, *The Patron's Payoff: Conspicuous Commissions in Italian Renaissance Art* (Princeton: Princeton University Press, 2008).

13 See Francesco De Sanctis, *Storia della letteratura italiana,* ed. Niccolò Gallo with an introduction by Giorgio Ficara (Turin: Einaudi-Gallimard, 1996). An English translation is available: Francesco De Sanctis, *History of Italian Literature*, trans. Joan Redfern (New York: Basic Books, 1960).

14 Virginia Cox, *The Prodigious Muse: Women's Writing in Counter-Reformation Italy* (Baltimore: Johns Hopkins University Press, 2011), pp. xiv–xv.

15 Mary Laven, 'Encountering the Counter-Reformation', *Renaissance Quarterly*, 59/3 (2006), pp. 706–20.

16 The essay is reprinted in *Women, History and Theory: The Essays of Joan Kelly* (Chicago: University of Chicago Press, 1984).

17 See Brian Jeffrey Maxson, *The Humanist World of Renaissance Florence* (Cambridge: Cambridge University Press, 2014).

18 On the editorial history of Ariosto, see Daniel Javitch, *Proclaiming a Classic: The Canonization of* Orlando Furioso (Princeton: Princeton University Press, 1991).

19 'Descrittione della vita del Croce', in *Storia di vita popolare nelle canzoni di piazza di G.C. Croce*, ed. Monique Rauch (Bologna: CLUEBB, 1982), p. 46.

Chapter 2: The Renaissance and the Ancient

1 The letter is cited from *Two Renaissance Book Hunters: The Letters of Poggius Bracciolini to Nicolaus de Niccolis*, trans. Phyllis Walter Goodhart Gordan (New York: Columbia University Press, 1991), pp. 193–5.

2 The phrase is from a metrical epistle of Lovati's, to a certain Bellinus, cited in Ronald G. Witt, *In the Footsteps of the Ancients: The Origins of Humanism From Lovato to Bruni* (Leiden: Brill, 2000), p. 53.

3 David Wray, *Catullus and the Poetics of Roman Manhood* (Cambridge: Cambridge University Press, 2001), p. 5.

4 Valuable as overviews of Petrarch's and Boccaccio's very diverse literary production are Victoria Kirkham and Armando Maggi (eds), *Petrarch: A Critical Guide to the Complete Works* (Chicago: University of Chicago Press, 2009), and Victoria Kirkham, Michael Sherberg, and Janet Levarie Smarr (eds), *Boccaccio: A Critical Guide to the Complete Works* (Chicago: University of Chicago Press, 2013).

5 ('Homerus ... apud me mutus, immo vero ego apud illum surdus sum'). Petrarch, *Le familiari*, ed. Vittorio Rossi and Umberto Bosco (Florence: Sansoni, 1933–42), Vol. 3, p. 277 (letter 18. 2, of January 1354). Petrarch's letters are available in English: *Rerum familiarum libri*, trans. Aldo S. Bernardo, 3 vols (New York: Italica Press, 2005).

6 Marianne Pade, 'The *fortuna* of Leontius Pilatus's Homer', in F. T. Coulson and A. A. Grotans (eds), *Classica et Beneventana: Essays Presented to Virginia Brown on the Occasion of her 65th Birthday* (Turnhout: Brepols, 2008), p. 150.
7 The text may be found in Craig W. Kallendorf (ed.), *Humanist Educational Treatises* (Cambridge, MA: Harvard University Press, 2002).
8 For discussion of the term and its history, see James Hankins, 'Humanism, scholasticism, and Renaissance philosophy', in James Hankins (ed.), *The Cambridge Companion to Renaissance Philosophy* (Cambridge: Cambridge University Press, 2007), pp. 30–2.
9 Maxson, *Humanist World.*
10 For a brief overview, see Hankins, 'Humanism', pp. 32–6.
11 Ibid., pp. 39–45.
12 See Salvatore Camporeale, *Christianity, Latinity, and Culture: Two Studies on Lorenzo Valla*, ed. Patrick Barker and Christopher S. Celenza (Leiden: Brill, 2014), esp. pp. 184–6.
13 Benvenuto Cellini, *Vita*, ed. Ettore Camesasca (Milan: Rizzoli, 2009), pp. 240–4 (Bk 64). For a translation, see *The Autobiography of Benvenuto Cellini*, trans. George Bull (Harmondsworth: Penguin, 1956).
14 Carrie E. Beneš, *Urban Legends: Civic Identity and the Classical Past in Northern Italy, 1250–1350* (University Park, PA: Pennsylvania State University Press, 2011), pp. 47–52.
15 ('In vestibulo Iustine virginis et ante ipsum sepulcri tui lapidem'). Petrarch, *Le familiari*, Vol. 4, p. 245 (24. 8).
16 Beneš, *Urban Legends*, pp. 122–5.
17 Ibid., pp. 63–88.
18 ('Aliquot sibi aureas argenteasque nostrorum principum effigies minutissimis ac veteribus literis inscriptas, quas in delitiis habebam, dono dedi, in quibus et Augusti Cesaris vultus erat pene spirans'). Petrarch, *Le familiari*, Vol. 3, p. 315 (29. 3).
19 ('Et ecce ... Cesar, quibus successisti; ecce quos imitari studeas et mirari'). Petrarch, *Le familiari*, Vol. 3, p. 315 (19. 3).
20 Suetonius, *The Lives of the Caesars*, trans. J.C. Rolfe (Cambridge, MA: Harvard University Press, 1989), Vol. 1, pp. 240–1 (2.75). On Petrarch's use of Suetonius in his autobiographical writings, see Gur Zak, 'Modes of self-writing from antiquity to the later Middle Ages', in Ralph Hexter et al. (eds), *The Oxford Handbook of Medieval Latin Literature* (Oxford: Oxford University Press, 2012), p. 498.
21 Diana Norman, 'Splendid models and examples from the past: Carrara patronage of art', in Diana Norman (ed.), *Siena, Florence, and Padua: Art, Society, and Religion, 1280–1400*, 2 vols (New Haven: Yale University Press, 1995), Vol. I, pp. 164–71.
22 Petrarch, *Le familiari*, Vol. 4, p. 205 (23.19).
23 ('Senza precettori, senza essemplo alcuno'). *Il nuovo* De Pictura *di Leon Battista Alberti*, ed. and trans. Rocco Sinisgalli (Rome: Edizioni Kappa, 2006), p. 89.
24 Michael Wyatt, 'Technologies', in Michael Wyatt (ed.), *The Cambridge Companion to the Italian Renaissance* (Cambridge: Cambridge University Press, 2014), p. 110.

25 Dora Thornton, *The Scholar in his Study: Ownership and Experience in Renaissance Italy* (New Haven: Yale University Press, 1998).
26 Charles Dempsey, *The Portrayal of Love: Botticelli's* Primavera *and Humanist Culture at the Time of Lorenzo the Magnificent* (Princeton: Princeton University Press, 1992).
27 On domestic furnishing, see Marta Ajmar and Flora Dennis, *At Home in Renaissance Italy* (London: Victoria and Albert Museum, 2006). On *cassone* painting, see Cristelle Baskins, *Cassone Painting, Humanism, and Gender in Early Modern Italy* (Cambridge: Cambridge University Press, 1998).
28 See James M. Saslow, *Ganymede in the Renaissance* (New Haven: Yale University Press, 1986); Michael Rocke, *Forbidden Friendships: Homosexuality and Male Culture in Renaissance Florence* (Oxford: Oxford University Press, 1998).
29 Hans Baron, 'Cicero and the Roman civic spirit in the Middle Ages and early Renaissance', *Bulletin of the John Rylands Library*, 22/1 (1938), pp. 72–97. For discussion of the 'civic humanist' tradition, see James Hankins (ed.), *Renaissance Civic Humanism: Reappraisals and Reflections* (Cambridge: Cambridge University Press, 2004).
30 The best study of Traversari remains Charles L. Stinger, *Humanism and the Church Fathers: Ambrogio Traversari (1386–1439) and Christian Antiquity in the Italian Renaissance* (Albany, NY: State University of New York Press, 1977).
31 See Craig Martin, *Subverting Aristotle: Religion, History and Philosophy in Early Modern Science* (Baltimore: Johns Hopkins University Press, 2014).
32 See Jill Kraye, 'The revival of Hellenistic philosophies', in Hankins (ed.), *Cambridge Companion*, p. 108; also ibid., p. 103 on Valla.
33 Martin, *Subverting Aristotle*, pp. 124–6.
34 See Brian Richardson, '*The Prince* and its early Italian readers', in Martin Coyle (ed.), *Niccolò Machiavelli's* The Prince*: New Interdisciplinary Essays* (Manchester: Manchester University Press, 1995).
35 ('contro alla fede, contro alla carità, contro alla umanità, contro alla religione'). Machiavelli, *Il principe*, ed. Giorgio Inglese (Turin: Einaudi, 1995), p. 118 (ch. 18). For an English edition, see Machiavelli, *The Prince and Other Political Writings*, trans. Stephen J. Milner (London: Everyman, 1995).
36 ('una lunga esperienza delle cose moderne e una continua lezione delle antiche'). Machiavelli, *Il principe*, p. 4.
37 For Lucretius's influence on Machiavelli, see Alison Brown, *The Return of Lucretius to Renaissance Florence* (Cambridge, MA: Harvard University Press, 2010), pp. 68–87.
38 Virginia Cox, 'Rhetoric and political ethics', in John Najemy (ed.), *The Cambridge Companion to Machiavelli* (Cambridge: Cambridge University Press, 2010), esp. pp. 179–81.

Chapter 3: The Renaissance and the Modern

1 *Il nuovo* De Pictura, pp. 165–6.
2 Pliny, *Natural History*, Bk 7, 4. On the status of artists in ancient Rome, see Peter Stewart, *The Social History of Roman Art* (Cambridge: Cambridge University Press, 2008), pp. 18–21.
3 Cennino Cennini, *Il libro dell'arte*, ed. Fabio Frezzato (Vicenza: Neri Pozza, 2003), ch. 2, p. 63. An English translation is available: Cennino Cennini, *The Craftsman's Handbook (Il libro dell'arte)*, trans. Daniel V. Thompson (New York: Dover, 1960).
4 Moderata Fonte, *The Worth of Women*, ed. and trans. Virginia Cox (Chicago: University of Chicago Press, 1997), p. 101 and n. 67. On the 'famous women' tradition generally, see Cox, *Women's Writing in Italy, 1400–1650* (Baltimore: Johns Hopkins University Press, 2008), pp. 20–1, 24–6.
5 The key *loci* for this are Chapter 25 of *Il principe*, and Machiavelli's letter of September 1506 to Giovanni Battista Soderini, known as the *ghiribizzi* ('scribblings'). See, for the latter, *Machiavelli and His Friends: Their Personal Correspondence*, ed. and trans. James B. Atkinson and David Sices (Delkalb: Northern Illinois University Press, 1996), pp. 134–6.
6 Javitch, *Proclaiming a Classic.*
7 See Susan Mosher Stuard, *Gilding the Market: Luxury and Fashion in Fourteenth-Century Italy* (Philadelphia: University of Pennsylvania Press, 2006); Carole Collier Frick, *Dressing Renaissance Florence: Families, Fortunes and Fine Clothing* (Baltimore: Johns Hopkins University Press, 2002); Eugenia Paulicelli, *Writing Fashion in Early Modern Italy: From Sprezzatura to Satire* (Aldershot: Ashgate, 2014).
8 Elizabeth Currie, 'Diversity and design in the Florentine tailoring trade, 1550–1620', in Michelle O' Malley and Evelyn Welch (eds), *The Material Renaissance* (Manchester: Manchester University Press, 2007), esp. p. 157.
9 Catherine Atkinson, *Inventing Inventors: Polydore Vergil's* De inventoribus rerum (Tübingen: Mohr Siebeck, 2007).
10 Alessandra Baroni and Manfred Sellink, *Stradanus (1523–1605): Court Artist to the Medici* (Turnhout: Brepols, 2012).
11 Burckhardt, *The Civilization of the Renaissance in Italy*, Part IV ('The Discovery of the World and Man'), pp. 185–229.
12 See Ann R. Jones and Margaret Rosenthal, *The Clothing of the Renaissance World: Cesare Vecellio's* Habiti antichi et moderni (New York: Thames and Hudson, 2008).
13 Paula Findlen, *Possessing Nature: Museums, Collecting, and Scientific Culture in Early Modern Italy* (Berkeley and Los Angeles: University of California Press, 1996).
14 See Michel Foucault, *The Order of Things: An Archaeology of the Human Sciences* (London: Routledge, 1970), especially pp. 17–33.
15 Marjorie O'Rourke Boyle, *Loyola's Acts: The Rhetoric of the Self* (Berkeley and Los Angeles: University of California Press, 1997), pp. 117–19.
16 ('non vogliate negar l'esperïenza/di retro al sol, del mondo senza gente'). Dante, *Inferno*, XXVI, 116–17.

17 ('Errorem sane circa locorum notitiam multa pariunt, atque hec inter cetera: regionum inaccessarum nostris hominibus longinquitas, nominum mutatio, scriptorum raritas obscuritasque eorumdemque nonnunquam dissensio, sed super omnia incuriositas ingeniorum ac segnities nichil omnino curantium nisi quod ante oculos est'). Cited from Giancarlo Petrella, *L'officina del geografo. La* Descrittione di tutta Italia *di Leandro Alberti e gli studi geografico-antiquari tra Quattro e Cinquecento* (Milan: Vita e Pensiero, 2004), p. 27.

18 ('tam apud scriptores presertim cosmographos quam in descriptionibus terrarum et quibusdam cartis vetustissimis que ad manus nostras venerunt'). Ibid.

19 Fra Mauro made two sets of Ptolemaic maps, one for the Venetian government (surviving in the Marciana Library in Venice), *c.* 1448–53; the other for King Afonso V of Portugal, *c.* 1457–9. See Piero Falchetta, *Fra Mauro's World Map*, trans. Jeremy Scott; foreword by Marino Zorzi (Turnhout: Brepols, 2006); also, more generally, Evelyn Edson, *The World Map, 1300–1492* (Baltimore: Johns Hopkins University Press, 2007).

20 C. H. Clough, 'The New World and the Italian Renaissance', in C. H. Clough and P. E. H. Hair (eds), *The European Outthrust and Encounter: The First Phase c. 1400–c. 1700* (Liverpool: Liverpool University Press, 1994), pp. 291–328.

21 Claudia Lazzaro, *The Italian Renaissance Garden: From the Conventions of Planting, Design, and Ornament to the Grand Gardens of Sixteenth-Century Central Italy* (New Haven: Yale University Press, 1990), p. 11, n. 29.

22 See Jules Janick and Harry S. Paris, 'The Cucurbit images (1515–1518) of the Villa Farnesina, Rome', *Annals of Botany*, 97/2 (2006), pp. 165–76.

23 Cited from Anthony Grafton, with April Shelton and Nancy Siraisi, *New Worlds, Ancient Texts: The Power of Tradition and the Shock of Discovery* (Cambridge, MA: Harvard University Press, 1992), p. 84.

24 ('Gli huomini de' tempi presenti che si dilettano di saper li siti della terra deono rendere infinite grazie al nostro Signore Iddio che gli ha fatti nascere in questa età'). Giovanni Battista Ramusio, *Navigazioni e viaggi*, ed. Marica Milanesi (Turin: Einaudi, 1978–88), Vol. 2, p. 502.

25 On the early history of medical dissection in Italy, see Nancy Siraisi, *Medieval and Early Renaissance Medicine: An Introduction to Knowledge and Practice* (Chicago: University of Chicago Press, 1990), pp. 86–96.

26 Katharine Park, 'The criminal and the saintly body: autopsy and dissection in late medieval Europe', *Renaissance Quarterly*, 47/1 (1994), pp. 1–33.

27 Bernard Schultz, *Art and Anatomy in Renaissance Italy* (Ann Arbor: UMI Research Press), pp. 61–3.

28 Further on this subject see Vivian Nutton, 'Hellenism postponed: some aspects of Renaissance medicine, 1490–1530', *Sudhoffs Archiv*, 81/2 (1997) pp. 158–70.

29 Giorgio Vasari, *Le vite de' più eccellenti pittori scultori e architettori nelle redazioni del 1550 e 1568*, ed. Rosanna Bettarini and Paola Barocchi (Florence: Sansoni [later S.P.E.S.], 1966–97), Vol. 3, p. 506. The *Vite* are cited from the 1568 edition unless otherwise noted. For an English translation, see Giorgio Vasari, *Lives of the Painters, Sculptors and*

Architects, trans. Gaston C. De Vere, with an introduction and notes by David Ekserdjian (New York: Knopf, 1996).

30 See Domenico Laurenza, *Art and Anatomy in Renaissance Italy: Images from a Scientific Revolution* (New York: Metropolitan Museum of Art, 2012), pp. 8–10; Shelley R. Langdale, *Battle of the Nudes: Pollaiuolo's Renaissance Masterpiece* (Cleveland, OH: Cleveland Museum of Art, 2002) , p. 54; Schultz, *Art and Anatomy*, pp. 51–9.

31 The mention of the 'book' is found in Windsor Castle, Royal Collection, RCIN 9190599r. See Martin Clayton and Ron Philo, *Leonardo da Vinci: Anatomist* (London: Royal Collection Enterprises, 2012), p. 48. On the techniques employed in Leonardo's anatomical drawings, see ibid., p. 22.

32 Windsor Castle, Royal Collection, RCIN 919027v. See Clayton and Philo, *Leonardo*, pp. 17 and 82.

33 Ibid., pp. 20–3.

34 See, for example, ibid., pp. 240–4.

35 Cited from Brian Ogilvie, *The Science of Describing: Natural History in Renaissance Europe* (Chicago: University of Chicago Press, 2006), p. 129.

36 Andrea Carlino, *Books of the Body: Anatomical Ritual and Renaissance Learning*, trans. John Tedeschi and Anne Tedeschi (Chicago: University of Chicago Press, 1999), pp. 198–9.

37 Ibid., pp. 202–7.

38 Ibid., pp. 207–10.

39 Ibid., p. 135.

40 This text is available in an English edition: Lilio Gregorio Giraldi, *Modern Poets*, ed. and trans. John N. Grant (Cambridge, MA: Harvard University Press, 2011).

41 See Alina Payne, 'Vasari, architecture, and the origins of historicizing art', *Anthropology and Aesthetics*, 40 (2001), pp. 51–76.

42 The Guardaroba project is examined in Francesca Fiorani, *The Marvel of Maps: Art, Cartography, and Politics in Renaissance Italy* (New Haven: Yale University Press, 2005).

43 ('... misurate perfettamente tutte, e ricorrette secondo gli autori nuovi'; 'non è stata mai per tempo nessuno fatta nè la maggiore nè la più perfetta'). Vasari, *Vite*, Vol. 6, pp. 250–1. The discussion forms part of Vasari's chapter on the Florentine Academicians.

44 Javitch, *Proclaiming a Classic*, pp. 21–6.

45 Virginia Cox, *The Prodigious Muse: Women's Writing in Counter-Reformation Italy* (Baltimore: Johns Hopkins University Press, 2011), pp. 32–45.

46 Brian Richardson, *Printing, Writers, and Readers in Renaissance Italy* (Cambridge: Cambridge University Press, 1999), p. 117.

47 Brian Pullan, 'Wage-earners and the Venetian economy', *The Economic History Review,* 16/3 (1964), esp. p. 415.

48 Carlo Ginzburg, *The Cheese and the Worms* (1976), trans. John Tedeschi and Anne Tedeschi (Baltimore, 1980), pp. 29–30.

49 On the increase in the size of libraries in this period, see Richardson, *Printing*, pp. 118–21.

50 On Luther and print culture, see Mark U. Edwards, *Printing, Propaganda, and Martin Luther* (Berkeley and Los Angeles: University of Chicago Press,

1995). For an overview of ephemeral print culture in Renaissance Italy, see Ottavia Niccoli, 'Italy', in Joad Raymond (ed.), *The Oxford History of Popular Print Culture*. Vol. 1. *Cheap Print in Britain and Ireland to 1660* (Oxford: Oxford University Press, 2011).

51 Mario Infelise, 'Roman *avvisi*: information and politics in the seventeenth century', in Gianvittorio Signorotto and Maria Antonietta Visceglia (eds), *Court and Politics in Papal Rome, 1492–1700* (Cambridge: Cambridge University Press, 2002), p. 216 (translation slightly amended). See also Andrew Pettegree, *The Invention of News: How the World Came to Know About Itself* (New Haven: Yale University Press, 2014), pp. 107–13.

52 Pierangelo Bellettini, 'Pietro Vecchi e il suo progetto di lettura pubblica, con ascolto a pagamento, delle notizie periodiche di attualità (Bologna 1596)', in Pierangelo Bellettini et al. (eds), *Una città in piazza. Comunicazione e vita quotidiana a Bologna tra Cinque e Seicento* (Bologna: Compositori, 2000), pp. 68–76.

53 Brian Richardson, 'The debates on printing in Renaissance Italy', *La bibliofilia*, 100/2–3 (1998), pp. 148–51.

54 Humfrey C. Butters, 'Conflicting attitudes towards Machiavelli's works in Spain, Rome, and Florence', in Law and Patton (eds), *Communes and Despots*, pp. 81–5.

55 ('Cum igitur haud ita pridem in Urbe nostra, secta quaedam emerserit hominum improbe curiosorum, qui quoscunque de publicis privatisque negociis, vel aliunde rimari possunt, vel ipsi etiam pro sua libidine comminiscuntur, domi, forisque facta, infecta, vera, falsa, nullo discrimine proponunt, recipiunt, et scriptitant, ita ut huius rei iam artem quasi quandam instituerint'). Bellettini, 'Pietro Vecchi', p. 70.

56 Amedeo Quondam, 'Saggio di bibliografia della poesia religiosa', in *Paradigmi e tradizioni* (Rome: Bulzoni, 2005), pp. 213–82, gives a sense of the range of this as yet little-studied literature. See also Cox, *Prodigious Muse,* pp. 32–41 on the more elite traditions of Counter-Reformation religious literature, and Niccoli, 'Italy', p. 194, for brief mention of popular religious literature at this time.

57 See Paolo Cherchi, *Polimatia di riuso. Mezzo secolo di plagio (1539–89)* (Rome: Bulzoni, 1998), pp. 74–7, 211–33; Cox, *Prodigious Muse*, pp. 246–7.

58 ('... perche in quei tempi era grandissima carestia di libri, e come uno sapeva un poco parlare per *bus*, e per *bas*, veniva adorato, come un Profeta, e gli era creduto ciò che egli diceva: ma di poi che questa benedetta stampa è venuta in luce, i libri sono multiplicati di sorte tale, che ogni uno può studiare; e massime che la maggior parte si stampano in lingua nostra materna'). Leonardo Fioravanti, *Dello specchio di scientia universale* (Venice: Vincenzo Valgrisi, 1564), 37v.

59 ('Ella [l'arte della stampa] è stata causa di risvegliare il mondo; il quale era addormentato nell'ignoranza'). Ibid., 61v.

60 ('la maggior parte delle genti tanto huomini quanto donne sanno leggere'; 'forse un giorno verrà tempo, che tutti saremo Dottori a un modo'). Ibid., 62r.

61 ('e così i gattesini hanno aperti gli occhi'). Ibid., 37v.

Chapter 4: Identity and the Self

1 Robert C. Davis, *The War of the Fists: Popular Culture and Public Violence in Late Renaissance Venice* (Oxford: Oxford University Press, 1994).
2 On the latter ritual, see Edward Muir, *Civic Ritual in Renaissance Venice* (Princeton: Princeton University Press, 1986), pp. 119–34.
3 Marilynn B. Brewer and Constantine Sedikides (eds), *Individual Self, Relational Self, Collective Self* (Philadelphia: Psychology Press, 2001). The definitions are from the editors' introduction, at pp. 1–2.
4 Shihui Han and Ying Zhu, 'Cultural differences in the self: from philosophy to psychology and neuroscience', *Social and Personality Psychology Compass*, 2/5 (2008), pp. 1799–811.
5 Leon Battista Alberti, *I libri della famiglia*, ed. Ruggiero Romano, Alberto Tenenti, and Francesco Furlan (Turin: Einaudi, 1994), pp. 321–428. An English translation is available: Leon Battista Alberti, *The Family in Renaissance Florence*, trans. Renée Neu Watkins (Columbia, SC: University of South Carolina Press, 1969).
6 ('essere a tutti riverenti'). Alberti, *Della famiglia*, p. 58.
7 ('Ob[servantissimo] fi[glio] et servitor'). Castiglione, *Lettere inedite e rare*, ed. Guglielmo Gorni (Milan: Ricciardi, 1969), p. 68 (letter 49).
8 ('acciò ch'el impara a bonhora ad esser humano'). Ibid.
9 See Jerry Root, *'Space to Speke': The Confessional Subject in Medieval Literature* (New York: Peter Lang, 1997).
10 Sara J. Schechner, 'Between knowing and doing: mirrors and their imperfections in the Renaissance', in *Early Science and Medicine*, 20/2 (2005), pp. 141–54.
11 Laura Jacobus, 'A knight in the Arena: Enrico Scrovegni and his "true image"', in Mary Rogers (ed.), *Fashioning Identities in Renaissance Art* (Aldershot: Ashgate, 2000), esp. p. 23; ead., 'The tomb of Enrico Scrovegni in the Arena Chapel, Padua', *The Burlington Magazine*, 1311/154 (2012), esp. pp. 408–409.
12 Catherine King, 'The arts of carving and casting', in Norman (ed.), *Siena*, Vol. 1, p. 118. The medals date from 1390.
13 ('credo che ad ognuno sia licito vestirsi a modo suo'). Baldassare Castiglione, *Il libro del Cortegiano*, ed. Nicola Longo, with an introduction by Amedeo Quondam (Milan: Garzanti, 1987), p. 158 (2.26). For an English translation, see Baldassare Castiglione, *The Book of the Courtier: The Singleton Translation*, trans. Charles S. Singleton, ed. Daniel Javitch (New York: Norton, 2002).
14 ('… debba fra se stesso deliberar ciò che vol parere e di quella sorte che desidera esser estimato, della medesima vestirsi'). Castiglione, *Cortegiano*, p. 160 (2.27).
15 ('Dapoi ch'io feci quella mia fodera de martore, l'usanza è venuta q[ui] de fare magiore le veste, trovo che adesso, alle veste che si usano, me li manca uno grande pezzo'). Castiglione, *Lettere*, ed. Guido La Rocca (Milan: Mondadori, 1978), Vol. 1, p. 236 (no. 162).
16 See Anthony Grafton, *Leon Battista Alberti: Master Builder of the Italian Renaissance* (Cambridge, MA: Harvard University Press, 2002), pp. 105–106.

17 See Rose Marie San Juan, 'The court lady's dilemma: Isabella d'Este and art collecting in the Renaissance', *Oxford Art Journal*, 14/1 (1991), pp. 67–78.
18 Stephen Campbell, *The Cabinet of Eros: Renaissance Mythological Painting and the Studiolo of Isabella d'Este* (New Haven: Yale University Press, 2006).
19 ('el pictore ne ha tanto mal facta che non ha alcuna de le nostre simiglie'). Letter of 20 April 1493, cited in Joanna Woods-Marsden, 'Theorizing Renaissance portraiture', in James Elkins and Robert Williams (eds), *Renaissance Theory (The Art Seminar)* (New York: Routledge, 2007), p. 363.
20 ('una puva vestita alla fogia che va lei de camisa, di maniche, de veste di sotto, et di sopra, et de abiliamenti, et aconciatura di testa, et deli capili, come la porta'). Cited in Yassana C. Croizat, '"Living dolls": François 1er dresses his women', *Renaissance Quarterly*, 60/1 (2007), p. 97, n. 6.
21 ('li profumi in bona quantità per donar a queste madimiselle ... et guanti assai, et un albarello di savonetto da mane, che sia grande per darne a molte et ancor olio, polvere et acque'). Cited in Evelyn Welch, *Shopping in the Renaissance: Consumer Cultures in Italy 1400–1600* (New Haven: Yale University Press, 2005), p. 359 n. 81.
22 Ibid., p. 359 n. 82.
23 ('grande inzegno'). Cited in Luke Syson, 'Reading faces: Gian Cristoforo Romano's medal of Isabella d'Este', in Cesare Mozzarelli et al. (eds), *La corte di Mantova nell'età di Mantegna, 1450–1550/The Court of the Gonzaga in the Age of Mantegna*, 1450–1550 (Rome: Bulzoni, 1997), p. 287.
24 ('neque actor ... alienae personae, sed auctor meae'). Cicero, *De oratore*, trans. E. W. Sutton and H. Rackman (Cambridge, MA: Harvard University Press, 1976), Vol. 1, p. 338 (2.194).
25 ('Nec te celestem neque terrenum, neque mortalem neque immortalem fecimus, ut tui ipsius quasi arbitrarius honorariusque plastes et fictor, in quam malueris tute formam effingas'). Giovanni Pico della Mirandola, *Discorso della dignità dell'uomo*, ed. Francesco Bausi (Parma: Ugo Guanda, 2003), p. 10. The translation quoted is that of Elizabeth Livermore Forbes in Ernst Cassirer et al., *The Renaissance Philosophy of Man* (Chicago: University of Chicago Press, 1956). The title 'On the Dignity of Man' was an invention of later editors; the original has no title.
26 ('negli animi nostri sono tante latebre e tanti recessi, che impossibil è che prudenzia umana possa conoscer quelle simulazioni, che dentro nascose vi sono'). Castiglione, *Cortegiano*, p. 163 (2.29). The phrasing echoes a passage in Cicero's *Pro Marcello*, 22.
27 John Jeffries Martin, *Myths of Renaissance Individualism* (Basingstoke: Palgrave MacMillan, 2004). See also Jon R. Snyder, *Dissimulation and the Culture of Secrecy in Early Modern Europe* (Berkeley and Los Angeles: University of California Press, 2012).
28 Machiavelli, *Il principe*, pp. 115–16 (ch. 18).
29 Luba Freedman, *Titian's Portraits Through Aretino's Lens* (University Park, PA: Pennsylvania State University Press, 1995), pp. 69–90.

30 Further on this point, see Virginia Cox (ed.), *Lyric Poetry by Women of the Italian Renaissance* (Baltimore: Johns Hopkins University Press, 2013), p. 20.
31 Stephen Greenblatt, *Renaissance Self-Fashioning: From More to Shakespeare* (Chicago: University of Chicago Press, 1980).
32 The detail is found in Carlo Dionisotti's entry on Bembo in the *Dizionario biografico*.
33 See Guido Beltramini et al. (eds), *Pietro Bembo e l'invenzione del Rinascimento* (Venice: Marsilio, 2013), pp. 208–209, which conjecturally identifies a painting in Besançon as the portrait by Titian mentioned by Vasari. The Cellini medal request is mentioned at ibid., p. 324.
34 On the Virgil codex, see Luba Freedman, *Classical Myths in Italian Renaissance Painting* (Cambridge: Cambridge University Press, 2011), p. 6. More generally, on Bembo's collecting and interiors, see Susan Nalezyty, 'From Padua to Rome: Pietro Bembo's mobile objects and convivial interiors', in Erin J. Campbell et al. (eds), *The Early Modern Italian Domestic Sphere, 1400–1700: Objects, Spaces, Domesticities* (Aldershot: Ashgate, 2014).
35 Raymond Waddington, *Aretino's Satyr: Sexuality, Satire, and Self-Projection in Sixteenth-Century Italy* (Toronto: University of Toronto Press, 2004).
36 ('La natura stessa, della cui semplicità son secretario, mi detta ciò che io compongo'). Pietro Aretino, *Lettere. Libro primo*, ed. Francesco Erspamer (Parma: Ugo Guanda, 1995), p. 156 (letter of 25 June 1537 to Lodovico Dolce).
37 Paula Hohti, 'Domestic space and identity: artisans, shopkeepers and traders in sixteenth-century Siena', *Urban History*, 37/3 (2010), pp. 337–8.
38 Patricia Allerston, 'Clothing and early modern Venetian society', *Continuity and Change*, 15/3 (2000), p. 377; Paulicelli, *Writing Fashion*, pp. 39 and 157.
39 Cited in Woods-Marsden, 'Theorizing', p. 362.

Chapter 5: Renaissance Man

1 Thomas Greene, 'The flexibility of the self in Renaissance literature,' in Peter Demetz et al. (eds), *The Disciplines of Criticism: Essays in Literary Theory, Interpretation, and History* (New Haven: Yale University Press, 1968), pp. 241–64.
2 Alberti, *I libri della famiglia*, p. 218. Giannozzo attributes the saying to the merchant-statesman Benedetto Alberti (d. 1388).
3 For more on merchants' writings, see Vittore Branca, *Merchant Writers of the Italian Renaissance from Boccaccio to Machiavelli*, trans. Murtha Baca (New York: Marsilio, 1999).
4 Benedetto Cotrugli, *Il libro dell'arte della mercatura*, ed. Ugo Tucci (Venice: Arsenale, 1990), pp. 206–207 .
5 ('egli è sommamente utile et ancora necessario l'avere il corpo in buona disposizione, atto a simile essercitio, il quale a questa opera della consequition del fine concorrerà come instrumento adacto, non altrimenti che si facci il martello che concorre come dextro instrumento del fabbro'). Ibid., p. 145.

6 Alberti, *Della famiglia*, pp. 213–18.
7 Mark Phillips, *The Memoir of Marco Parenti: A Life in Medici Florence* (Princeton: Princeton University Press, 1987), p. 36.
8 Cotrugli, *Della mercatura*, p. 103.
9 ('mai non perdé punto di tempo, sempre attento in acquistare l'amore del suo creatore Idio pelle sue limosine e buone operazioni, appresso in acquistare amicizia di buoni uomini e da bene e potenti'). Giovanni Morelli, *Ricordi*, ed. Vittore Branca (Florence: Le Monnier, 1956).
10 Maxson, *Humanist World*.
11 Eugenio Refini, '"Aristotile in parlare materno": vernacular readings of the *Ethics* in the Quattrocento', *I Tatti Studies in the Italian Renaissance*, 16/1–2 (2013), pp. 311–41.
12 ('molte città: e molti costume de homeni'). Ibid., p. 334 and n. 99.
13 ('li mercanti gravi et valenti non debbono essere come l'ago, che è vile strumento, perché non sa se non cucire'). Cotrugli, *Il libro*, p. 211.
14 Vittore Branca, 'L'epopea mercantile', in *Boccaccio medievale* (Florence: Sansoni, 1965), pp. 71–99.
15 Guido Guerzoni, 'The demand for arts of an Italian Renaissance court: the case of d'Este of Ferrara (1471–1560)', in Clara Eugenia Nuñez (ed.), *Markets for Art, 1400–1600* (Seville: Universidad de Sevilla, 1998), p. 56. See also Guerzoni, *Apollo*, pp. 47–9.
16 Lauro Martines, *Power and Imagination: City-States in Renaissance Italy* (New York: Knopf, 1979), p. 221.
17 See Christopher S. Celenza, *Renaissance Humanism and the Papal Curia: Lapo da Castiglionchio the Younger's* De curiae commodis (Ann Arbor: University of Michigan Press, 1999).
18 ('furti, omicidii, odi, vendette, et ire'). See *The Satires of Ludovico Ariosto: A Renaissance Autobiography*, ed. and trans. Peter DeSa Wiggins (Athens, OH: Ohio University Press, 1976), pp. 10–12 (Satire 1, ll. 97–9, 109–14), for unwelcome diplomatic missions and p. 106 (Satire 4, l. 147) for the Garfagnana.
19 Castiglione, *Cortegiano*, p. 280 (3.16).
20 Ibid., pp. 59–61 (1.26).
21 Cicero, *Brutus. Orator*, trans. G. L. Hendrickson and H. M. Hubbell (Cambridge, MA: Harvard University Press, 1939), p. 362 (23.78).
22 Castiglione, *Cortegiano*, p. 92 (1.43).
23 Ibid., pp. 53–5 (1.21–2).
24 For the term, see Lisa K. Regan, 'Ariosto's threshold patron: Isabella d'Este in the *Orlando Furioso*', *MLN*, 120/1 (2005), pp. 50–69.
25 ('Ma perché par che la fortuna, come in molte altre cose, così ancora abbia grandissima forza nelle opinioni degli omini ...'). Castiglione, *Cortegiano*, p. 167 (2.32).
26 Ibid., pp. 128–30 (2.8).
27 Ibid. p. 179 (2.39).
28 Norbert Elias, *The Civilizing Process* (Oxford: Blackwell, 1994).
29 See Peter Burke, *The Fortunes of the* Courtier*: The European Reception of Castiglione's* Cortegiano (University Park, PA: Pennsylvania State University Press, 1996).

30 ('mercatura autem, si tenuis est, sordida putanda est; sin magna et copiosa ... non est admodum vituperanda'). Cicero, *De officiis*, 1.151.
31 The title of count awarded in such cases was a personal, rather than a hereditary, honour, and involved no grant of estates or land.
32 Molly Bourne, 'Signs of success: Leone Leoni's signposting in sixteenth-century Milan', in Nelson and Zechauser (eds), *The Patron's Payoff*.
33 ('la qual oggidì forsi par mecanica e poco conveniente a gentilomo'). Castiglione, *Cortegiano*, p. 102 (1.49).
34 ('lo specchio della vita umana'). Vasari, *Vite*, Vol. 3, p. 4.
35 ('non si curò egli mai di freddo, di fame, di disagio, di incomodità, di fatica, né di vergogna'). Ibid., Vol. 3, p. 528.
36 ('e mostrerà agl'artefici che chi lavora e studia continuamente e non a ghiribizzi, lascia opere, nome, facultà et amici'). Ibid., Vol. 3, p. 614.
37 Ibid., Vol. 4, p. 641.
38 ('[il] non meno eccellente che grazioso Raffael Sanzio da Urbino'). Ibid., Vol. 4, p. 610.
39 See especially Antonio Natali, *Andrea del Sarto* (New York: Abbeville, 1999).
40 Guerzoni, *Apollo*, p. 50. The calculation excludes years in which there was important ephemeral expenditure on events such as weddings and funerals.
41 Gregory Lubkin, *A Renaissance Court: Milan Under Galeazzo Maria Sforza* (Berkeley and Los Angeles: University of California Press, 1994), pp. 91, 138.
42 ('che debbio far io qui, poi ch'io non vaglio/smembrar su la forcina in aria starne,/né so a sparvier, né a can metter guinzaglio?'). *Satires*, p. 12 (Satire 1, ll. 142–4).
43 Castiglione, *Cortegiano*, p. 60 (1.26).
44 See on this Wayne A. Rebhorn, 'Baldesar Castiglione, Thomas Wilson, and the courtly body of Renaissance rhetoric', *Rhetorica*, 11/3 (1993), pp. 249–50.
45 On Scappi's life, see Terence Scully, *The* Opera *of Bartolomeo Scappi: L'arte e prudenza d'un maestro cuoco (The Art and Craft of a Master Cook)* (Toronto: University of Toronto Press, 2008), pp. 12–25. On his honours, see p. 20.
46 Vincenzo Cervio, *Il Trinciante, con l'aggiunta di Reale Fusoritto*, ed. Emilio Faccioli (Florence: Il Portolano, 1979), pp. 30–31 (ch. 1).
47 On fifteenth-century dance manuals and their authors, see Jennifer Nevile, *The Eloquent Body: Dance and Humanist Culture in Fifteenth-Century Italy* (Bloomington, IN: Indiana University Press, 2004).
48 A modern English edition exists: Martino da Como, *The Art of Cooking, with Fifty Modernized Recipes by Stefania Barzini*, ed. Luigi Ballerini; trans. Jeremy Parzen (Berkeley and Los Angeles: University of California Press, 2005).
49 The writings of the table professionals are discussed in Katherine A. McIver, *From Kitchen to Table: Cooking and Eating in Renaissance Italy* (Lanham, MD: Rowman and Littlefield, 2015). On horsemanship, see Federico Grisone's *The Rules of Riding: An Edited Translation of the First Renaissance Treatise on Classical Horsemanship*, ed. and trans. Elizabeth

M. Tobey (Tempe, AZ: Arizona Center for Medieval and Renaissance Studies, 2014).

50 Cervio, *Il Trinciante*, p. 31.

51 ('se ne trovano di quelli, che nati ignobilmente hanno nondimeno maniere d'huomini nobilissimi'). Claudio Corte, *Il cavallarizzo* (Venice: Giordano Ziletti, 1562), 115r. Corte acknowledges at 118v that the majority of *cavallarizzi* are in practice non-noble.

52 Corte, *Il cavallarizzo*, 114v.

53 Domenico Romoli, *La singolare dottrina ... dell'ufficio dello scalco* (Venice: Giovanni Battista Bonfadino, 1593), 14r–v.

54 Corte, *Il cavallarizzo*, 121r.

55 On the culture of instrument-making, see Alexander Marr, *From Raphael to Galileo: Mutio Oddi and the Mathematical Culture of Late Renaissance Italy* (Chicago: University of Chicago Press, 2011).

56 Silvio Leydi, 'The swordsmiths of Milan, c. 1525–1630', in Tobias Capwell, Sydney Anglo et al., *The Noble Art of the Sword: Fashion and Fencing in Renaissance Europe 1520–1630* (London: Wallace Collection, 2012), pp. 177–201, esp. pp. 186–7.

57 See Joseph Connors, '*Ars tornandi*: Baroque architecture and the lathe', *Journal of the Warburg and Courtauld Institutes*, 53 (1990), p. 220.

58 ('il disegno è la chiave che apre le porte non solo a l'oro, ma a tutti gli essercitii'). Vannoccio Biringuccio, *La pirotechnia* (Venice: Girolamo Gigli, 1559), 279v (Bk 9, ch. IV: 'L'arte del fabro orefice' ('The art of the goldsmith')). All subsequent references will be to this edition, which is more accurate than the first edition. An English edition is available: *The Pirotechnica of Vannoccio Biringuccio*, ed. and trans. Cyril Stanley Smith and Martha Teach Gnudi (New York: The American Institute of Mining and Metallurgical Engineers, 1943).

59 Biringuccio, *La pirotechnia*, 301r (Bk 9, ch. XIV: 'Discorso sopra l'arte figolina, con alcuni suoi secreti').

60 See Marta Ajmar, 'Mechanical Disegno', *RIHA Journal*, 0084 (2014).

61 ('tali artefici son gente senza dissegno e per il più, gente rustica, e grossa'). Biringuccio, *La pirotechnia*, 285v (Bk 9, ch. VI: 'Dell'arte del fabro ferario').

62 ('Tal che (se non fusse essercitio tanto fatigoso, e senza aluna dilicatezza), direi ch'il fusse esercitio da molto esaltare, perche quando considero che li maestri di tale arte fanno li lor lavori senza forma, o disegno, o stampa, ma col bastargli solo veder con l'occhio, et col giudicio, e poi col battere li fanno giusti, e garbeggiati, mi par gran cosa'). Ibid., 287v.

63 These examples are added in the 1583 edition of the text (at 28v–29r), where Fioravanti generally expands his personal tributes to practitioners of non-elite arts; see George W. McClure, *The Culture of Profession in Late Renaissance Italy* (Toronto: University of Toronto Press, 2004), p. 73 and pp. 268-69, nn. 21 and 23.

64 McClure, *Culture*, pp. 214–15.

65 ('non vi gloriate però tanto in questa vostra arte, se bene ella è bella, e vaga ... perche non è però di quello ingegno et di quel grado che voi pensate'). On the rising status of tailors in later sixteenth-century Italy, see Currie, 'Diversity and design'.

66 See especially, in English, John Jeffries Martin, 'The imaginary piazza: Tommaso Garzoni and the late Italian Renaissance', in Samuel K. Cohn, Jr. and Steven A. Epstein (eds), *Portraits of Medieval and Renaissance Living: Essays in Memory of David Herlihy* (Ann Arbor: University of Michigan Press, 1996), pp. 439–54; McClure, *Culture*, pp. 70–140.
67 ('quelle cose che con l'ingegno e la mano insieme si fanno'; 'E non tutti gli artefici tritti e vulgari son da esser detti propriamente mecanici, ma quelli solo che con l'ingegno soccorrono alle difficoltà grandissime emergenti, ad utilità commune'). Tommaso Garzoni, *La piazza universale di tutte le professioni del mondo,* ed. Paolo Cerchi and Beatrice Collina, 2 vols (Turin: Einaudi, 1996), Vol. 2, p. 1216.
68 ('solazzo mondano'). Garzoni, *La piazza*, Vol. 2, p. 1423.
69 Ibid., 1285–6.
70 ('superfluità ... pompa'; 'non più capanne, ma case, palazzi, castelli, et grandissime città'). Biringuccio, *La pirotechnia*, 304r.
71 ('stimolati ... dal natural desiderio dell'insatiabilità, che sempre vuole più di quello che si ha, e non mai contentasi di quello che ha'). Ibid.
72 ('assai più divina, che humana, considerando gli effetti'). Biringuccio, *La pirotechnia*, 306r.
73 ('le notitie nuove sempre partoriscon inventioni nuove negli intelletti e nuove notitie'). Biringuccio, *La pirotechnia*, 14v.
74 Pamela Long, *Openness, Secrecy, Authorship: Technical Arts and the Culture of Knowledge from Antiquity to the Renaissance* (Baltimore: Johns Hopkins University Press, 2001). Long discusses Biringuccio's treatise at pp. 178–82.
75 For a description of the scheme, see Larry J. Feinberg, 'The *Studiolo* of Francesco I reconsidered', in Cristina Acidini Luchinat et al., *The Medici, Michelangelo, and the Art of Late Renaissance Florence* (New Haven: Yale University Press, 2002), pp. 47–65.
76 Guerzoni, *Apollo*, p. 118. The quotation in the text is taken from the account of the spectacle in Tommaso Porcacchi, *Attioni d'Arrigo Terzo, re di Francia, e di Polonia, descritte in dialogo* (Venice: Giorgio Angelieri, 1574), 28r.
77 See Lisa Sampson, *Pastoral Drama in Early Modern Italy: The Making of a New Genre* (Oxford: Legenda, 2006).
78 See Guerzoni, *Apollo*; and compare Richard A. Goldthwaite, *The Building of Renaissance Florence: An Economic and Social History* (Baltimore: Johns Hopkins University Press, 1980), pp. 397–425, on similar dynamics at work in fifteenth-century Florence.

Chapter 6: Renaissance Woman

1 *Rime diverse d'alcune nobilissime e virtuosissime donne*, ed. Lodovico Domenichi (Lucca: Vincenzo Busdraghi, 1559); Francesco Agostino della Chiesa, *Theatro delle donne letterate, con un breve discorso della preminenza e perfettione del sesso donnesco* (Mondovì: Giovanni Gislandi and Giovanni Tommaso Rossi, 1620). For discussion, see Cox (ed.), *Lyric Poetry*, p. 26; ead., *Prodigious Muse*, pp. 22–3.

2 Fonte, *Worth of Women*, pp. 261–3.
3 Sharon T. Strocchia, 'Learning the virtues: convent schools and female culture in Renaissance Florence', in Barbara J. Whitehead (ed.), *Women's Education in Early Modern Europe. A History, 1500–1800* (New York: Garland, 1999).
4 See Margaret L. King, 'Book-lined cells: women and humanism in the early Italian Renaissance', in Patricia H. Labalme (ed.), *Beyond Their Sex: Learned Women of the European Past* (New York: New York University Press, 1980).
5 See Cox, *Women's Writing*, p. 9.
6 An English edition is available: Annibale Guasco, *Discourse to Lady Lavinia his Daughter*, ed. and trans. Peggy Osborn (Chicago: University of Chicago Press, 2003).
7 On the *concerto delle donne*, see Anthony Newcomb, *The Madrigal at Ferrara, 1579–97* (Princeton: Princeton University Press, 1980); on the *balletto*, Nina Treadwell, '"Simil combattimento fatto da Dame": the musico-theatrical entertainments of Margherita Gonzaga's *balletto delle donne* and the female warrior in Ferrarese cultural history', in Todd C. Borgerding (ed.), *Gender, Sexuality, and Early Music* (New York: Routledge, 2002), pp. 27–40.
8 See Prudence Allen, *The Concept of Woman Vol. I. The Aristotelian Revolution, 750 B.C.–1250 A.D.* (Grand Rapids, MI: William B. Eerdman, 1997); Ian Maclean, *The Renaissance Notion of Woman: A Study in the Fortunes of Scholasticism and Medical Science in European Intellectual Life* (Cambridge: Cambridge University Press, 1980).
9 Alberti, *I libri della famiglia*, pp. 268–81.
10 For an exhaustive overview of the humanist response to the Aristotelian position on women, see Prudence Allen, *The Concept of Woman. Vol. II. The Early Humanist Reformation, 1250–1500* (Grand Rapids, MI: William B. Eerdman, 2002). For a historically contextualized summary, see Cox, *Women's Writing*, pp. 17–36.
11 The early part of the tradition has been surveyed in Stephen Kolsky, *The Genealogy of Women: Studies in Boccaccio's* De claris mulieribus (New York: Peter Lang, 2003), and id., *The Ghost of Boccaccio: Writings on Famous Women in Renaissance Italy* (Turnhout: Brepols, 2005). Boccaccio's *Famous Women* is available in a modern bilingual edition, ed. and trans. Virginia Brown (Cambridge, MA: Harvard University Press, 2001).
12 ('Le meschine non desiderano l'esser omo per farsi più perfette, ma per aver libertà e fuggir quel dominio che gli omini si hanno vendicato sopra esse per sua propria autorità'). Castiglione, *Cortegiano*, p. 279 (3.16).
13 Ibid., pp. 274–86 (3.12–18).
14 Ibid., p. 266 (3.5).
15 ('giocare a palla, maneggiar l'arme, cavalcare, andar a caccia, e far quasi tutti gli esercizi che possa fare un cavaliero'). Ibid., p. 270 (3.7).
16 Paolo Giovio, *Notable Men and Women of Our Time*, ed. and trans. Kenneth Gouwens (Cambridge, MA: Harvard University Press, 2013), pp. 512–14.
17 *Gynevera* has not yet been translated into English. The most accessible Italian edition remains that of Corrado Ricchi and Alberto Bacchi della

Lega (Bologna: Romagnoli-Dall'Acqua, 1888). All subsequent references are to this edition. For a study, see Carolyn James, *Giovanni Sabadino degli Arienti: a Literary Career* (Florence: Olschki, 1996), ch. 4.

18 ('Il suo piacere, presso il motevole parlare di honestà pieno, era la foresta'). Arienti, *Gynevera*, p. 332.

19 ('fu virago in molti aspetti'). Ibid., p. 195.

20 ('prati de diversi fiori et vaghe herbette et boschi de varii albori, cum animali dentro relevati, come naturali'). Ibid., p. 155.

21 ('grandissima arte e calliditá'). Ibid., p. 129.

22 ('iocunda e grata in ricevere li amici e parenti, in forma che ogni uccellino facea parere falcone'). Ibid., p. 365.

23 See Margaret Franklin, *Boccaccio's Heroines: Power and Virtue in Renaissance Society* (Aldershot: Ashgate, 2006), 131–74; also, for the Roberti paintings, Virginia Cox, 'Gender and eloquence in Ercole de' Roberti's *Portia and Brutus*', *Rhetorica*, 62 (2009), pp. 61–101.

24 On gender and the genealogical theme in Ariosto, see Eleonora Stoppino, *Genealogies of Fiction: Women Warriors and the Dynastic Imagination in the* Orlando Furioso (New York: Fordham University Press, 2012).

25 On the history of women's writing in this period, see Cox, *Women's Writing*. On the significance of Colonna and Gambara in particular, see ibid., pp. 64–79.

26 For the text of the poem, see Cox (ed.), *Lyric Poetry*, pp. 77–82.

27 ('Seguir se deve il sposo dentro o fore ... a quel che arrisca l'un l'altro s'arrisca/equali in vita, equali siano in morte'). Ibid., p. 79.

28 See Virginia Cox, 'The exemplary Vittoria Colonna', in Abigail Brundin et al. (eds), *A Companion to Vittoria Colonna* (Leiden: Brill, forthcoming).

29 See Virginia Cox, 'Women writers and the canon: the case of Vittoria Colonna', in Pamela J. Benson and Victoria Kirkham (eds), *Strong Voices, Weak History: Women Writers and Canons in England, France, and Italy* (Ann Arbor: University of Michigan Press, 2005), pp. 17–19.

30 On the gender microculture of Siena in these years, see Konrad Eisenbichler, *The Sword and the Pen: Women, Politics, and Poetry in Sixteenth-Century Siena* (Notre Dame: University of Notre Dame Press, 2012); George McClure, *Parlour Games and the Public Life of Women in Renaissance Italy* (Toronto: University of Toronto Press, 2013), pp. 29–54.

31 See Virginia Cox, 'The female voice in Italian Renaissance dialogue', *MLN*, 128/1 (2013), pp. 53–78 for an overview; ead., 'Il commento paradossale: un microgenere senese', in Massimo Danzi and Roberto Leporatti (eds), *Il poeta e il suo pubblico: lettura e commento dei testi lirici nel Cinquecento* (Geneva: Droz, 2012), for the Atalanta Donati dialogue.

32 *The Travels and Life of Sir Thomas Hoby of Bisham Abbey, Written by Himself, 1547–1564*, ed. Edgar Powell (London: Royal Historical Society, 1902), p. 19.

33 ('eroica e libera maniera di procedere'). Cox, 'Il commento paradossale', p. 335.

34 On this phase in the history of Italian women's writing, see Cox, *Women's Writing*, pp. 80–120.

35 ('vederemo certamente che non l'antiquità de' sangui, né 'l soggiogar de' popoli, non l'oro né la porpora, ma l'animo di virtù splendido far l'uomo

veramente nobile'). Chiara Matraini, *Rime e lettere*, ed. Giovanna Rabitti (Bologna: Commissione per i Testi di Lingua, 1989), p. 94. Matraini's *Rime* are available in translation: *Selected Poetry and Prose*, ed. and trans. Eleanor Maclachlan, with an introduction by Giovanna Rabitti (Chicago: University of Chicago Press, 2008).

36 Gaspara Stampa, *The Complete Poems. The 1554 Edition of the* Rime*: A Bilingual Edition,* ed. Troy Tower and Jane Tylus; trans. with an introduction by Jane Tylus (Chicago: University of Chicago Press, 2010).

37 On the figure of the courtesan in Italy, see Margaret F. Rosenthal, *The Honest Courtesan: Veronica Franco, Citizen and Writer in Sixteenth-Century Venice* (Chicago: University of Chicago Press, 1992). On the broader culture of prostitution, see Tessa Storey, *Carnal Commerce in Counter-Reformation Rome* (Cambridge: Cambridge University Press, 2008).

38 The works of both are available in English translation. See *The Poems and Letters of Tullia d'Aragona and Others: A Bilingual Edition*, ed. and trans. Julia Hairston (Toronto: University of Toronto Press, 2014), and Veronica Franco, *Poems and Selected Letters*, ed. and trans. Ann Rosalind Jones and Margaret F. Rosenthal (Chicago: University of Chicago Press, 1998).

39 By, respectively, Victoria Kirkham and Ann Rosalind Jones; see Cox., *Women's Writing*, p. 109.

40 On this episode, see Deanna Basile, '*Fasseli gratia per poetessa*: Duke Cosimo I de' Medici's role in the Florentine literary circles of Tullia d'Aragona', in Konrad Eisenbichler (ed.), *The Cultural Politics of Duke Cosimo I de' Medici* (Aldershot: Ashgate, 2001).

41 Cox, *Prodigious Muse*, pp. 253–70. For an overview of this period, see ead., *Women's Writing*, pp. 131–65.

42 ('per l'abuso, che corre oggidì in questa città, che non si vol veder donna virtuosa in altro, che nel governo della casa'). Moderata Fonte, *Il merito delle donne*, ed. Adriana Chemello (Venice: EIDOS, 1988), p. 9. An English translation is available: Fonte, *Worth of Women*.

43 See Virginia Cox, 'The single self: feminist thought and the marriage market in early modern Venice', in John Jeffries Martin (ed.), *The Renaissance: Italy and Abroad* (London: Routledge, 2002).

44 On women's role in musical and dramatic culture at this time, see, for example, Tim Carter, 'Finding a voice: Vittoria Archilei and the Florentine "New Music"', in Lorna Hutson (ed.), *Feminism and Renaissance Studies* (Oxford: Oxford University Press, 1999); Anne McNeil, *Women and Music in the* Commedia dell'Arte (Oxford: Oxford University Press, 2003); Suzanne G. Cusick, *Francesca Caccini and the Medici Court: Music and the Circulation of Power* (Chicago: University of Chicago Press, 2009).

45 On women artists in this period, see Frederika H. Jacobs, *Defining the Renaissance Virtuosa: Women Artists and the Language of Art History and Criticism* (Cambridge: Cambridge University Press, 1997); Caroline P. Murphy, *Lavinia Fontana: A Painter and her Patrons in Renaissance Bologna* (New Haven: Yale University Press, 2003).

46 On sixteenth-century Italian actresses, see Robert Henke, *Performance and Literature in the* Commedia dell'Arte (Cambridge: Cambridge University Press, 2002), pp. 85–105; Rosalind Kerr, *The Rise of the Diva on the*

Sixteenth-Century Commedia dell'Arte *Stage* (Toronto: University of Toronto Press, 2015).

47 For discussion, see Cox, *Women's Writing*, pp. 97–8.

48 Adriano Valerini, *Oratione in morte della divina signora Vincenza Armani comica eccellentissima [...]* (Verona: Sebastiano and Giovanni Dalle Donne, 1570), 5r. Subsequent parenthetical references are to this edition. For discussion of Valerini's text, see Kerr, *Rise of the Diva*, 71–4.

49 ('ella non solo nella scenica attione haveva il vanto, ma nel componer gli istessi Poemi, e nell'insegnare all'Interlocutore il vero modo dell'arte'). Valerini, *Oratione*, 9r.

50 See MacNeil, *Music and Women*, pp. 50–51; Kerr, *Rise of the Diva*, pp. 123–7.

51 On Fontana, see Murphy, *Lavinia Fontana*; on Mantuana, Evelyn Lincoln, *The Invention of the Italian Renaissance Printmaker* (New Haven: Yale University Press, 2000), pp. 111–45; on Elisabetta and Girolama Parasole, Cox, *Women's Writing*, pp. 160–1.

52 Victoria Kirkham, 'Creative partners: the marriage of Laura Battiferra and Bartolomeo Ammannati', *Renaissance Quarterly*, 55/2 (2002), pp. 498–558.

53 The painting and the commission are discussed in Murphy, *Lavinia Fontana*, pp. 73–6.

54 On Strozzi's *Hymns*, see Cox, *Prodigious Muse*, pp. 58–9.

55 Elissa Weaver, *Convent Theatre in Early Modern Italy: Spiritual Fun and Learning* (Cambridge: Cambridge University Press, 2002).

56 Jonathan K. Nelson (ed.), *Plautilla Nelli (1524–1588): The Painter-Prioress of Florence* (Syracuse, NY: Syracuse University Press, 2008).

57 Robert L. Kendrick, *Celestial Sirens: Nuns and their Music in Early Modern Milan* (Oxford: Oxford University Press, 1996). See also, on other centres, Craig A. Monson, *Disembodied Voices: Music and Culture in an Early Modern Convent* (Berkeley and Los Angeles: University of Chicago Press, 1995); Colleen Reardon, *Holy Concord Within Sacred Walls: Nuns and Music in Siena, 1500–1700* (Oxford: Oxford University Press, 2001).

58 Cox, *Prodigious Muse*, pp. 7–9.

59 Monique Frize, *Laura Bassi and Science in 18th Century Europe* (Heidelberg: Springer, 2013), pp. 32–3.

60 Sharon T. Strocchia, 'The nun apothecaries of Renaissance Florence: marketing medicines in the convent', *Renaissance Studies*, 25/5 (2011), pp. 627–47. On nuns and history-writing, see K. P. Lowe, *Nuns' Chronicles and Convent Culture in Renaissance and Counter-Reformation Italy* (Cambridge: Cambridge University Press, 2003).

Conclusion

1 On Marino's literary impact and the coming of the Baroque, see Cox, *Women's Writing*, p. 177.

2 On the seventeenth-century misogynistic backlash, see Cox, *Women's Writing*, pp. 166–227. On Arcadia, see ibid., pp. 229–33.

3 Cox (ed.), *Lyric Poetry*, pp. 38–40.

Bibliography

Primary works

Alberti, Leon Battista, *The Family in Renaissance Florence*, trans. Renée Neu Watkins (Columbia, SC: University of South Carolina Press, 1969).

——— *I libri della famiglia*, ed. Ruggiero Romano, Alberto Tenenti, and Francesco Furlan (Turin: Einaudi, 1994).

——— *Il nuovo* De Pictura *di Leon Battista Alberti*, ed. and trans. Rocco Sinisgalli (Rome: Edizioni Kappa, 2006).

Alighieri, Dante, *The Divine Comedy*, trans. Robert M. Durling; ed. Robert M. Durling and Ronald L. Martinez, 3 vols (New York: Oxford University Press, 1996–2013).

Aretino, Pietro, *Lettere. Libro primo*, ed. Francesco Erspamer (Parma: Ugo Guanda, 1995).

Arienti, Giovanni Sabadino degli, *Gynevera, de le clare donne*, ed. Corrado Ricchi and Alberto Bacchi della Lega (Bologna: Romagnoli-Dall'Acqua, 1888).

Ariosto, Lodovico, *The Satires of Lodovico Ariosto: An Autobiography*, trans. Peter DeSa Wiggins (Athens, OH: Ohio University Press, 1976).

Biringuccio, Vannoccio, *La pirotechnia* (Venice: Girolamo Giglio, 1559).

——— *The Pirotechnia of Vannoccio Biringuccio*, ed. and trans. Cyril Stanley Smith and Martha Teach Gnudi (New York: The American Institute of Mining and Metallurgical Engineers, 1943).

Boccaccio, Giovanni, *Famous Women*, ed. and trans. Virginia Brown (Cambridge, MA: Harvard University Press, 2001).

Bracciolini, Poggio, *Two Renaissance Book Hunters: The Letters of Poggius Bracciolini to Nicolaus de Niccolis*, trans. Phyllis Walter Goodhart Gordan (New York: Columbia University Press, 1991).

Castiglione, Baldassare, *Lettere inedite e rare*, ed. Guglielmo Gorni (Milan: Ricciardi, 1969).

——— *Lettere*, ed. Guido La Rocca (Milan: Mondadori, 1978).

——— *Il libro del cortegiano*, ed. Amedeo Quondam (Milan: Garzanti, 1987).

——— *The Book of the Courtier: The Singleton Translation*, ed. Daniel Javitch (New York: Norton, 2002).

Cellini, Benvenuto, *The Autobiography of Benvenuto Cellini*, trans. George Bull (Harmondsworth: Penguin, 1956).

——— *Vita*, ed. Ettore Camesasca (Milan: Rizzoli, 2009).

Cennini, Cennino, *Il libro dell'arte*, ed. Fabio Frezzato (Vicenza: Neri Pozza, 2003).

——— *The Craftsman's Handbook (Il libro dell'arte)*, trans. Daniel V. Thompson (New York: Dover, 1960).

Cervio, Vincenzo, *Il Trinciante, con l'aggiunta di Reale Fusoritto*, ed. Emilio Faccioli (Florence: Il Portolano, 1979).

Cicero, *Brutus. Orator*, trans. G. L. Hendrickson and H. M. Hubbell (Cambridge, MA: Harvard University Press, 1939).

——— *De officiis*, trans. Walter Miller (Cambridge, MA: Harvard University Press, 1913).

——— *De oratore*, trans. E. W. Sutton and H. Rackman (Cambridge, MA: Harvard University Press, 1976).

Corte, Claudio, *Il cavallarizzo* (Venice: Giordano Ziletti, 1562).

Cotrugli, Benedetto, *Il libro dell'arte della mercatura*, ed. Ugo Tucci (Venice: Arsenale, 1990).

Cox, Virginia (ed.), *Lyric Poetry by Women of the Italian Renaissance* (Baltimore: Johns Hopkins University Press, 2013).

Croce, Giulio Cesare, 'Descrittione della vita del Croce', in *Storia di vita popolare nelle canzoni di piazza di G.C. Croce*, ed. Monique Rauch (Bologna: CLUEB, 1982).

d'Aragona, Tullia, *The Poems and Letters of Tullia d'Aragona and Others: A Bilingual Edition*, ed. and trans. Julia Hairston (Toronto: Centre for Reformation and Renaissance Studies, 2014).

da Como, Martino, *The Art of Cooking, with Fifty Modernized Recipes by Stefania Barzini*, ed. Luigi Ballerini; trans. Jeremy Parzen (Berkeley and Los Angeles: University of California Press, 2005).

della Chiesa, Francesco Agostino, *Theatro delle donne letterate, con un breve discorso della preminenza e perfettione del sesso donnesco* (Mondovì: Giovanni Gislandi and Giovanni Tommaso Rossi, 1620).

Domenichi, Lodovico (ed.), *Rime diverse d'alcune nobilissime e virtuosissime donne* (Lucca: Vincenzo Busdraghi, 1559).

Fioravanti, Leonardo, *Dello specchio di scientia universale* (Venice: Vincenzo Valgrisi, 1564).

——— *Dello specchio di scientia universale* (Venice: Heirs of Melchiorre Sessa, 1583).

Fonte, Moderata [Modesta Pozzo], *Il merito delle donne*, ed. Adriana Chemello (Venice: EIDOS, 1988).

——— *The Worth of Women*, ed. and trans. Virginia Cox (Chicago: University of Chicago Press, 1997).

Franco, Veronica, *Poems and Selected Letters*, ed. and trans. Ann Rosalind Jones and Margaret F. Rosenthal (Chicago: University of Chicago Press, 1998).

Garzoni, Tommaso, *La piazza universale di tutte le professioni del mondo*, ed. Paolo Cherchi and Beatrice Collina (Turin: Einaudi, 1996).

Giovio, Paolo, *Notable Men and Women of Our Time*, ed. and trans. Kenneth Gouwens (Cambridge, MA: Harvard University Press, 2013).

Giraldi, Lilio Gregorio, *Modern Poets*, ed. and trans. John N. Grant (Cambridge, MA: Harvard University Press, 2011).

Grisone, Federico, *Federico Grisone's* The Rules of Riding*: An Edited Translation of the First Renaissance Treatise on Classical Horsemanship*, ed. and trans. Elizabeth M. Tobey (Tempe, AZ: Arizona Center for Medieval and Renaissance Studies, 2014).

Guasco, Annibale, *Discourse to Lady Lavinia his Daughter*, ed. and trans. Peggy Osborn (Chicago: University of Chicago Press, 2003).

Hoby, Thomas, *The Travels and Life of Sir Thomas Hoby of Bisham Abbey, Written by Himself, 1547–1564*, ed. Edgar Powell (London: Royal Historical Society, 1902).

Kallendorf, Craig W. (ed.), *Humanist Educational Treatises* (Cambridge, MA: Harvard University Press, 2002).

Machiavelli, Niccolò, *The Prince and Other Political Writings*, trans. Stephen J. Milner (London: Everyman, 1995).

——— *Il principe*, ed. Giorgio Inglese (Turin: Einaudi, 1995).

——— et al., *Machiavelli and His Friends: Their Personal Correspondence*, ed. and trans. James B. Atkinson and David Sices (Dekalb, IL: Northern Illinois University Press, 1996).

Matraini, Chiara, *Rime e lettere*, ed. Giovanna Rabitti (Bologna: Commissione per i Testi di Lingua, 1989).

——— *Selected Poetry and Prose*, trans. and ed. Eleanor Maclachlan, with an introduction by Giovanna Rabitti (Chicago: University of Chicago Press, 2008).

Morelli, Giovanni, *Ricordi*, ed. Vittore Branca (Florence: Le Monnier, 1956).

Petrarca, Francesco, *Le familiari*, ed. Vittorio Rossi and Umberto Bosco, 4 vols (Florence: Sansoni, 1933–42).

——— *Rerum familiarum libri*, trans. Aldo S. Bernardo, 3 vols (New York: Italica Press, 2005).

Pico della Mirandola, Giovanni, 'On the Dignity of Man', trans. Elizabeth Livermore Forbes, in Ernst Cassirer et al., *The Renaissance Philosophy of Man* (Chicago: University of Chicago Press, 1956).

——— *Discorso della dignità dell'uomo*, ed. Francesco Bausi (Parma: Ugo Guanda, 2003).

Pliny, *Natural History*, 2 vols (Cambridge, MA: Harvard University Press, 1942).

Porcacchi, Tommaso, *Attioni d'Arrigo Terzo, re di Francia, e di Polonia, descritte in dialogo* (Venice: Giorgio Angelieri, 1574).

Ramusio, Giovanni Battista, *Navigazioni e viaggi*, ed. Marica Milanesi (Turin: Einaudi, 1978–88).

Romoli, Domenico, *La singolare dottrina ... dell'ufficio dello scalco* (Venice: Giovanni Battista Bonfadino, 1593).

Segre, Cesare (ed.), *Volgarizzamenti del Duecento e Trecento* (Turin: UTET, 1953).

Stampa, Gaspara, *The Complete Poems. The 1554 Edition of the* Rime*: a Bilingual Edition*, ed. Troy Tower and Jane Tylus; trans. with an introduction by Jane Tylus (Chicago: University of Chicago Press, 2010).

Suetonius, *The Lives of the Caesars*, trans. J. C. Rolfe, 2 vols (Cambridge, MA: Harvard University Press, 1989).

Valerini, Adriano, *Oratione in morte della divina signora Vincenza Armani comica eccellentissima [...]* (Verona: Sebastiano and Giovanni Dalle Donne, 1570).

Vasari, Giorgio, *Le vite de' più eccellenti pittori scultori e architettori nelle redazioni del 1550 e 1568*, ed. Rosanna Bettarini and Paola Barocchi (Florence: Sansoni [later S.P.E.S.], 1966–97).

——— *Lives of the Painters, Sculptors and Architects*, trans. Gaston C. De Vere, with an introduction and notes by David Ekserdjian (New York: Knopf, 1996).

Secondary works

Ajmar, Marta, 'Mechanical Disegno', *RIHA Journal* 0084 (2014). Online publication.

——— and Flora Dennis, *At Home in Renaissance Italy* (London: Victoria and Albert Museum, 2006).

Allen, Prudence, *The Concept of Woman. Vol. I. The Aristotelian Revolution, 750 B.C.–1250 A.D.* (Grand Rapids, MI: William B. Eerdman, 1997).

——— *The Concept of Woman. Vol. II. The Early Humanist Reformation, 1250–1500* (Grand Rapids, MI: William B. Eerdman, 2002).

Allerston, Patricia, 'Clothing and early modern Venetian society', *Continuity and Change*, 15/3 (2000), pp. 367–90.

Atkinson, Catherine, *Inventing Inventors: Polydore Vergil's* De inventoribus rerum (Tübingen: Mohr Siebeck, 2007).

Baron, Hans, 'Cicero and the Roman civic spirit in the Middle Ages and early Renaissance', in *Bulletin of the John Rylands Library*, 22/1 (1938), pp. 72–97.

Baroni, Alessandra, and Manfred Sellink, *Stradanus (1523–1605): Court Artist to the Medici* (Turnhout: Brepols, 2012).

Basile, Deanna, '*Fasseli gratia per poetessa*: Duke Cosimo I de' Medici's role in the Florentine literary circles of Tullia d'Aragona', in Konrad Eisenbichler, ed., *The Cultural Politics of Duke Cosimo I de' Medici* (Aldershot: Ashgate, 2001).

Baskins, Cristelle, *Cassone Painting, Humanism, and Gender in Early Modern Italy* (Cambridge: Cambridge University Press, 1998).

Bellettini, Pierangelo, 'Pietro Vecchi e il suo progetto di lettura pubblica, con ascolto a pagamento, delle notizie periodiche di attualità (Bologna 1596)', in Pierangelo Bellettini et al. (eds), *Una città in piazza. Comunicazione e vita quotidiana a Bologna tra Cinque e Seicento* (Bologna: Compositori, 2000).

Beltramini, Guido, et al. (eds), *Pietro Bembo e l'invenzione del Rinascimento* (Venice: Marsilio, 2013).

Beneš, Carrie E., *Urban Legends: Civic Identity and the Classical Past in Northern Italy, 1250–1350* (University Park, PA: Pennsylvania State University Press, 2011).

Black, Robert, 'Education and the emergence of a literate society', in Najemy (ed.), *Italy*.

Bourne, Molly, 'Signs of success: Leone Leoni's signposting in sixteenth-century Milan', in Nelson and Zeckhauser (eds), *The Patron's Payoff*.

Branca, Vittore, *Boccaccio medievale* (Florence: Sansoni, 1965).

——— (ed.), *Merchant Writers of the Italian Renaissance from Boccaccio to Machiavelli*, trans. Murtha Baca (New York: Marsilio, 1999).

Brewer, Marilynn B. and Constantine Sedikides (eds), *Individual Self, Relational Self, Collective Self* (Philadelphia: Psychology Press, 2001).

Brown, Alison, *The Return of Lucretius to Renaissance Florence* (Cambridge, MA: Harvard University Press, 2010).

Burckhardt, Jacob, *The Civilization of the Renaissance in Italy* (1860), trans. S. G. C. Middlemore, with an introduction by Peter Burke (London: Penguin, 2004).

Burke, Peter, *The Fortunes of the* Courtier*: The European Reception of Castiglione's* Cortegiano (University Park, PA: Pennsylvania State University Press, 1996).

Butters, Humfrey C., 'Conflicting attitudes towards Machiavelli's works in Spain, Rome, and Florence', in Law and Patton (eds), *Communes and Despots*.

Caffero, William, *Contesting the Renaissance* (Chichester: Wiley-Blackwell, 2010).

Campbell, Stephen, *The Cabinet of Eros: Renaissance Mythological Painting and the Studiolo of Isabella d'Este* (New Haven: Yale University Press, 2006).

——— and Michael W. Cole, *A New History of Italian Renaissance Art* (London: Thames and Hudson, 2012).

Camporeale, Salvatore, *Christianity, Latinity, and Culture: Two Studies on Lorenzo Valla*, ed. Patrick Barker and Christopher S. Celenza (Leiden: Brill, 2014).

Carlino, Andrea, *Books of the Body: Anatomical Ritual and Renaissance Learning*, trans. John Tedeschi and Anne Tedeschi (Chicago: University of Chicago Press, 1999).

Carter, Tim, 'Finding a voice: Vittoria Archilei and the Florentine "New Music"', in Lorna Hutson (ed.), *Feminism and Renaissance Studies* (Oxford: Oxford University Press, 1999).

Celenza, Christopher S., *Renaissance Humanism and the Papal Curia: Lapo da Castiglionchio the Younger's* De curiae commodis (Ann Arbor: University of Michigan Press, 1999).

Cherchi, Paolo, *Polimatia di riuso. Mezzo secolo di plagio (1539–89)* (Rome: Bulzoni, 1998).

Clayton, Martin and Ronald Philo, *Leonardo da Vinci: Anatomist* (London: Royal Collection, 2012).

Clough, C. H. 'The New World and the Italian Renaissance', in C. H. Clough and P. E. H. Hair (eds), *The European Outthrust and Encounter: the First Phase c. 1400–c. 1700* (Liverpool: Liverpool University Press, 1994).

Cochrane, Eric, *Italy, 1530–1630* (London: Longman, 1989).

Connors, Joseph, '*Ars tornandi*: Baroque architecture and the lathe', *Journal of the Warburg and Courtauld Institutes*, 53 (1990), pp. 217–36.

Cornish, Alison, *Vernacular Translation in Dante's Italy: Illiterate Literature* (Cambridge: Cambridge University Press, 2013).

Cox, Virginia, 'The single self: feminist thought and the marriage market in early modern Venice', in John Jeffries Martin, ed., *The Renaissance: Italy and Abroad* (London: Routledge, 2002).

——— 'Women writers and the canon: the case of Vittoria Colonna', in Pamela J. Benson and Victoria Kirkham (eds), *Strong Voices, Weak History: Early*

Women Writers and Canons in England, France and Italy (Ann Arbor: University of Michigan Press, 2005).
——— *Women's Writing in Italy, 1400–1650* (Baltimore: Johns Hopkins University Press, 2008).
——— 'Gender and eloquence in Ercole de' Roberti's *Portia and Brutus*', *Rhetorica*, 62 (2009), pp. 61–101.
——— 'Rhetoric and political ethics', in John Najemy (ed.), *The Cambridge Companion to Machiavelli* (Cambridge: Cambridge University Press, 2010).
——— *The Prodigious Muse: Women's Writing in Counter-Reformation Italy* (Baltimore: Johns Hopkins University Press, 2011).
——— 'Il commento paradossale: un microgenere senese', in Massimo Danzi and Roberto Leporatti (eds), *Il poeta e il suo pubblico: lettura e commento dei testi lirici nel Cinquecento* (Geneva: Droz, 2012).
——— 'The female voice in Italian Renaissance dialogue', *MLN*, 128/1 (2013), pp. 53–78.
——— 'The exemplary Vittoria Colonna', in Abigail Brundin et al. (eds), *A Companion to Vittoria Colonna* (Leiden: Brill, forthcoming).
Croizat, Yassana C., '"Living dolls": François 1er dresses his women', *Renaissance Quarterly*, 60/1 (2007), pp. 94–130.
Currie, Elizabeth, 'Diversity and design in the Florentine tailoring trade, 1550–1620', in O' Malley and Welch (eds), *The Material Renaissance*.
Cusick, Suzanne G., *Francesca Caccini and the Medici Court: Music and the Circulation of Power* (Chicago: Chicago University Press, 2009).
Davis, Robert C., *The War of the Fists: Popular Culture and Public Violence in Late Renaissance Venice* (Oxford: Oxford University Press, 1994).
De Sanctis, Francesco, *History of Italian Literature,* trans. Joan Redfern (New York: Basic Books, 1960).
——— *Storia della letteratura italiana,* ed. Niccolò Gallo, with an introduction by Giorgio Ficara (Turin: Einaudi-Gallimard, 1996).
Dempsey, Charles, *The Portrayal of Love: Botticelli's* Primavera *and Humanist Culture at the Time of Lorenzo the Magnificent* (Princeton: Princeton University Press, 1992).
Dizionario biografico degli italiani (Rome: Istituto dell'Enciclopedia Italiana, 1960–).
Edson, Evelyn, *The World Map, 1300–1492* (Baltimore: Johns Hopkins University Press, 2007).
Edwards, Mark U., *Printing, Propaganda, and Martin Luther* (Berkeley and Los Angeles: University of California Press, 1995).
Eisenbichler, Konrad, *The Sword and the Pen: Women, Politics, and Poetry in Sixteenth-Century Siena* (Notre Dame: University of Notre Dame Press, 2012).
Elias, Norbert, *The Civilizing Process* (Oxford: Blackwell, 1994).
Falchetta, Piero, *Fra Mauro's World Map*, trans. Jeremy Scott; foreword by Marino Zorzi (Turnhout: Brepols, 2006).
Feinberg, Larry J., 'The *Studiolo* of Francesco I reconsidered', in Cristina Acidini Luchinat et al. (eds), *The Medici, Michelangelo, and the Art of Late Renaissance Florence* (New Haven: Yale University Press, 2002).

Findlen, Paula, *Possessing Nature: Museums, Collecting, and Scientific Culture in Early Modern Italy* (Berkeley and Los Angeles: University of California Press, 1996).

Fiorani, Francesca, *The Marvel of Maps: Art, Cartography, and Politics in Renaissance Italy* (New Haven: Yale University Press, 2005).

Foucault, Michel, *The Order of Things: An Archaeology of the Human Sciences* (London: Routledge, 1970).

Franklin, Margaret, *Boccaccio's Heroines: Power and Virtue in Renaissance Society* (Aldershot: Ashgate, 2006).

Freedman, Luba, *Titian's Portraits through Aretino's Lens* (University Park, PA: Pennsylvania State University Press, 1995).

——— *Classical Myths in Italian Renaissance Painting* (Cambridge: Cambridge University Press, 2011).

Frick, Carole Collier, *Dressing Renaissance Florence: Families, Fortunes and Fine Clothing* (Baltimore: Johns Hopkins University Press, 2002).

Frize, Monique, *Laura Bassi and Science in 18th Century Europe* (Heidelberg: Springer, 2013).

Ginzburg, Carlo, *The Cheese and the Worms,* trans. John Tedeschi and Anne Tedeschi (Baltimore: Johns Hopkins University Press, 1980).

Goldthwaite, Richard A., *The Building of Renaissance Florence: An Economic and Social History* (Baltimore: Johns Hopkins University Press, 1980).

——— *Wealth and the Demand for Art in Italy, 1300–1600* (Baltimore: Johns Hopkins University Press, 1993).

Grafton, Anthony, *Leon Battista Alberti: Master Builder of the Italian Renaissance* (Cambridge, MA: Harvard University Press, 2002).

Grafton, Anthony, with April Shelton and Nancy Siraisi, *New Worlds, Ancient Texts: The Power of Tradition and the Shock of Discovery* (Cambridge, MA: Harvard University Press, 1992).

Greenblatt, Stephen, *Renaissance Self-Fashioning: From More to Shakespeare* (Chicago: University of Chicago Press, 1980).

Greene, Thomas M., 'The flexibility of the self in Renaissance literature', in Peter Demetz et al. (eds), *The Disciplines of Criticism: Essays in Literary Theory, Interpretation, and History* (New Haven: Yale University Press, 1968).

Guerzoni, Guido, 'The demand for arts of an Italian Renaissance court: the case of d'Este of Ferrara (1471–1560)', in Clara Eugenia Nuñez (ed.), *Markets for Art, 1400–1600* (Seville: Universidad de Sevilla, 1998).

——— *Apollo and Vulcan: The Art Markets in Italy, 1400–1700* (East Lansing: Michigan State University Press, 2011).

Hale, John, *The Civilization of Europe in the Renaissance* (London: HarperCollins, 1994).

Han, Shihui, and Ying Zhu, 'Cultural differences in the self: from philosophy to psychology and neuroscience', *Social and Personality Psychology Compass*, 2/5 (2008), pp. 1799–1811.

Hankins, James, 'Humanism, scholasticism, and Renaissance philosophy', in Hankins (ed.), *Cambridge Companion.*

Hankins, James (ed.), *Renaissance Civic Humanism: Reappraisals and Reflections* (Cambridge: Cambridge University Press, 2004).

——— *The Cambridge Companion to Renaissance Philosophy* (Cambridge: Cambridge University Press, 2007).

Hay, Denis, and John Law, *Italy in the Age of the Renaissance, 1380–1530* (London: Longman, 1989).

Henke, Robert, *Performance and Literature in the* Commedia dell'Arte (Cambridge: Cambridge University Press, 2002).

Hohti, Paula, 'Domestic space and identity: artisans, shopkeepers and traders in sixteenth-century Siena', *Urban History*, 37/3 (2010), pp. 372–85.

Howard, Peter, *Creating Magnificence in Renaissance Florence* (Toronto: University of Toronto Press, 2012).

Infelise, Mario, 'Roman *avvisi*: information and politics in the seventeenth century', in Gianvittorio Signorotto and Maria Antonietta Visceglia (eds), *Court and Politics in Papal Rome, 1492–1700* (Cambridge: Cambridge University Press, 2002).

Jacobs, Frederika, *Defining the Renaissance Virtuosa: Women Artists and the Language of Art History and Criticism* (Cambridge: Cambridge University Press, 1997).

Jacobus, Laura, 'A knight in the Arena: Enrico Scrovegni and his "true image"', in Mary Rogers (ed.), *Fashioning Identities in Renaissance Art* (Aldershot: Ashgate, 2000).

——— 'The tomb of Enrico Scrovegni in the Arena Chapel, Padua', *The Burlington Magazine*, 1311/154 (2012), pp. 403–409.

James, Carolyn, *Giovanni Sabadino degli Arienti: a Literary Career* (Florence: Olschki, 1996).

Janick, Jules, and Harry S. Paris, 'The Cucurbit images (1515–1518) of the Villa Farnesina, Rome', *Annals of Botany*, 97/2 (2006), pp. 165–76.

Javitch, Daniel, *Proclaiming a Classic: The Canonization of* Orlando Furioso (Princeton: Princeton University Press, 1991).

Jones, Ann R. and Margaret Rosenthal, *The Clothing of the Renaissance World: Cesare Vecellio's* Habiti antichi et moderni (New York: Thames and Hudson, 2008).

Jones, Philip, *The Italian City-State: From Commune to Signoria* (Oxford: Oxford University Press, 1997).

Kelly, Joan, 'Did women have a Renaissance?', in *Women, History, and Theory: The Essays of Joan Kelly* (Chicago: University of Chicago Press, 1984).

Kendrick, Robert L., *Celestial Sirens: Nuns and their Music in Early Modern Milan* (Oxford: Oxford University Press, 1996).

Kerr, Rosalind, *The Rise of the Diva on the Sixteenth-Century* Commedia dell'Arte *Stage* (Toronto: University of Toronto Press, 2015).

King, Catherine, 'The arts of carving and casting', in Norman (ed.), *Siena*, Vol. 1.

King, Margaret L., 'Book-lined cells: women and humanism in the early Italian Renaissance', in Patricia H. Labalme (ed.), *Beyond Their Sex: Learned Women of the European Past* (New York: New York University Press, 1980).

Kirkham, Victoria, 'Creative partners: the marriage of Laura Battiferra and Bartolomeo Ammannati,' *Renaissance Quarterly*, 55/2 (2002), pp. 498–558.

——— and Armando Maggi (eds), *Petrarch: A Critical Guide to the Complete Works* (Chicago: University of Chicago Press, 2009).

——, Michael Sherberg, and Janet Levarie Smarr (eds), *Boccaccio: A Critical Guide to the Complete Works* (Chicago: University of Chicago Press, 2013).

Kohl, Benjamin G., 'The myth of the Renaissance despot', in Law and Patton (eds), *Communes and Despots.*

Kolsky, Stephen, *The Genealogy of Women: Studies in Boccaccio's* De claris mulieribus (New York: Peter Lang, 2003).

—— *The Ghost of Boccaccio: Writings on Famous Women in Renaissance Italy* (Turnhout: Brepols, 2005).

Kraye, Jill, 'The revival of Hellenistic philosophies', in Hankins (ed.), *Cambridge Companion.*

Langdale, Shelley R., *Battle of the Nudes: Pollaiuolo's Renaissance Masterpiece* (Cleveland, OH: Cleveland Museum of Art, 2002).

Laurenza, Domenico, *Art and Anatomy in Renaissance Italy: Images from a Scientific Revolution* (New York: Metropolitan Museum of Art, 2012).

Laven, Mary, 'Encountering the Counter-Reformation', *Renaissance Quarterly*, 59/3 (2006), pp. 706–20.

Law, John Easton and Bernadette Patton (eds), *Communes and Despots in Medieval and Renaissance Italy* (Aldershot: Ashgate, 2010).

Lazzaro, Claudia, *The Italian Renaissance Garden: From the Conventions of Planting, Design, and Ornament to the Grand Gardens of Sixteenth-Century Central Italy* (New Haven: Yale University Press, 1990).

Leydi, Silvio, 'The swordsmiths of Milan, c. 1525–1630', in Tobias Capwell, Sydney Anglo et al., *The Noble Art of the Sword: Fashion and Fencing in Renaissance Europe 1520–1630* (London: Wallace Collection, 2012).

Lincoln, Evelyn, *The Invention of the Italian Renaissance Printmaker* (New Haven: Yale University Press, 2000).

Long, Pamela, *Openness, Secrecy, Authorship: Technical Arts and the Culture of Knowledge from Antiquity to the Renaissance* (Baltimore: Johns Hopkins University Press, 2001).

Lowe, K. P., *Nuns' Chronicles and Convent Culture in Renaissance and Counter-Reformation Italy* (Cambridge: Cambridge University Press, 2003).

Lubkin, Gregory, *A Renaissance Court: Milan under Galeazzo Maria Sforza* (Berkeley and Los Angeles: University of California Press, 1994).

Maclean, Ian, *The Renaissance Notion of Woman: A Study in the Fortunes of Scholasticism and Medical Science in European Intellectual Life* (Cambridge: Cambridge University Press, 1980).

Malanima, Paolo, 'Urbanisation and the Italian economy during the last millennium', *European Review of Economic History*, 9/1 (2005), pp. 97–122.

Marr, Alexander, *From Raphael to Galileo: Mutio Oddi and the Mathematical Culture of Late Renaissance Italy* (Chicago: University of Chicago Press, 2011).

Martin, Craig, *Subverting Aristotle: Religion, History and Philosophy in Early Modern Science* (Baltimore: Johns Hopkins University Press, 2014).

Martin, John Jeffries, 'The imaginary piazza: Tommaso Garzoni and the late Italian Renaissance', in Samuel K. Cohn Jr. and Steven A. Epstein (eds), *Portraits of Medieval and Renaissance Living: Essays in Memory of David Herlihy* (Ann Arbor: University of Michigan Press, 1996).

——— *Myths of Renaissance Individualism* (Basingstoke: Palgrave MacMillan, 2004).

Martines, Lauro, *Power and Imagination: City-States in Renaissance Italy* (New York: Knopf, 1979).

Maxson, Brian Jeffrey, *The Humanist World of Renaissance Florence* (Cambridge: Cambridge University Press, 2014).

McClure, George W., *The Culture of Profession in Late Renaissance Italy* (Toronto: University of Toronto Press, 2004).

——— *Parlour Games and the Public Life of Women in Renaissance Italy* (Toronto: University of Toronto Press, 2013).

McIver, Katherine A., *From Kitchen to Table: Cooking and Eating in Renaissance Italy* (Lanham, MD: Rowman and Littlefield, 2015).

McNeil, Anne, *Women and Music in the* Commedia dell'Arte (Oxford: Oxford University Press, 2003).

Mirabella, Bella (ed.), *Ornamentalism: The Art of Renaissance Accessories* (Ann Arbor: University of Michigan Press, 2011).

Monson, Craig A., *Disembodied Voices: Music and Culture in an Early Modern Convent* (Berkeley and Los Angeles: University of California Press, 1995).

Muir, Edward, *Civic Ritual in Renaissance Venice* (Princeton: Princeton University Press, 1981).

Murphy, Caroline P., *Lavinia Fontana: A Painter and Her Patrons in Renaissance Bologna* (New Haven: Yale University Press, 2003).

Najemy, John M. (ed.), *Italy in the Age of the Renaissance: 1300–1550* (Oxford: Oxford University Press, 2004).

——— *A History of Florence, 1200–1575* (Oxford: Blackwell, 2006).

Nalezyty, Susan, 'From Padua to Rome: Pietro Bembo's mobile objects and convivial interiors', in Erin J. Campbell et al. (eds), *The Early Modern Italian Domestic Sphere, 1400–1700: Objects, Spaces, Domesticities* (Aldershot: Ashgate, 2014).

Natali, Antonio, *Andrea del Sarto* (New York: Abbeville, 1999).

Nelson, Jonathan K. (ed.), *Plautilla Nelli (1524–1588): The Painter-Prioress of Florence* (Syracuse, NY: Syracuse University Press, 2008).

——— and Richard J. Zeckhauser, *The Patron's Payoff: Conspicuous Commissions in Italian Renaissance Art* (Princeton: Princeton University Press, 2008).

Nevile, Jennifer, *The Eloquent Body: Dance and Humanist Culture in Fifteenth-Century Italy* (Bloomington, IN: Indiana University Press, 2004).

Newcomb, Anthony *The Madrigal at Ferrara, 1579–97* (Princeton: Princeton University Press, 1980).

Niccoli, Ottavia, 'Italy', in Joad Raymond (ed.), *The Oxford History of Popular Print Culture*. Vol. 1: *Cheap Print in Britain and Ireland to 1660* (Oxford: Oxford University Press, 2011).

Norman, Diana (ed.), *Siena, Florence, and Padua: Art, Society, and Religion, 1280–1400*, 2 vols (New Haven: Yale University Press, 1995).

——— 'Splendid models and examples from the past: Carrara patronage of art', in Norman (ed.), *Siena*, Vol. 1.

Nutton, Vivian, 'Hellenism postponed: some aspects of Renaissance medicine, 1490–1530,' *Sudhoffs Archiv*, 81/2 (1997) pp. 158–70.

Ogilvie, Brian, *The Science of Describing: Natural History in Renaissance Europe* (Chicago: University of Chicago Press, 2006).

O'Malley, Michelle and Evelyn Welch, eds, *The Material Renaissance* (Manchester: Manchester University Press, 2007).

O'Rourke Boyle, Marjorie, *Loyola's Acts: The Rhetoric of the Self* (Berkeley and Los Angeles: University of California Press, 1997).

Pade, Marianne, 'The *fortuna* of Leontius Pilatus's Homer', in F. T. Coulson and A. A. Grotans (eds), *Classica et Beneventana: Essays Presented to Virginia Brown on the Occasion of her 65th Birthday* (Turnhout: Brepols, 2008).

Park, Katharine, 'The criminal and the saintly body: autopsy and dissection in late medieval Europe', *Renaissance Quarterly*, 47/1 (1994) pp. 1–33.

Patton, Bernadette and John Easton Law (eds), *Communes and Despots in Medieval and Renaissance Italy* (Aldershot: Ashgate, 2010).

Paulicelli, Eugenia, *Writing Fashion in Early Modern Italy: From Sprezzatura to Satire* (Aldershot: Ashgate, 2014).

Payne, Alina, 'Vasari, architecture, and the origins of historicizing art', *Anthropology and Aesthetics*, 40 (2001), pp. 51–76.

Petrella, Giancarlo, *L'officina del geografo. La* Descrittione di tutta Italia *di Leandro Alberti e gli studi geografico-antiquari tra Quattro e Cinquecento* (Milan: Vita e Pensiero, 2004).

Pettegree, Andrew, *The Invention of News: How the World Came to Know About Itself* (New Haven: Yale University Press, 2014).

Phillips, Mark, *The Memoir of Marco Parenti: A Life in Medici Florence* (Princeton: Princeton University Press, 1987).

Pullan, Brian, 'Wage-earners and the Venetian economy', *The Economic History Review*, 16/3 (1964), pp. 407–26.

Quondam, Amedeo, 'Saggio di bibliografia della poesia religiosa', in *Paradigmi e tradizioni* (Rome: Bulzoni, 2005).

Reardon, Colleen, *Holy Concord Within Sacred Walls: Nuns and Music in Siena, 1500–1700* (Oxford: Oxford University Press, 2001).

Rebhorn, Wayne A., 'Baldesar Castiglione, Thomas Wilson, and the courtly body of Renaissance rhetoric', *Rhetorica*, 11/3 (1993), pp. 241–74.

Refini, Eugenio, '"Aristotile in parlare materno": vernacular readings of the *Ethics* in the Quattrocento', *I Tatti Studies in the Italian Renaissance*, 16/1–2 (2013), pp. 311–41.

Regan, Lisa K., 'Ariosto's threshold patron: Isabella d'Este in the *Orlando Furioso*', *MLN*, 120/1 (2005), pp. 50–69.

Richardson, Brian, '*The Prince* and its early Italian readers', in Martin Coyle (ed.), *Niccolò Machiavelli's* The Prince*: New Interdisciplinary Essays* (Manchester: Manchester University Press, 1995).

——— 'The debates on printing in Renaissance Italy', *La bibliofilia*, 100/2–3 (1998), pp. 148–51.

——— *Printing, Writers, and Readers in Renaissance Italy* (Cambridge: Cambridge University Press, 1999).

Rocke, Michael, *Forbidden Friendships: Homosexuality and Male Culture in Renaissance Florence* (Oxford: Oxford University Press, 1998).

Root, Jerry, *'Space to Speke': The Confessional Subject in Medieval Literature* (New York: Peter Lang, 1997).

Rosenthal, Margaret F., *The Honest Courtesan: Veronica Franco, Citizen and Writer in Sixteenth-Century Venice* (Chicago: University of Chicago Press, 1992).

Ruggiero, Guido (ed.), *A Companion to the Worlds of the Renaissance* (Chichester: Wiley-Blackwell, 2008).

Sampson, Lisa, *Pastoral Drama in Early Modern Italy: The Making of a New Genre* (Oxford: Legenda, 2006).

San Juan, Rose Marie, 'The court lady's dilemma: Isabella d'Este and art collecting in the Renaissance', *Oxford Art Journal*, 14/1 (1991), pp. 67–78.

Saslow, James M., *Ganymede in the Renaissance* (New Haven: Yale University Press, 1986).

Schechner, Sara J., 'Between knowing and doing: mirrors and their imperfections in the Renaissance', *Early Science and Medicine*, 20/2 (2005), pp. 137–62.

Schultz, Bernard, *Art and Anatomy in Renaissance Italy* (Ann Arbor: UMI Research Press, 1985).

Scully, Terence, *The* Opera *of Bartolomeo Scappi: L'arte e prudenza d'un maestro cuoco (The Art and Craft of a Master Cook)* (Toronto: University of Toronto Press, 2008).

Siraisi, Nancy, *Medieval and Early Renaissance Medicine: An Introduction to Knowledge and Practice* (Chicago: University of Chicago Press, 1990).

Snyder, Jon R., *Dissimulation and the Culture of Secrecy in Early Modern Europe* (Berkeley and Los Angeles: University of California Press, 2012).

Stewart, Peter, *The Social History of Roman Art* (Cambridge: Cambridge University Press, 2008).

Stinger, Charles L., *Humanism and the Church Fathers: Ambrogio Traversari (1386–1439) and Christian Antiquity in the Italian Renaissance* (Albany, NY: State University of New York Press, 1977).

Stoppino, Eleonora, *Genealogies of Fiction: Women Warriors and the Dynastic Imagination in the* Orlando Furioso (New York: Fordham University Press, 2012).

Storey, Tessa, *Carnal Commerce in Counter-Reformation Rome* (Cambridge: Cambridge University Press, 2008).

Strocchia, Sharon T., 'Learning the virtues: convent schools and female culture in Renaissance Florence', in Barbara J. Whitehead (ed.), *Women's Education in Early Modern Europe. A History, 1500–1800* (New York: Garland, 1999).

——— 'The nun apothecaries of Renaissance Florence: marketing medicines in the convent', *Renaissance Studies* 25/5 (2011), pp. 627–47.

Stuard, Susan Mosher, *Gilding the Market: Luxury and Fashion in Fourteenth-Century Italy* (Philadelphia: University of Pennsylvania Press, 2006).

Syson, Luke, 'Reading faces: Gian Cristoforo Romano's medal of Isabella d'Este', in Cesare Mozzarelli et al. (eds), *La corte di Mantova nell'età di Mantegna, 1450–1550/The Court of the Gonzaga in the Age of Mantegna, 1450–1550* (Rome: Bulzoni, 1997).

Thornton, Dora, *The Scholar in his Study: Ownership and Experience in Renaissance Italy* (New Haven: Yale University Press, 1998).

Treadgold, Warren (ed.), *Renaissances Before the Renaissance: Classical Revivals of Late Antiquity and the Middle Ages* (Stanford: Stanford University Press, 1984).

Treadwell, Nina, '"Simil combattimento fatto da dame": the musico-theatrical entertainments of Margherita Gonzaga's *balletto delle donne* and the female warrior in Ferrarese cultural history', in Todd C. Borgerding (ed.), *Gender, Sexuality, and Early Music* (New York: Routledge, 2002).

Waddington, Raymond, *Aretino's Satyr: Sexuality, Satire, and Self-Projection in Sixteenth-Century Italy* (Toronto: University of Toronto Press, 2004).

Weaver, Elissa, *Convent Theatre in Early Modern Italy: Spiritual Fun and Learning* (Cambridge: Cambridge University Press, 2002).

Welch, Evelyn, *Art and Authority in Renaissance Milan* (New Haven: Yale University Press, 1997).

——— *Shopping in the Renaissance: Consumer Cultures in Italy 1400–1600* (New Haven: Yale University Press, 2005).

Witt, Ronald G., 'What did Giovannino read and write? Literacy in early Renaissance Florence', *I Tatti Studies*, 6 (1995), pp. 83–114.

——— *In the Footsteps of the Ancients: The Origins of Humanism From Lovato to Bruni* (Leiden: Brill, 2000).

Woods-Marsden, Joanna, 'Theorizing Renaissance portraiture', in James Elkins and Robert Williams (eds), *Renaissance Theory (The Art Seminar)* (New York: Routledge, 2007).

Wray, David, *Catullus and the Poetics of Roman Manhood* (Cambridge: Cambridge University Press, 2001).

Wyatt, Michael (ed.), *The Cambridge Companion to the Italian Renaissance* (Cambridge: Cambridge University Press, 2014).

——— 'Technologies', in Wyatt (ed.), *Cambridge Companion.*

Zak, Gur, 'Modes of self-writing from antiquity to the later Middle Ages', in Ralph Hexter et al. (eds), *The Oxford Handbook of Medieval Latin Literature* (Oxford: Oxford University Press, 2012).

Index